IMPACT

HOW THE PRESS AFFECTS FEDERAL POLICYMAKING

IMPACT

HOW THE PRESS AFFECTS FEDERAL POLICYMAKING

MARTIN LINSKY

W · W · NORTON & COMPANY

New York · *London*

Copyright © 1986 by
The Institute of Politics at Harvard University

All rights reserved.

Published simultaneously in Canada by Penguin Books Canada Ltd,
2801 John Street, Markham, Ontario L3R 1B4
Printed in the United States of America.

The text of this book is composed in Times Roman,
with display type set in Times Roman.
Composition and manufacturing by the Maple-Vail Book Manufacturing Group.
Book design by Jacques Chazaud

First Edition

Library of Congress Cataloging-in-Publication Data

Linsky, Martin.
Impact: how the press affects federal policymaking.

Includes index.
1. Government and the press—United States.
I. Title.
PN4745.L5   1986   302.2'3'0973   85–31060

ISBN 0-393-02327-3

W. W. Norton & Company, Inc., 500 Fifth Avenue, New York, N. Y. 10110
W. W. Norton & Company Ltd., 37 Great Russell Street, London WC1B 3NU

1 2 3 4 5 6 7 8 9 0

For my Dad

Our special thanks to
the Charles H. Revson Foundation
for its generous support

CONTENTS

ACKNOWLEDGMENTS

For this book, recognizing the contributions of others takes on a particular significance. Although I bear the responsibility for what is written, this work has truly been a shared enterprise.

There would have been no enterprise at all if it were not for the generous assistance of the Charles H. Revson Foundation. Our original program officer, Carol Japha Weiland, believed in this project from the beginning. She and her successor, Lisa Goldberg, provided helpful guidance throughout its duration. Special thanks are due to Eli Evans, president of the Charles H. Revson Foundation, who gave whatever was asked of him at every stage of the project: keen vision, sage advice, and necessary support, of both the financial and moral varieties. The Alfred P. Sloan Foundation provided additional support for the work of Gary R. Orren in connection with the project.

If the Revson Foundation launched this ship, it was the senior staff of the project, Wendy O'Donnell and David Whitman, who kept it afloat. They are first-rate talents with substantial accomplishments behind them and great careers ahead of them. They taught me more than they can imagine. Thanks, too, to Carol Colborn, Todd Peterson, and Cheryl Wires, who served on the staff in the early stages.

At the end, in the final year, when the results of the research were beginning to be distilled, several of my students made contributions to the process which added to the quality of the final product: Catherine Allen, Karen Bonner, Changyin Chung, Clark Gaulding, Marcia Petrini, Robert Samors, Cynthia Sloan, Joan Toole, and Andrew Wolf. Some of them went well beyond the call of duty and deserve special mention: Thomas Gardner, Steven Nicholas, Robert Shepardson, H. Bailey Spencer, Hon. Michael Stinziano, and Robert Tatar.

Special thanks are due to friends who were cajoled into reading some or all of this manuscript under tight deadlines and the severe constraint of having to be supportive and critical at the same time: Edwin Chin, Elizabeth Coulter, Russ Hoyle, John Hubner, William Kovach, Caroline McCarley, Jean Richards, and William Ury, and to my running partners, H. James Brown, Stephen Rothstein, and Gregory Treverton, who not only had to read the manuscript, but also had to listen to me talk about it mile after mile.

Friends had only to respond to the call when there were words on paper;

my colleagues on the faculty study group for the project were on duty for three years. Each is a distinguished professional. Individually, they helped in their own ways. Collectively, they had an incaculable influence on the final result. They were teachers, mentors, friends, resources, and confidants. They saved me from my own mistakes again and again, and they added new dimensions to the conventional notion of collegiality as it is practiced in an intensely competitive world. That they have been willing to give so much of themselves, to share their experience, insight, and expertise not only made an enormous substantive difference but was an energizing inspiration to me and to the rest of the staff all along the way. I thank them all: Richard Neustadt, who served as vice-chairman, F. Christopher Arterton, Hale Champion, John Chancellor, Stephen Hess, Albert Hunt, Mark Moore, Gary Orren, Eileen Shanahan, James C. Thomson, Jr., John William Ward, and Lewis W. Wolfson. Bill Ward died as this project came to a close. He commented extensively on early drafts of the manuscript. Much of his counsel is reflected in this book. He was a special person and I will treasure the memory of having worked with him.

As always, the staff at the Institute of Politics was extraordinarily supportive, somehow organizing the disorganized and managing the unmanageable. At the Institute, everyone helped. Two wonderful people, Betsy Pleasants Whitehead and Mary McTigue, were there whenever I needed them . . . which was most of the time. Esmé McTighe did wonders with the footnotes. Elizabeth Marsh began working with me near the completion of this work and helped me very much in tying together all the loose ends I had left dangling during the past two years.

My editor, Linda Healey, made the agony of rewriting almost a pleasure. She and Katie Nelson, and all the others at Norton were indispensable to getting the work done.

My wife, Lynn Staley, and my children, Alison, Sam, and Max, had to do without me too much over the course of these three years, especially during the last eight months. Funny, they seemed to have survived all right; I was the one who realized again how difficult it is to survive and do well without them.

Finally, there is Jonathan Moore. His presence in this book is as pervasive as the media's in Washington. His impact has been as enormous as that of the press on policymaking. He is so much a part of this work in every respect that I cannot imagine what it would have been like without him. My name is on the cover, but his fingerprints are on every page.

Martin Linsky
Cambridge, Massachusetts
September 3, 1985

INTRODUCTION

This book is the principal product of a three-year research effort on "How the Press Affects Federal Policymaking" undertaken by the Institute of Politics of the John F. Kennedy School of Government at Harvard University and funded by the Charles H. Revson Foundation. Along with its responsibilities for research about electoral politics and for innovative programming to benefit political practitioners, the institute has for a long time sponsored various activities relating to the interaction of the media and government. During the past few years it has taken the lead in developing a new Center on the Press, Politics, and Public Policy, an enterprise which encompasses "The Revson Project."

Back in 1981, recognizing that it was inadequate to attempt to understand political decision making in this country without understanding the role played by the media, that the press had an impact on the forming of public policy and the performance of political institutions, and that very little was known about how that impact was felt, we decided to seek assistance in trying to learn more about the subject. In our submission to the Revson Foundation, we wrote:

"A new body of information about how the press affects policymaking could generate a dialogue between the media and the governors which progresses beyond the instinctive adversary approach and faces up to questions of responsibility and accountability. It could help public officials understand that the press can play a constructive role in developing more sound public policies; and it could help those in the press understand that they, too, are participants in the governmental process."

We hoped we could see better the impact of the press on individual public officials, the institutions and processes of government, and policies themselves. Our work would have three principal purposes: reaching out to the general public to increase understanding about the real impact of the media on government decision making, enlightening present and future public policymakers and journalism professionals about the role of the media, and assisting faculty interested in developing curricula and teaching in this area.

We sought throughout this project to understand how the press affects policymaking from the perspective of the policymaker. That is, this is a study about aspects of government, not a study of the press. We did not set out to try to define what is good coverage of government, nor what are good policies or even what is good policymaking, although we believe that what we found has implications for all of these areas.

In this book, by "government" we mean the national government; by "press" or "media" we mean editors and reporters who cover Washington for general circulation print media or for network television. We mean no disrespect for or lack of interest in trade publications, periodicals, or state and local government. We simply had to start and stop somewhere.

In limiting ourselves to the interaction between the press and government in Washington itself, we know that much of what happens in government is affected by people and events outside the nation's capital. And we realize that Washington is not like any other place because the business of the city is the federal government. But the role of the press in what goes on there has significance far beyond the nation's capital.

A faculty study group was established to guide and oversee the project, made up of fourteen men and women with extensive experience in the federal government, in Washington-based journalism, and in academic-based writing and research in government and press matters. Its membership included: F. Christopher Arterton, associate professor of political science, Yale University; Hale Champion, executive dean, Kennedy School of Government; John Chancellor, network correspondent, NBC News; Stephen Hess, senior fellow, The Brookings Institution; Albert Hunt, national political correspondent, *The Wall Street Journal;* Mark Moore, Guggenheim Professor of criminal justice policy and management, Kennedy School of Government; Gary Orren, associate professor, Kennedy School of Government; Eileen Shanahan, senior assistant managing editor, *Pittsburgh Post-Gazette;* James

C. Thomson, Jr., curator of the Neiman Foundation; John William Ward, president, American Council of Learned Societies; and Lewis Wolfson, professor of communication, American University. Richard E. Neustadt, Lucius N. Littauer Professor of public administration at the Kennedy school, served as vice-chairman of the study group, and I was its chairman. Martin Linsky, assistant director of the Institute of Politics, was named project director and became the principal author of this book.

This body helped develop a research and work plan, set priorities and monitored progress of the research, and reviewed the products. It kept in touch with the project through correspondence, written reports, exchanging drafts, telephone consultations, a variety of special tasks, rump sessions, and four extended meetings of the entire group—on January 31, 1983, June 6, 1983, January 16, 1984, and September 23–24, 1984. Research and writing of the kind aspired to in this project could not be accomplished without a collaborative, collegial process, and this faculty study group and its members provided exactly the authority, dedication, resourcefulness, and sagacity which it was designed to. Although the book was made possible by funds granted by the Revson Foundation, the statements made and views expressed are solely the responsibility of the author.

There were five fundamental components to the overall research effort which produced this book. First, there was an exposition of central hypotheses and principles, the essential questions to be addressed, comprising the conceptual framework of the project. Second, we undertook a broad survey by mail of all senior federal policymakers from the last twenty years. Third, lengthy interviews were done with 20 policymakers and 16 journalists nominated by their peers as having been particularly competent in making policy and covering the federal government, respectively. Fourth, six case studies were written, providing detailed examination of differing press roles and impacts in significant federal policy decisions over the past two decades. And fifth, we reached some findings and conclusions, drawing from what we discovered or generated that was of particular value—for future analytical inquiry as well as for better public understanding, strengthened performance of practitioners, and improved teaching.

Professor Gary Orren's conceptual treatment in the Prologue notes the significance of the growth in both the press and the government, discusses in theoretical terms the role of the press in our democratic system, and observes that the changes in the relationship in the last twenty-five years go far beyond what most observers and participants would have predicted. Material from the survey and interviews is woven throughout the book's narrative and analysis, and appendices are included to elucidate our methodology and results. Overall findings are discussed in the opening and closing chapters.

The case studies are even more extensively drawn upon in the following chapters, and deserve further comment. In selecting cases that would provide illuminating insights into the subject matter, we employed a range of variables. We sought cases in different time frames and administrations, in different executive branch departments involving both domestic and foreign policy issues, and in Congress. We looked for stories to demonstrate government officials reacting to and anticipating press coverage and using the press. And we chose cases showing different kinds of impact on policymaking procedures and on policy content, and focusing on the specific role of television.

Each of the cases developed is a single exposition of significant press–policymaking interaction: the 1969 reorganization of the Postal Department, the resignation of Vice-President Agnew, the decision of President Carter not to deploy the neutron bomb, the relocation of 700 families from the Love Canal area in New York State, the Reagan administration's support of a tax exemption for Bob Jones University, and the 1984 suspension of Social Security Disability reviews. David Whitman wrote the neutron bomb, Bob Jones, Social Security, and postal reorganization cases; Wendy O'Donnell the Agnew case; and Martin Linsky the Love Canal case.

The six case studies are published in full in a separate book published by W. W. Norton entitled *How the Press Affects Federal Policymaking: Six Case Studies*.

Harvard's new Press–Politics Center, mentioned above, will encourage more understanding by government officials about the role and value of the media, better coverage by media professionals of government and politics, better analysis of public policies affecting the media, and more knowledge of how the media influence our political processes and governmental institutions. It will pursue these goals through teaching of present and future public managers and policy-makers, applied research, educational programs for print and television practitioners, and conferences and symposia for joint consideration of media–government problems. This book is an early manifestation, in motivation, strategy, and product, of what the new center is all about.

Jonathan Moore
Director, Institute of Politics
August 1985

THINKING ABOUT THE PRESS AND GOVERNMENT

GARY R. ORREN

66 IF A TREE falls in the forest, and the media are not there to cover it, has the tree really fallen?"

That caption from a *Saturday Review* cartoon conveys a significant truth: the press has become one of the most potent institutions in contemporary society.

This is a particularly opportune time to engage the issue of press–government relations. First, we are experiencing the convergence of two important trends in recent American history: revolutionary changes in the size and sophistication of both government and the press. As these two institutions have grown in complexity and influence, the importance of understanding their interplay has risen as well. Second, there is no lack of lively debate on the subject. Yet the dialogue— however heated—invariably rests on anecdotal evidence and personal impressions. It is often wide of the mark.

The Growth of Government and the Media

We are so accustomed to the ubiquity of government and the press in daily life that we tend to take their presence for granted. We must remind ourselves that the prominence of the press and the federal bureaucracy has in fact sprung from quite recent transformations, so rapid and complete as to have dimmed our collective memory of the world left behind. The first development has been the unprecedented growth of the federal government. Prior to World War I, the total number of appointed civilian officials employed by the government rose at a steady but modest pace: from 3,000 at the end of the Federalist period, to 95,000 as Grover Cleveland assumed office in 1881, to nearly half a million by 1925. The subsequent growth in the number of administrative agencies and employees during the Depression and World War II was explosive: the federal government now employs more than 2.7 million civilians.[1]

While the number of federal employees has risen relatively little in the last forty years, the responsibilities that the government has assumed have proliferated beyond anyone's prediction. Before World War II, public officials in general and federal officials in particular played an extremely limited role in the administration of American life. Since then, the government has launched a sweeping array of economic and social initiatives (in health, civil rights, education, housing, manpower, consumer protection, the environment, energy, and transportation, to name just a few). At the same time, the government jettisoned its isolationism in the international arena. Greater involvement in world affairs and the widening scope of domestic concerns is evident in the amount of money spent and the volume of regulations issued by the federal government: since 1955, national spending has doubled in constant dollars and the number of federal regulations has risen sixfold.[2]

During the same years of government expansion, the news media too began to assume an unprecedented level of influence in American life. The growing democratization of a government previously dominated by an elite minority was both cause and consequence of greater public access to news of national affairs. With the advent of the broadcast media, the evolution of the news industry accelerated sharply. This increase in the degree and immediacy of the average American's access to information has been as sudden as it is significant. As William Rivers acutely observed, "Thirty years ago, when D. W. Brogan wrote his classic *Politics in America,* he did not consider it necessary even to mention the role of the media in the American political process."[3]

Within the span of a single generation, the American press has been transformed from a nearly invisible spectator to a principal actor in the American political arena, one frequently described as the "fourth branch" of American government. We have become a society fueled by information, fast approaching what has been dubbed the "first amendment regime."

The enhanced role of the media stems in part from the greater education of the public; it was not until 1970 that a majority of Americans had completed at least four years of high school. With education comes both an interest in news and a greater capacity to assimilate it. Equally significant is the technological progress in mass communication systems, especially in the last fifty years. The United States has known truly national media only since the development of radio in the 1930s. Before then, the media consisted almost entirely of newspapers, which are by nature parochial and decentralized. Radio broadcasts, unheard of sixty years ago, now command a daily audience of 92 million people. In 1950, fewer than 10 percent of American households owned television sets; today 98 percent of American households have at least one television set (which is tuned in, on average, more than seven hours a day). The evening news programs on the three networks have an average daily viewership of 56 million people.

Inevitably, the vast audience for news has influenced the size of the press corps that collects and presents the news. The Washington press corps has tripled in number since the end of World War II, with a more than fourfold growth in radio and TV reporters over the last twenty years.[4] There are now approximately 10,000 news journalists from more than 3,000 news organizations operating in Washington alone. Not only has their number expanded, but the press corps has also changed its approach to covering the news. As recently as the 1930s, a president could restrict his exposure through the media by holding press conferences off the record, or by arranging for the press not to write about or photograph his physical disability.[5] In the age of fiercely independent journalism, such attempts to define the scope of news coverage sound strangely primitive. Today journalists are much less restrained by government and far more intrusive.

With the expansion of both the government and the media over the past fifty years, special governmental units devoted to communications—variously labeled public relations, public information, public liaison, and press offices—have grown apace. Such offices are certainly not unique to the post–New Deal period; even Thomas Jefferson, an outspoken champion of a press completely free of government interference, established a newspaper under governmental auspices to promulgate his views. Nevertheless, the growth of public relations activities in the government since Franklin Roosevelt's time has been staggering.

Only four or five White House staff members were engaged in public relations under Roosevelt, about 5 percent of his staff. In Ronald Reagan's White House the public relations staff numbers at least fifty, or approximately 25 percent of the senior staff. Congress attempted one of the first head counts of public relations officials throughout the government during Roosevelt's first term: 146 full-time and 124 part-time government employees. By 1964, about 3,000 federal government employees worked in the public information field, according to one study; in 1976, the number of public relations people in the government had swelled to 19,000, according to another.[6]

In 1978, the federal government ranked as America's twenty-fifth largest advertiser. The amount of government money spent to produce media messages and buy media time and space exceeded the combined expenditures of such highly visible commercial advertisers as Exxon, American Airlines, and Schlitz.[7] All in all, the government currently spends more money and uses more people to disseminate news than news organizations do to collect it.

In short, the last fifty years have witnessed the rise of both the bureaucratic state and the media state, a rise more dramatic than anything contemplated by observers a half century ago, let alone by the Founding Fathers. However, the issue of press impact on the government has not suddenly appeared. Its roots can be traced to the history and traditions of this country, to the theory of democracy, and to the nature of decision making in the public sector. To advance our understanding of the interconnections between the press and government, then, let us consider three connections—historical, democratic, and managerial ones—that bear heavily on the linkage between journalism and public affairs.

The Historical Connection

There has always been a close link between the technology of the media and the operation of the American government.[8] In the first years of the nation, newspaper circulation was severely limited, a pattern consistent with a political system in which influence was confined to a small group of political leaders. In the early 1800s mass readership local newspapers (the penny press) appeared, fostering the emergence of mass political parties and widespread public participation. In the late nineteenth century, the growth of national magazines of opinion encouraged the development of national policy-oriented interest groups such as the Progressive reformers. Finally, the invention of electronic journalism in the twentieth century allowed public officials to build independent, personal followings, one of the key features of contemporary government and politics.

We are often tempted to assume that contemporary society is fundamentally different from the past, thinking that we live in the best or the worst of times. While modern American policymakers now court the national press, it would be a mistake to conclude that this relationship was struck up only with the emergence of network television. Indeed, the ties between the federal government and the media were probably never more intimate than in the infancy of the Republic when the press was part of the normal machinery of government—in fact, an instrument of government. The Congressional Act of 1789, which created the State Department, explicitly authorized the secretary of state to select at least three newspapers to serve as official heralds of new laws and resolutions. This provision gradually grew into a system through which government officials bestowed financial rewards and prestige on their allies in the press. Newspapers were frequently created, sponsored, and controlled by political leaders. During the Washington administration, for example, Alexander Hamilton and the Federalists created the *Gazette of the United States* to carry their views. Thomas Jefferson retaliated by creating the *National Gazette* with the assistance of the Republican Party. Each man accused the other of abusing the press for personal benefit.[9]

Press–government ties were quite close during those early days, but the interplay of the two has been substantial throughout the full span of American history. Until the middle of the nineteenth century, the ardent partisanship of American journalism was its most notable quality; neutral or independent newspapers were an anomaly. Government leaders and politicians continued to maintain close alliances with newspapers as official or semi-official propaganda organs. Indeed,

President Andrew Jackson's famous Kitchen Cabinet was actually composed of a trio of newspapermen who ran the *Washington Globe,* a paper which served as government spokesman during the Jackson and Van Buren administrations.

After the Civil War, the press–government relationship gradually became less incestuous. The impact of the press on government affairs, however, was hardly less potent. Horace Greely's antislavery editorials in the New York *Weekly Tribune* were immensely influential during the national debate of the 1850s and 1860s. In the decades just before and after 1900, many newspapers launched effective assaults against municipal misgovernment, and the muckraking crusades of weekly and monthly magazines (like *McClure's, Cosmopolitan, and Collier's*) sparked government reforms. Around the same time, the reckless jingoism and yellow journalism of papers like Pulitzer's *World* and Hearst's *Journal* fed the popular fervor for the Spanish American War, overcoming government reluctance for involvement.

Long before Ronald Reagan became the Great Communicator, administrations thus were highly news-conscious. Teddy Roosevelt, who had once made his living as a writer, felt right at home with the press and artfully courted its support. Warren Harding had in fact been a newspaperman before he was elected president. And Franklin Roosevelt—as publicity-minded as any modern-day politician—made skillful use of the print press and radio.

The historical connection between the press and government also grows out of shifting public moods. In a nation with a free, commercial, and highly competitive press, the climate of public opinion crucially shapes what messages the audience reads and hears, for in the end popular tastes are the final arbiter of survival for mass circulation news organizations. Furthermore, journalists themselves usually reflect the prevailing sentiments and values of society. Thus, for example, the surge of chauvinism and appetite for imperialism which gripped the country in the 1890s established a ripe climate for newspapers locked in a struggle for circulation to preach the gospel of manifest destiny and clamor for war.

The temper of the public in our own times has a quite different though no less powerful influence on the press. Over the last twenty years, Americans have expressed growing feelings of disenchantment, distrust, and cynicism toward government. This upsurge of alienation began around 1964, paralleling a stream of political disappointments— political assassinations, race riots, the Vietnam War, Watergate, the energy crisis, hostage takings, and economic recession. It is no accident that press–government relations during these years acquired some adversarial qualities, with press coverage often displaying a negative or condescending tone.

Historians will debate whether the rough correlation between public moods and news coverage means that reporters pander to popular tastes or merely reflect public sentiments, or even whether the press itself creates these public moods. All three possibilities are probably true. From our perspective, however, it is sufficient to emphasize that changing public moods strongly condition the relationship between the press and government.

The Democratic Connection

Debate over the actual and proper relationship between the press and the government has assumed new urgency as the media have gained a more commanding role in public affairs. That role has expanded as democracy has moved from "classical" democracy, to "party / elite" democracy, to the current stage of "media" democracy.

The classical doctrine of democracy was rooted in the idea of popular sovereignty: the power to govern and decide political issues was vested in the public. Government was not only for the people but also of and by the people. This 18th century vision, with its presumption that citizens could discover a common good through rational argument and debate, is the one that permeates American civics books and dominates popular discourse.

In this populist view of democracy, the media play a key role as "middlemen" between the government and the governed. At one time or another, most of the Founding Fathers agreed with Madison's observation that "a popular government, without popular information, or the means of acquiring it, is but a prologue to a farce or a tragedy; or perhaps both."[10] From time to time we hear less eloquent echoes of this image of the press—statements like "American democracy simply would not work if the American people were not informed [by the

7

press] about what government is doing.''[11] Presumably, the process is that the press tells the public what they need to know, the people then decide what they want, and the press helps communicate these decisions back to policymakers.

One of the main contributions of American political science was the discovery that in fact this is not what happens. A diverse group of distinguished thinkers—including V. O. Key, Jr., E. E. Schattschneider, Joseph Schumpeter, and Walter Lippmann—offered critical reexaminations of classical democratic theory. Despite their different starting points, methodologies, ideological leanings, and even ultimate prescriptions, they all came to the conclusion that classical theory provided a simplistic and erroneous description of the democratic process. What evolved from these analyses was what we might call a party / elite model of democracy.

Empirical research indicated that the American public had neither the knowledge nor the interest to perform the tasks assigned by classical democracy. Some observers expressed a deep distrust of the citizens' capacity for democratic citizenship. Lippmann, for example, argued that citizens were shackled by preconceptions, stereotypes, and selective perceptions that distorted their political judgments, and that few citizens had either the time or the ability to adjust these attitudes. Lippmann the newspaperman did not trust the press to correct this problem; he put his faith instead in an elite cadre of political experts.[12] For many of the same reasons, Schumpeter doubted the public's capacity for self-government; but he argued that democracies nevertheless managed to operate tolerably well because citizens did not have to settle issues themselves. They needed only to choose among political elites in periodic competitive elections. Elected representatives would then do the deciding.[13]

Other critics, such as Key and Schattschneider, agreed that the public lacked many of the requisite skills of democratic citizenship, but emphasized that people did not need to know all that traditional democratic theory required. Like Lippmann and Schumpeter, Key acknowledged the crucial importance of leadership; one of the missing pieces of the classical model was the upper layer of political activists who guided and shaped public opinion.[14] Government leaders therefore enjoy wide discretion in formulating policy. The public exercises

its role chiefly, as Schumpeter suggested, by appraising past government performance, mostly in elections.

According to Key, the main instrumental locus for this political
leadership was the political party. The party provided the mechanism
for change (a crowd of outs booting the ins from office) and an indispensable source of stability (creating "loyalties that transcend and neu-
tralize the vagaries of the opinion of the moment.").[15]

Schattschneider also recognized the limitations of the public, but
agreed with Key that the citizenry probably did not need to know as
much as classical democratic theorists suggested: "It is not necessary
to be an automobile engineer to buy an automobile or an obstetrician
in order to have a baby." He also believed, like Key, that democracy
did not require the public to issue prescriptions for future policy but
"to judge things by their results" and "to establish relations of confidence and responsibility so that [citizens] can take advantage of what
other people know." Similarly, he saw political competition among
political leaders who define and embody alternatives as central to
democracy. The institutional locus for the necessary leadership, organization, and competition was, again, the political party.[16]

The party / elite model of democracy granted the press an important role, but not the eyes and ears of the public as in classical democracy. The same empirical studies that questioned the democratic capacity
of individual citizens also cast doubt on the informing powers of the
press. For example, the public turned out to rely far less on press
information in making its choices than generally assumed. A number
of powerful buffers (including intentional exclusion, selective perception, and lack of understanding) softened the potential impact of media
messages on the general public. Evidence suggested that individuals
were firmly anchored in their original sets of beliefs and more strongly
swayed by friends, family and other groups than by media messages.
The mass media, it appeared, was a rather blunt and surprisingly ineffective weapon for changing public opinion.[17] The media *did,* however, strongly influence the attitudes and behavior of political elites—
those leaders and activists who Lippmann, Schumpeter, Key, and
Schattschneider identified as so central to democracy.

Over the past two decades or so, we have moved to yet a third
stage of democracy, one we might call media democracy. The extraor-

dinary growth of both the federal government and the mass media has expanded the role of the press and limited the influence of other traditional political institutions, particularly political parties. "The media in the United States are the new political parties," according to James David Barber. "The old political parties are gone. What we now have are television and print."[18]

The media now serve as the main, and in many cases the only, source of information for citizens about what is happening in the government and the primary mechanism by which government learns what is happening in the public—two traditional functions of political parties. The media also have replaced the party apparatus as the internal arm of government action, i.e., as the means of communication within the government and among political groups outside the government. Increasingly, the media are even involved in the process of recruiting government officials, as they define the personal attributes required for effective governing and assess future leaders' potential. The media have assumed a greater role in setting the policy agenda, once the exclusive terrain of parties and political leaders. While earlier evidence showed that the media had surprisingly little effect on what people *think,* more recent studies have suggested that the media strongly shape what people think *about.*[19]

Finally, the media have come to perform the quintessential partisan task of scrutinizing and evaluating government performance, even setting the standards of success and failure. The roles of communicator, recruiter, and scorekeeper which political parties once shared are more and more the responsibilities of the media alone. The media have become the forum for policy discussion and debate, both inside and outside the government.

This progression to the third stage of democracy is due largely to the ubiquity of television. In addition to accelerating the long-term decline of political parties, television has profoundly altered the way the press covers public affairs. The intrinsic nature of the technology fosters an emphasis on stories with dramatic (some say melodramatic) and visual appeal. Television has brought with it a more intense, intrusive, and sustained scrutiny of government and government officials; it has personalized news coverage, focusing on the manner, motivations, and emotions of public figures. By vastly accelerating the speed and immediacy of reporting, television has compressed the response time for government leaders and magnified the risks (and consequences) of their mistakes. And with its enormous broadcasting reach, television has significantly widened the potential audience for public affairs. Public officials have had to adjust to the demands and opportunities of this new style of news coverage, one of the hallmarks of media democracy.

The Managerial Connection

The very nature of public management in the United States, particularly those qualities which distinguish the public from the private sector, invites the media to play a crucial role in governmental decision making. Public management in the American system is characterized by fragmentation and diffusion of authority, responsibility that far exceeds control, the need to be responsive to many public and political pressures, and accountability to multiple sources of oversight.[20] In this kind of setting, the media are one of the few available levers for building and sustaining political support inside and outside the government. Government officials must therefore display a degree of sensitivity to the press that is usually not demanded of their private-sector counterparts.

Of course, attention to the press is particularly crucial for those government officials running for office; since their mandates derive entirely and directly from the public, they must cultivate public support through the press. However, even for the vast majority of government appointees, a receptive public and a favorable political environment are essential for the performance of day-to-day tasks. In our political system where power is so fragmented and dispersed, creating such an environment must include dealing with the press. Effective policymakers must be aware of the opinions of various groups and individuals as well as of the public as a whole, and they must be able to communicate their views to these constituencies. That is just as it ought to be; democracy demands that those wielding public power be subjected to continuing and close scrutiny. The press is an indispensable vehicle for fulfilling that requirement.

Changing Connections

We have highlighted three connections between the press and government: historical, democratic, and managerial. Over the last twenty-five years each of these has changed in ways that have intensified the press–government relationship.

Historically, the ties between the press and government always have been close, although their nature has altered and their strength has ebbed and flowed over the years. In the period since 1960 those ties have grown particularly strong. The expanding army of public affairs and communication specialists in government, and the parallel growth in the Washington press corps, have produced ever-greater interconnection. History bears on the connection between reporters and officials in another way. We have noted how the tenor of the times shapes news coverage. The public mood since 1964—cynicism and distrust of public officials—has colored all relations between the press and government.

As for the democratic linkage, during the last quarter century American society has progressed to the third stage of democracy in which the press has usurped many functions once reserved for political parties. The media have become the principal intermediary between the public and its leaders.

Finally, the already fragmented world of public management in the United States has grown still more atomized over the past two decades. Power in Congress has become more widely dispersed, interest groups have proliferated, central party organizations have lost control over the selection of candidates, and the formal authority of the President has waned.[21] Thus, those very properties of our political system which encourage the media's involvement in government affairs have been magnified.

The Current Debate

Just how the press is involved in government affairs is a favorite topic of the principals themselves, both journalists and policymakers. It summons their self-interest and provokes their passions like few other subjects. These discussions inevitably center on the extent, and the quality, of interaction between the two "estates."

- To what extent are the press and the government involved in each other's worlds? Does the press take an active role in shaping government policies or does it simply report what happens? Does the government manipulate the press, or does it just respond to press initiatives?
- Is the relationship between the government and the press friendly or hostile?

Discourse about the press and government naturally covers a wide range of issues. But the dialogue invariably gravitates to these two questions. The debate is waged both on a descriptive level (How actively are the press and government actually involved in each other's affairs, and how amicable are their relations?) and a normative one (What is the proper degree of press–government involvement, and should reporters and officials deal with each other as adversaries or friends?)

Extent of Interaction. Perceptions of the extent of press involvement in the affairs of government might be arrayed along the following continuum:

Neutral Transmitter	Selective Transmitter	Interpreter	Active Participant

Those whose views lie at one extreme see the media as a neutral messenger, simply reporting the news as it occurs and taking no active role in shaping events. Although the media's actions may affect government policy, such effects are considered the inevitable result of objective and unbiased reporting. This view of the press as a dispassionate transmission belt has met with growing skepticism in recent years, and is probably less widespread than it once was, but it has not entirely lost its appeal to journalists. Many reporters style themselves as objective observers charged with conveying the news, not as interpreters of or participants in public affairs. Walter Cronkite ritualized this belief in his famous summation of each evening's newscast, "And that's the way it is."

A slight modification of that view sees the media as selectively transmitting news. This view holds that journalists generally report the news in a neutral way, but that they use criteria other than space considerations in choosing what to report. The bias introduced in this manner may be extremely subtle but also extremely important. From this perspective, an event in government that fails to attract press coverage might never have taken place.

Next along the continuum is the notion that the press typically goes beyond mere reporting and introduces its own subjective interpretations of events. Of course, this is what columnists are paid to do; the idea here, however, is that even those whose job it is to report the facts do so from their own perspective. Reporters are seen as more than play-by-play announcers. They are more analogous to the color commentators of sportscasting who let their personal impressions slip into the narration.[22]

Finally, at the other end of the spectrum from the neutral transmitter, the press is viewed as an active participant in shaping public affairs. Journalists are seen not simply as narrators or even interpreters of events in the governmental arena; they are actors in the performance. According to this argument, the presence and style of press coverage itself has become a significant factor in determining how government officials do their jobs.[23]

The question of the extent of press-government interaction is a two-sided coin; it also involves what the government is doing. A corresponding set of distinctions guides thinking about government vis-à-vis the press. Here the argument ranges from the view that government officials adopt a fairly passive relationship with the press—responding or reacting to press inquiries and coverage, to the view that they are actively engaged in news management—initiating, orchestrating, and manipulating how the news is reported. Again, the debate is waged as often over what the proper degree of involvement should be as over the question of what actually happens.

Friends or Foes?

The other prominent question that dominates thinking on this subject is whether the press and government operate mainly as friends or foes. On that question, the possibilities may be arrayed as follows:

| Enemy | Adversary | Symbiant | Ally |

Very few observers or participants adopt either of the extreme positions, casting the press and the government as enemies locked in bitter combat or as staunch allies.[24] Many do, however, see the media and the government engaged in an adversarial relationship, where each side inhibits the other's ability to meet its objectives. The other dominant view sees the relationship as more symbiotic, with the media and the government supporting each other's pursuit of their respective goals. The emphasis here is on cooperation and mutual benefit.

Although the adversary relationship is also a two-way street, it is generally the adversary press which is emphasized. Some prominent journalists have emphatically endorsed this adversarial stance. Tom Wicker, for example, has stressed "the necessity to encourage the developing tendency of the press to shake off the encumbrance of a falsely objective journalism and to take on an adversary position toward the most powerful institutions of American life."[25] In the same spirit, Max Frankel has hailed the "clean and desirable adversary relationship between the government and the media."[26]

Some people both inside and outside of journalism have condemned this tendency as detrimental to democracy. One of the most controversial critiques of the hostility between the press and government has come from Daniel Patrick Moynihan, who has argued that journalistic practice has become infected with what Lionel Trilling once called the "'adversary culture." Consequently, the press has grown increasingly antagonistic toward American government and society, setting a tone of pervasive dissatisfaction with public policies.[27] More recently, Michael J. O'Neill echoed this criticism in his valedictory address as president of the American Society of Newspaper Editors. "The press has become so adversarial in its relationship with government," he said, "that it threatens the democratic process."[28]

Among those who see press–government relations as primarily adversarial, there is disagreement over the source of the conflict. Sometimes the source is attributed to ideological differences between the two groups (seen either in left–right terms or in anti-authority, anti-establishment terms).[29] Whatever adversarial relationship exists, however, is to a large extent a function of conflicting professional requirements of the two jobs, rather than a function of conflicting values. The task of newsgathering requires, or at least fosters, a probing and critical style. Newspeople want to present exciting, highly visible stories that will attract a large audience; the reporter's objective is to gather the maximum amount of information that departs from the audience's initial knowledge or expectation, i.e., the most "news." Simply put, as veteran media analyst Paul Weaver has said, a reporter's job is:

> to find news and then to write it up. The bigger and more earthshaking the news, the better things are for him and the happier he is . . . when nothing in particular is happening—no scandal, no conflict, no controversy, no dramatic change—then there is no news, there is nothing to write about, and he is out of work.[30]

The professional needs of the journalist (not necessarily a reporter's urge to advocate a particular point of view) thus tend to be at odds with the professional needs of the official. When the bureaucrat's interest in secrecy or a positive story, for example, are pushed up against the interest of the reporter in conflict, controversy, and the unexpected, each are doing their jobs, but tensions are inevitable.

From time to time, attention is called to the government's participation in this conflict. Ithiel de Sola Pool once described that side of the struggle as follows:

> The politician seeks to lull the people with pleasantries of government. The journalist seeks the cold, hard facts of government. Sometimes these don't jibe, whereupon the politician reaches for the nearest microphone and assures the people that the journalist is the worst sort of skunk.[31]

According to this view, the government jousts daily with the press, withholding information, releasing misleading or false statements, censoring the news, and criticizing the press to the public.

Many observers downplay such examples of conflict and instead discern a close institutional bond between reporters and officials. In the words of William Rivers, "The two governments—the official government and the national news media—increasingly form part of a single, symbiotic unit."[32] With mutual suspicion that the government manipulates and lies while the press distorts and entraps, the potential for adversarial relations may be ever-present. In the symbiotic scheme, however, open battles rarely erupt because each side recognizes that the other holds strong cards that it sorely needs. For example, Michael Grossman and Martha Kumar concluded in their study of the news media and the White House, that ''it would be a mistake to view the relationship as basically antagonistic. The adversary elements of the relationship tend to be its most highly visible aspects. Cooperation and continuity are at its core.'' They found that news organizations and public officials go to great lengths to maintain cooperative, cordial relations because both sides gain.[33]

Occupational imperatives—like the strong desire to get exclusive stories and not jeopardize routine channels and sources—cause reporters to curry favor with government officials and cultivate cooperation. Not only does the press get its stories, but the government also benefits: policies are publicized, and the media transmit important information from one part of the government to another, or from the government to the nongovernmental world. This symbiosis includes the reporting of authorized, as well as unauthorized information. As William Lanouette commented in the *National Journal,* ''Leaks are typical of the usual relationship between the government and the press— a relationship in which both sides benefit. They supply the press with accounts of government intrigue at the same time they serve government officials who are working for particular policy objectives.''[34]

Some analysts describe the relationship between the press and government as both adversarial and symbiotic. Ithiel de Sola Pool used two metaphors to illuminate the mixed roles of cronies and combatants:

> The whole relationship of reporter and politician resembles a bad marriage. They cannot live without each other, nor can they live without hostility. It is also like the relationship of competing athletic teams that are part of the same league. It is conflict within a shared system.[35]

Rarely, according to this view, are the press or the government merely spectators; more often they both are active players on the field, including the other team's field, albeit with different interests and different stakes. Even more rarely does hostility break out between the two teams as a result of their adversariness. More often they are, as Edwin Diamond once described them, adversaries in the manner of professional wrestlers: they know each other's moves, understand each other's language, and realize that they must cooperate to perform their respective jobs. Most of their interaction is governed by ritual and convention, although occasionally someone gets hurt almost by accident as a by-product of each doing their jobs in such close quarters.[36]

The relationship thus might be characterized as alternating between "stroking" and "poking."

The Inadequacy of the Debate

Again and again, discussions about the press and government are drawn back to these two basic questions: how extensive and how friendly is the interaction? The answers journalists and officials provide serve as short-hand images for interpreting their worlds. Yet, the more one probes, the more it is clear that these common conceptualizations are inadequate to the task of assessing with precision the impact of the press on federal policymaking.

First, like many if not most simplifications, the distinction between neutral transmitter and active participant, and that between friend and foe, fail to capture what actually occurs. Reality is not as separable and immutable as the distinctions imply. Different journalists have different relationships with various people in government. Those relationships are extremely fluid. They may change over time or even in the course of a single story or a single contact. A journalist might be a neutral transmitter today and an active participant tomorrow, adversarial on one story and cooperative on the next.

Second, there are problems with these conceptions which stem from the answers frequently given to the two questions. Many reporters and officials cling to the view that the press and government are not closely intertwined. They each suggest that their side acts in a proper and professional (i.e., neutral) way and keeps the other at arm's length. Even more often, each side describes the press–government relationship as fundamentally adversarial. However, their private actions usually do not match their public rhetoric.

It is not hard to imagine where these myths originate, and why they are so dearly held by reporters and officials even though they bear little relationship to reality. The rhetoric is consistent with the norms of both journalism and public service. The image of a press corps that avoids active participation in public affairs while striking a skeptical if not adversarial stance toward government fits with the ideals of a free, independent, and objective press that guards the public interest but does not bear any responsibility for the consequences of policymaking.[37] The idea of bureaucrats eschewing active engagement with the press flows from the traditional creed of public administration that emphasizes efficiency, strict adherence to formal grants of authority, technical and substantive expertise, limited discretion, and neutral political competence.[38] These myths persist because they work for their adherents. For journalists the notions of distance and adversariness enable them to do their work without worrying about the impact of what they write and broadcast, and therefore without agonizing beforehand over what may result. For officials, distance and adversariness provide an excuse for not engaging with the press and an explanation other than their own passivity for news coverage which does not serve their interests.

Third, even if we could somehow resolve the debate over how extensive and how friendly the press–government relationship is and ought to be, we still would not advance far toward answering the question of impact, which is the central mission of this study. At the extremes, we could make some logical assumptions: if reporters and officials are intimate and active participants in each other's business, it is likely that the press has a substantial impact. Similarly, if hostility is the norm in their relations, it is likely that from the perspective of policymakers the press hinders their doing their jobs. But even that would tell us relatively little with much precision; and further, our experience and observations suggest that few press–government relationships exist at those extremes. For everything but the extremes, pinpointing the press–government relationship on the continua of distance or friendliness hardly advances our understanding of impact. The press may wield great influence even if it confines itself to transmitting neutral stories, just as any agenda-setting initiative that the press makes may have no impact. Similarly, the influence of the press may be great or small no matter if it is locked in a bitter struggle with the government or engaged in a friendly alliance.

Beyond that, the challenging question is not whether the press influences policymaking, or even in general terms how much it influences policymaking. Nearly everyone, including journalists (at least privately), acknowledges that the influence of the press is substantial.[39] "To be sure, we are fairly certain that there is a media influence," Paul Weaver noted. "What we do not know," he ruefully observed, "is the most important thing of all: what difference this influence makes in the way we . . . govern ourselves."

The Task at Hand

"[Edmund] Burke said there were three estates in Parliament. But in the reporters' gallery yonder there sat a fourth estate more important far than they all."[40] So Thomas Carlyle reckoned the power of the press nearly one hundred and fifty years ago. While many have echoed Carlyle's view, few have suggested with any precision the *nature* of the press effect on government.

And small wonder. The influence of the press is, in Rowland Evans's words, "so intangible, so difficult to define, that it is like catching grains of dust in a sunbeam."[41]

But the time is ripe. The historical, democratic, and managerial connections between the press and government are strong, and getting stronger. The parallel burgeoning of both government and the press over the last fifty years commands our attention. And our grasp of the subject must move beyond the current debate over the extent and friendliness of press–government relations.

Dust specks can be captured, with care and the right tools. And these aspects of the press's effects on democratic government are as crucial as they are elusive. Refining our understanding of the sources and import of these institutional interactions merits and demands our efforts.

CHAPTER ONE

THE PRESS–GOVERNMENT RELATIONSHIP TODAY

JUNE 6, 1977. 6 A.M. General Alfred Starbird scans the front page of his *Washington Post*. He is stunned to see a 14-paragraph story by Walter Pincus under the headline "Neutron Killer Warhead Buried in ERDA Budget," which reports that "The United States is about to begin production of its first nuclear battlefield weapon specifically designed to kill people through the release of neutrons rather than to destroy military installations through heat and blast." The fourth paragraph of the story, which was to become the most memorable, reads: "According to one nuclear weapons expert, the new warhead 'cuts down on blast and heat and thus total destruction, leaving buildings and tanks standing. But the great quantities of neutrons it releases kill people.' " By the time he gets to the end, Starbird is extremely upset.

Starbird is the assistant administrator for national security at the US Energy Research and Development Administration (ERDA), the agency responsible for the development of all US nuclear weapons. A few days before the story appeared, Pincus had been covering a hearing of the House Appropriations Committee. During a break in the testimony, Pincus began to read a just-published transcript of an earlier committee hearing which included testimony from Starbird on upcoming production in the atomic stockpile. Starbird's testimony contained a reference to enhanced radiation (ER) warheads. When the testimony was declassified, that reference had not been deleted, as it was supposed to have been. As Pincus saw it, this was the first public disclosure of the production of neutron weapons. He knew that a front page article in the *Post* would stir debate, although he says now that he did not foresee the scope of what was to emerge.

The development of the ER warhead, or neutron bomb as it came to be known, had begun over twenty years before. In 1955, as a result of war games which were designed to assess the effects of a "successful" defense of Europe, the NATO allies realized that the existing nuclear warheads then arrayed to repel an invasion by the Soviet Union would in the process also devastate friendly territory and civilian polulations, particularly in West Germany. Accordingly, US scientists then set out to develop a "clean" nuclear warhead, one that would limit collateral damage by killing primarily by prompt radiation, rather than by blast or radioactive fallout. A weapon that relied on a concentrated momentary burst of radiation for its effect would have at least the possibility of being able to defend Western Europe without destroying it as well. Before he had left office, President Gerald Ford had signed off on funding for production of the weapon, and Starbird's testimony was defending that appropriations request.

It soon became clear that Starbird was not the only person who was going to be upset by what Pincus had reported. During the next ten months, the list of those who would be concerned about the article and its implications would include many members of the US Senate, most of the leaders of the NATO countries, hundreds of thousands of political activists, and, of course, President Jimmy Carter. As Zbigniew Brzezinski, then the national security adviser, later put it, "The *Post* article touched off a political explosion that reverberated throughout the United States and Europe."

The initial White House reaction to the story on the morning it appeared was to concentrate on finding out more about the weapon and limiting Carter's connection with it. "The president," then-Press Secretary Jody Powell later recalled, "didn't know anything about the weapon at the time, so we initially chased around to get information on it. You could tell by the way the story was played that it was going to be a stinkeroo, although no one anticipated the trouble it eventually caused."[1] White House officials were able to establish quickly that Ford's decision to go ahead with production of the bomb had not been formally reviewed by President Carter. Later that afternoon, Powell told Pincus that Carter would delay the production decision until "he had specifically approved the program."

John Marcum of the NSC staff was asked by Brzezinski to prepare a briefing on the weapon with recommendations for a public response, and he was one of the first to begin to appreciate the dimensions of what was in store. Marcum was worried about the language in the fourth paragraph of Pincus's story, quoting an anonymous weapons expert:

> Our basic recommendation on press guidance was that we ought to provide a more rational perspective on this as an anti-tank weapon. We felt we had to remedy the absurd impression the initial stories created: that this weapon was some weird thing that hit a building, leaving the building intact but killing the people inside.[2]

At the State Department, only a handful of people had even heard of the enhanced radiation weapons, and there was no sense there that the weapons held any great military significance. The typical reaction at State, as Lou Finch, one of the desk officers recalled, was, "Is the neutron bomb a super killer that nobody ever heard of, and have these crazy guys at the Pentagon been hiding this in their back pocket all these years?"[3]

With the White House trying to establish distance and the State Department assuming it was someone else's problem, the task of dealing with the continuing story in the *Post* and with the other interested news organizations and their reporters initially was relegated to the Department of Defense. At Defense, where the neutron bomb was one of its own so to speak, responsibility for dealing with the issue was delegated. Secretary of Defense Harold Brown was not particularly concerned. Brown had once been director of the Livermore Laboratory, where the concept of enhanced radiation had first been worked on; he was thoroughly familiar with the weapons. His knowledge fed his response: "My reaction to the story was just that it cast ER weapons in the worst possible light, saying that they destroyed people and saved property, neglecting to say that the 'people' were Soviet tank crews and the 'property' was the houses in Germany that would fall on civilians and kill them if the property was destroyed. . . . I thought that since it was an incorrect characterization and there was nothing new in it, it wouldn't have a very big effect.[4] Brown's assistant secretary for public affairs, Thomas Ross, had never heard of neutron weapons, so the job of handling the press at the Pentagon was delegated primarily to Donald Cotter, Brown's special assistant for atomic energy. Cotter was a nuclear weapons engineer who was one of those most responsible for assuring that the ER program was fairly represented in the policy and budget process. His guidelines for ERDA and the Department of Defense (DOD) on dealing with the press did no more than confirm that ERDA was working on an enhanced radiation warhead, and had been doing so since the early 1960s.

The strongest and most public reaction in the government came from the US Senate. Senator Mark Hatfield (R–OR) quickly introduced an amendment to the appropriations bill to eliminate funding for ER weapons. The pending fight in the Senate helped Pincus and the *Post* keep the story alive. The *Post* editorialized against the weapon two days after the first Pincus story appeared. For the first ten days, the Senate debate and the *Post* fueled each other to keep the story going until the rest of the media began to get involved on their own. On June 10, the Defense Department drafted a 1½-page rationale for the weapon which tried to minimize the significance of the enhanced radiation warheads. Pincus was still essentially the only reporter covering the story and he saw the press guidance as disingenuous in the extreme: "The Pentagon wanted the money to produce the weapon, and the way they tried to kill the interest was to say 'there's nothing new about this, it's just a modernization program.' That line was passed to the White House, too. Now I had already talked to the people who were convincing the White House that there was nothing new. They had all told me previously that this was a new weapon and they thought it was the greatest thing since sliced bread. I knew they were playing both sides of the issue, so I just began to look for ways to prove what had already been told me by these very same people; that this was a special, new weapon system."[5]

Beginning in mid-June, Cotter began meeting with Pincus on a background basis. The interviews initially were reasonably cordial and constituted a kind of diplomatic minuet. But reaching a meeting of the minds was almost impossible. Cotter's executive officer, who sat in on several of the meetings, remembers it this way: "If Cotter told Pincus something in his story was inaccurate, then the presumption became that the sentence above must be accurate. Moreover, if we said something was inaccurate, then you had to justify what you said. It was very difficult to explain why some of what Pincus wrote was inaccurate without getting into classified information."[6]

One of the turning points in the coverage occurred on June 17, when NBC News ran a film clip, obtained from the Armed Forces Radiology Research Institute, showing what happened to monkeys when they were irradiated with 4,600 rads of neutron radiation. The results, not surprisingly, were quite gruesome. Pincus was then working half-time for NBC. NBC correspondent John Hart told him that the clip had spurred a big viewer reaction and, on June 22, Pincus wrote an article on the clip. ABC ran the clip on June 24, and NBC ran it again several weeks later on the *Today* show. Pincus's June 22 story spawned a phone call from a source who suggested that what Pincus had found in Starbird's testimony was just the tip of the iceberg of a plan to shift most nuclear artillery to an enhanced radiation basis. That information, particularly as it related to specific weapons, was highly classified and on that basis the Defense Department declined to comment when Pincus called to ask for confirmation.

Pincus's article with the new information about the broader implementation of enhanced radiation weaponry led the paper on June 24, and kicked off not only another wave of stories and editorials in the *Post,* but substantially heightened interest among the rest of the press as well. The continuing coverage consistently used some version of the language from Pincus's original story, namely that the bomb "killed people but left buildings intact." There was very little in the news or commentaries which reflected the Defense Department's view of the weapon or any perspective other than what Secretary Brown termed the "incorrect characterization" in that first article.

Cotter and Pincus had scheduled a meeting for June 24, and Cotter let his irritation show. He was deeply annoyed by Pincus's use of the phrase "killer warheads" and by the description of the appropriation as having been "buried" in the ERDA budget. He argued that Pincus knew that the enhanced radiation warheads had gone through normal and required channels so that buried was very misleading, and

25

that all warheads kill. Pincus describes Cotter as "livid" at that session, but defends the coverage: "I had no problem at all with saying that the warheads were 'buried.' I didn't say they were hidden; 99% of the people would not have known to have looked in ERDA's budget to find them. I also had no problem with the 'kills people and leaves buildings standing' tags; that was the beauty of the weapon and that was the way people at the labs talked about it. Those were their terms, not mine. The 'killer warhead' phrase was coined by a *Post* headline writer but I did use it a number of times. It's true that all weapons are killer weapons. To be brutally honest, I'd have to say that it helped people to focus on the weapon, so it didn't hurt the cause. You do develop slogans and it had a nice swing to it."[7]

At the meeting, Cotter tried to convince Pincus that secrecy about the weapons was important because Soviets would have a major re-equipment problem once they were deployed. Pincus went back and wrote a story about that, under the headline "Pentagon Wanted Secrecy On Neutron Bomb Production." The story prompted an editorial in the Sunday *Post* which said, "The whole thing has the look of a black bag job."[8]

Cotter was enraged and called the Pentagon's press expert, Thomas Ross, for advice. Ross discouraged a direct response, but Cotter went ahead anyway: "Ross, I think, regarded me as something of a wild man, running around with these plans to modernize the nuclear weapons that Jimmy Carter said we were going to get rid of. This was a serious $3 billion weapon program these guys were taking cracks at, saying it was being run in a dishonorable fashion. You can't take that shit when you're the guy responsible for the program. These stories were causing all sorts of problems for us, and promised to continue to; the Allies were nervous, the Russians were making hay out of it, and people on the Hill, like Scoop Jackson, were really pissed. With an article coming out every day I finally reached the end of my rope and went in to talk to Charlie Seib, the *Post* ombudsman."[9]

Unbeknownst to Cotter, Seib had already become disturbed by the *Post*'s use of the "killer warhead" phrase, and had written two memos to the paper's top editors questioning its use.[10] Cotter met with Seib with Pincus present. Seib listened and encouraged Cotter to send a letter to the editor. Pincus said nothing at all.

Back at the Pentagon, Ross urged Cotter not to send the letter. After several strongly worded drafts were toned down, Cotter sent a letter which the *Post* eventually published. In it he stated that ERDA had followed all the statutory procedures with regard to the enhanced radiation weapons, including keeping Congress informed, and that the degree of classification for the program was what was required, "no more, no less," to help prevent the spread of the technology to US adversaries.[11]

Early in July, the Defense Department began a low-key media campaign on behalf of the weapons in anticipation of the Senate vote on the Hatfield amendment. Brown was interviewed by NBC. Background briefings on the technical details of the enhanced radiation warhead and on how it compared to existing weapons were provided for Pentagon reporters. Senate supporters of the neutron bomb were worried and pressed for more help, particularly looking to the White House for a clearer commitment. Finally, on July 12, the eve of the Senate vote, President Carter made a crucial intervention. At a televised press conference, he asked for continuing funding while he was making up his mind. All three networks led the news with Carter's comments.

The next day the Senate voted 58–38 against the Hatfield amendment and in favor of a compromise which prohibited funds from being used to build enhanced radiation weapons until the president certified that they were in the national interest. Congress would then have 45 days to disapprove the weapons by a concurrent resolution of both houses. The debate in the Senate featured attacks on the press coverage by the supporters of the neutron bomb and ringing defenses of the press by opponents.

The Senate vote ended the first phase of the neutron bomb story, but the storm was just beginning to stir in Europe. After the Senate debate made it clear that the neutron bomb was to be deployed on European soil, there was increased interest abroad. Egon Bahr was an important figure in the liberal wing of the ruling party in the tenuous coalition government headed by Helmut Schmidt in West Germany. Four days after the vote in the Senate, Bahr published an article on the bomb in *Vorwearts,* the weekly party newspaper. Under the headline "Is Mankind Going Crazy,"[12] he picked up the themes of Pincus's original story. Other European columns and editorials echoed the view that the neutron warhead was a singularly perverse invention.

Soon the Soviets got into the act, generating a substantial propaganda campaign against the bomb which helped reinforce growing popular dismay. Beginning right after the Bahr article, one Soviet front organization after another began issuing denunciations of the neutron bomb. TASS and *Izvestia* published a steady diet of critical articles, culminating in a broad statement on US foreign policy and the bomb in TASS on July 30. It was the first such statement issued by TASS since 1974. The Soviet activity helped stir the pot, intensifying the concern that was already building among many noncommunists in Western European countries.

One of the problems that quickly became apparent was that the arguments which had worked for the Carter administration in the US Senate sounded very different in Europe. At home, the enhanced radiation warheads were justified as providing greater security for the United States by being a more credible threat. The neutron bomb killed people through the release of neutrons rather than heat or blast, thereby inflicting less collateral damage to the countryside than the weapons they were to replace. That would make it more conceivable than before that a Soviet invasion could be repelled without either nuclear escalation or the devastation of Europe. Thus, for example, at one point the Pentagon was distributing diagrams showing the radius of effect of the neutron warheads, with drawings of tanks being blown up and soldiers dying. In Europe that picture looked much less comforting than it did in the US; rather than increased security, the message to many people there reasonably appeared to be that deployment of the neutron bomb would lower the nuclear threshold and increase the chance of a limited nuclear war. To ordinary Europeans, the argument that is was a more credible deterrent because it was believable that it *could* actually be used, meant that it actually *might* be used.

Most allied leaders in Western Europe favored deployment as part of their NATO responsibilities, because the US government had favored it, and because they believed that deterrence was more likely a result than use. But the fuss about the weapon made them look to Washington for a strong commitment to produce the bomb before they tried to defend its deployment. This was particularly true for West German Chancellor Helmut Schmidt; West Germany was one of the three countries, along with Belgium and Holland, where US policy-makers actually wanted to deploy the weapons. Schmidt did not believe that he could maintain public support for deploying them, unless he could give the impression that they were being pushed on him by the Americans. Carter, on the other hand, was hoping for clearcut early commitments from the allies. He wanted to be able to say that *he* was the one being pushed, so that the decision to go ahead with production would not seem so harsh in light of his commitment in his inaugural address to "move this year a step toward our ultimate goal—the elimination of all nuclear weapons from this Earth."[13] On September 16, Schmidt and Carter talked about the bomb on the phone. Carter warned that he did not want to proceed with production and "get shot down as an international ogre."[14]

In November, with signs that the debate over the bomb was reviving the European peace movement, the Carter administration finally implemented a comprehensive strategy for building support, even though the president had yet to make his decision. Articles in government publications began to explain the policy considerations behind deployment. The Department of Defense began to generate pro-bomb material for consumption by the allies. There was even an ill-fated effort (exposed and ridiculed by Pincus in the *Post*) to change the name of the bomb from the neutron bomb to the "reduced blast / enhanced radiation weapon."[15]

Both the Soviets and the Americans stepped up propaganda efforts during the beginning of 1978. In January, prompted by the increasing success of Soviet diplomatic pressure against the bomb and the Soviet's covert and semicovert infiltration of the European anti-bomb movement, the US decided to institute its own covert action program. A plan was approved by Brzezinski and Vance which involved asking sympathizers and supporters in the European press corps to give more favorable coverage to the bomb. As explained by Leslie Gelb, then director of politico military affairs at the State Department, it was simply designed to produce some better stories about the bomb: "We weren't trying to disrupt the renting of convention halls [for anti-bomb rallies] or anything like that. This campaign was chosen to supplement our overt activities, like having the embassies talk to European journalists. We thought that more favorable press coverage might help show the

European public that we weren't trying to upset the nuclear balance, that the neutron bomb was a legitimate modernization move."[16]

The details of the covert action campaign have remained classified. A sampling of the British and German press coverage from the time indicates that coverage favorable to the neutron bomb and sharply critical of the Soviet propaganda campaign began appearing frequently in February and March. A March 1 report by the United States Information Agency noted that "a trend in Western European media toward the acceptance of the neutron bomb as part of the NATO defense arsenal was intensified in the last two weeks."[17]

The growing media support for neutron warheads seemed to create more latitude for key European leaders in handling the issue. While the US and the USSR were conducting a battle over public opinion and European press coverage of the bomb, the US and its NATO allies were quietly working out an agreement for production and deployment.

The discussions were taking place at the same time that the anti-bomb sentiment was reaching a peak in Europe. The high water mark of the protest movement was probably the International Forum, which was held in Amsterdam on March 18–19. Fifty thousand demonstrators listened to speeches by Daniel Ellsberg, among others, and then marched through the streets of the city in the rain, chanting "Ban the neutron bomb." Organizers of the rally sold 400,000 anti-neutron bomb window bills, stickers, and buttons and collected the signatures of 1.2 million Dutch citizens (there are only about 10 million Dutch voters in all) on anti-bomb petitions.

The US and the Allies worked out what Gelb called an "elaborately choreographed" scenario to make the NATO plan public.[18] It included a commitment to continued production by the US, an effort to make deferral dependent on a Soviet decision to defer the SS–20, and a consensus for deployment from NATO as a whole rather than support from each nation individually. On Saturday, March 18, with the agreement ready to go, Brzezinski sent a two-page decision memo to Carter, who was vacationing in Georgia. Vance says that they decided to send a decision memo rather than an information memo because they "wanted to make absolutely sure, one final time, that the president was really on board."

Carter read the memo and promptly sent word back that he was vetoing the deal. Gelb remembers being awakened early the next morning, Sunday, March 19, by a phone call from the senior NSC aide who was the first one to receive the message from Carter back at the White House. "You won't believe what happened," Gelb recalls him saying, "he checked the wrong box." [19]

Those involved have various theories as to what was the crucial factor in Carter's decision. Vance has speculated that when the president finally saw the memo, committing himself in effect to the deployment of a weapon in Europe that the allies, for whose security it had been developed, would accept but not individually request, his "innermost self rebelled." Brzezinski suggests that Carter "felt that the European governments . . . were attempting to push all the political costs on him." Journalists such as Richard Burt of the *New York Times,* Pincus of the *Post,* and some syndicated columnists speculated in print that Carter was persuaded by UN Ambassador Andrew Young, an opponent of the bomb, that putting it into production would weaken the US position at the upcoming UN Special Session on Disarmament. Yet it is clear that the way the bomb had been characterized was also an influential factor.

Carter returned to Washington and, on March 26, told his dismayed advisers that he was not only against the NATO arrangement, but that he had decided to cancel the bomb. Brzezinski, Vance, and others began preparing a plan for announcing the cancellation as they were simultaneously continuing to try to convince the president to change his mind.

For a week, they had more success at keeping the decision out of the news than they did at convincing Carter to reverse himself. Then, on April 4, the decision to cancel was reported in the *New York Times.* The information had been leaked to *Times* reporter Richard Burt. The White House responded with a wave of official denials that the decision had been made. An anonymous White House source was quoted as saying that the "genuine reappraisal" of the bomb was not yet over. [20] The leak generated a new onslaught of public and private pressure on the president from outside the White House, coming mostly from those in the press and in the Congress who thought it would be a terrible mistake not to go forward with production and deployment.

Finally, on April 7, Carter announced his decision. The characterization of what he was doing was modified; he described it as a deferral rather than outright cancellation of production of the weapon. But the effect was the same. Brzezinski noted at the time that Carter believed that if he had approved the neutron bomb, "his administration would be stamped forever as the administration which introduced bombs that kill people but leave buildings intact." Those words, of course, came almost verbatim from the anonymous nuclear weapons expert quoted ten months earlier in Walter Pincus's article that started it all.

It was the Pentagon that built the bomb and the government's own expert who coined the description that was so damaging, but it is obvious that the press was central to the policymaking here. It had a powerful influence on the process of decision making and the policy outcome. And the personal and political fallout from Carter's decision was substantial.

The whole saga began in the press, with Walter Pincus's story in the *Washington Post*. Responding to the story was the form that some of the policymaking took. The day it appeared, senior officials in the White House and the Department of Defense concentrated primarily on how to deal with the press, not on the merits or demerits of the neutron bomb. The issue was not what ought to be the administration's position on enhanced radiation warheads, but what ought to be the administration's position on the Pincus story. That pattern continued. The consideration of press strategies became a major focus of policymakers' time and energy throughout the ten months until the deferral was announced. The development of plans for trying to influence the coverage and thereby influence public perceptions about the issue, was not the exclusive prerogative of Jody Powell and Thomas Ross, whose job descriptions called for management of press relations. It was also given attention at the cabinet secretary level and at the highest levels of the White House staff.

The agreement with the NATO allies that Carter vetoed was as significantly a press strategy as a neutron bomb strategy. The Dutch, the Belgians, the Danes, and the Norwegians were not willing individually to support European deployment. It was all the rest of the allies could do to prevent them from opposing the decision. So the US, in consultation with the Germans and the British, developed the "elaborately choreographed" scenario to create what one of Gelb's aides characterized as "the appearances of a concerted alliance position" when none existed.[21] A carefully worded NATO communique was drafted which stressed that deployment of the neutron bomb was tied to the failure of the Soviets to defer the SS–20; in this way none of the NATO countries, including the US, would appear to be supporting the weapon in and of itself. After the statement was issued, the Americans, Germans, British, and Canadians were to issue their own statements explicitly endorsing it. The rest of the NATO allies would have no comment. Gelb's deputy co-authored the communique. It was, he said later, "more a diplomatic document than a public relations document, but it was all public relations. When I wrote the statement I was considering quite a bit how the press would cover it."[22] The goal was to have the press convey a very specific picture of the policy and its context, a picture which did not capture exactly what had taken place but was a view that the NATO countries were willing to present to the world. The whole plan was, as one senior Defense Department official said, "a sort of theater, where each side, after being rehearsed, would say just enough to satisfy the other side."

It may not be possible to prove that the Pincus story killed the neutron bomb, but without his story there might have been no issue at all. Questions about production and deployment had not yet been raised in the routine course of events by the Senate, the administration, or the allies. As Secretary of Defense Harold Brown later summed it up, "Without the Pincus articles, they [neutron warheads] would have been deployed and nobody would have noticed."[23] Once the coverage began, the dormant neutron bomb policy issue was very much awake. The intensity of the coverage itself made it a major issue. The press attention resonated with the response of some US Senators and among some elements of the public to put the issue high on the agenda for the Carter administration. The more the attention in the press, the less the Defense Department was able to deal with the issue alone and the more the White House, and the president, became directly involved.

The Ford and Carter administrations had done nothing to prepare the public for the neutron bomb debate. After the Pincus story was published, the government could never quite catch up with the momentum that the article created. The image from the initial article had blasted into the consciousness of Senators and the Washington press corps, and seeped its way into public opinion here and abroad. Reframing the issue was a much more difficult job than creating a favorable impression in the first place would have been. Government officials found themselves reacting, unable to seize the initiative. For a long period of time, part of the government, particularly at State and most of the policymakers at DOD except Cotter, adopted a strategy of not responding at all in the hope that the story would simply go away. As Ross reasoned later, "By creating campaigns, giving heavy rebuttals, you prolong the issue rather than get rid of it."[24] They only answered the questions they had to, and only with the minimum amount of information. Later, most of the government turned to a more affirmative but very low-key approach. This involved offering press guidance to other officials who might need to respond, writing articles in government publications laying out the argument in favor of the weapon, and briefing reporters. Only Don Cotter pursued an aggressive press strategy, although all of those involved worried about what to do. Even Cotter's approach was primarily reacting to coverage, rather than trying to influence it in advance. None of the approaches seemed to make much of a difference.

Some of those close to the president believe that one of the consequences of the story was damage to Carter's political future.[25] Brzezinski wrote in his memoirs that as a result of the neutron bomb controversy, "the President's credibility was damaged in Europe and at home." Jody Powell told us that "the neutron bomb fueled what came to be two of our biggest problems in Washington, the appearance of indecisiveness and the notion that Carter was weak on defense." "Politically," Vance wrote in his memoirs, "the costs were extremely high." What makes this question particularly interesting is that a press which saw the whole story in a light different than the one painted by Pincus's original article might have presented Carter in a very different way. Roger Morris, a former NSC aide, made this point in the *Columbia Journalism Review*. Without changing any of the facts, he suggested, "There were elements of another story, a story of Carter striving to discipline an autonomous and insubordinate bureaucracy, of Carter standing up to the Germans and insisting that they take their fair share of responsibility for mutual defense policies, of the President skillfully manipulating opponents at home and abroad.''[26]

When Carter finally decided to defer, there were significant consequences beyond his own political future. Brzezinski believes that: ''The neutron bomb affair was a major setback in US–European relations, particularly in our relations with West Germany. Personal relations between Carter and Schmidt took a further turn for the worse and never recovered.''[27] In the aftermath of the debate about the bomb, officials realized that they had to take the press into account in formulating nuclear weapons policy in Europe. The Reagan administration set up a cabinet-level interagency team for the sole purpose of coordinating the administration's public relations abroad; the team was to give special emphasis to obtaining favorable media coverage and influencing younger Europeans to adopt sympathetic attitudes toward the presence of nuclear weapons and US nuclear policy.

It is impossible to separate the role of the press from the policymaking here. The stakes were high and the press was very much a part of the story. Yet in one form or another, that pattern was repeated throughout our three years of research into how the press affects policymaking.

Finding that the press is central to what goes on in government should not be news, certainly not to those who work in Washington, but it may be an uncomfortable reality for them. Both journalists and reporters have their reasons for hanging on to an unrealistic view of their interaction. For the journalists, acknowledging their influence undermines their felt need to keep their distance from policymaking. Their own ethic demands that they report *on* government, not, in anything more than the most passive sense, be a part *of* it. Not only do journalistic practices, such as the value on objectivity, drive them to that position, but the consequences of understanding their influence are complicating. If they acknowledge to themselves the potential impact of what they are reporting and publishing in a specific case, then they may be said to have contributed to and be held partially responsible for the result. Walter Pincus would not be relieved of some responsibility for the neutron bomb deferral just because he is a reporter. Journalists fear that such a burden, if taken seriously, would undermine what they see as their primary reason for being, namely to tell the people what is going on.

Understanding the impact of the press on policymaking is uncomfortable for the officials as well. It challenges them to internalize that awareness and make it part of the way they conduct themselves in office. It means they can no longer blame the press for their own bad coverage. In the neutron bomb case, it means they cannot blame Pincus for their difficulties with the bomb.

However, the conclusions of our study go well beyond the centrality of the media to government. As viewers or readers, we cannot learn very much about the impact of the press on policymaking just by following the news. We cannot tell what is going on simply by watching. When we see the press and policymakers together on television, they are usually in formal roles and familiar situations, such as at a press conference or on an interview program. Sometimes we see journalists and officials or read about them in conflict at a time of particular tension, such as during the Iranian hostage crises in 1980, the aftermath of the invasion of Grenada in 1983, and the hostage taking at the Beruit airport in 1985. Each of these events generates heated debate about the press–government interaction in times of great moment, but sheds little light on influence of the press on policymaking under less dramatic conditions. Newspapers often comment on the way television covers the news, but very rarely do they comment on other newspapers; television stations almost never cover the print media. Sometimes, but only rarely, newspapers provide a glimpse of behind-the-scenes policymaking activity which shows how decision makers used the press or reacted to coverage.

These random and sporadic images of the press–government connection tend to stick in our minds and shape our opinions, however unrepresentative they might be. In this study we have probed deeper to discover how press and officials really interact, and the effect of their interaction on policymaking.

Overall, we found that the press and policymakers in Washington are engaged in a continuing struggle to control the view of reality that is presented to the American people. The engagement is highly competitive, but collegial nonetheless. When the media's view and the officials' view are more or less shared, the struggle is more like a waltz. When there is a wide gap, or when early on in a particular issue it is not clear which perspective will predominate or even what the perspectives are, toes are stepped on and there is tension between the partners. In either event, the interaction is important to both policy-makers and reporters because they believe that the stakes—the goals of governing and the ideals of journalism—are so high.

A minor footnote to recent history captures the essence of this relationship. It involves television, not print, and some of the particular qualities that the electronic media bring to coverage of public affairs, but it is a good metaphor for how press and officials often interact. The incident was reported by James Markham of the *New York Times* on May 4, 1985, as President Ronald Reagan was preparing to leave Washington for his controversial trip to the German military cemetary at Bitburg. White House staff and television newsmen were already at the cemetery site. Markham reported how the White House advance team and network advance teams were negotiating over the placement of the network cameras which would record the visit for posterity . . . and for the nightly news. The issue was whether the cameras would be located on tripods. CBS had won the draw among the networks and had the preferred position. They wanted to be able to pan in a single shot from the president to an SS grave. The White House people argued that tripods would unduly restrict the already limited space, although they clearly were interested in keeping the president as far away as possible from the SS graves in the eyes of the American people.

The CBS News producer was quoted in the story in the *Times* as acknowledging that the White House staff were trying to "manage the picture. . . . That is their job. Our job is to cope with the story." The CBS crew got their tripod, and the shot they wanted was shown to millions of Americans that night.

The interaction was intense, the interests were professional, and the stakes were high. Government officials representing an administration with a reputation for effective communication spared no details in trying to influence how the news was presented. They knew that without that time and effort, the news would be less reflective of the president's view of reality and more reflective of someone else's view. The journalists for their part, although they accepted the administration's agenda just by covering the trip, were not willing to accept the official perspective on events. They were not only skeptical, they had their own perspective as well and that's the one they wanted to put out on their air.

This was primarily a professional conflict, not a question of right and wrong. It is not at all clear who was right, the White House men or the CBS men. Is it fair to show the president and then pan over to the SS graves? Is it a picture of truth, or is it just good television? Should either CBS or the government have the power to determine how we are going to visualize the event? The struggle over the tripod is an inevitable consequence of both parties aggressively doing their jobs. The press is not disrupting the policymaking any more than the policymakers are disrupting the press. Each is getting in the other's way at the moment, but each needs the other in order to do their own jobs.

Markham acknowledges the influence the press can exert. He concluded that "The way this 10-minute event—and Mr. Reagan's ride through Bitburg to the cemetery—will look on television may determine whether the president's visit is judged a fiasco or a limited damage draw." We cannot know for sure what was the impact of that particular CBS picture; what is significant is that even the *New York Times* reporter thought that the way that little tussle at the Bitburg ceremony was played out had the potential for significant consequences as part of the whole controversy surrounding the trip.

Not only do the press and officials continually bump into each other in the course of doing their work, but the results of their doing so are substantial for the policies and processes of government and, as the neutron bomb case shows, not limited to the location of a tripod and the public assessment of a Presidential trip.

In this study, we sought to find out just what those consequences were. First, we wanted to know in what various ways the press affects the daily routines of senior federal officials: how much time these officials spend with the press and thinking about press matters; to what extent they actively seek coverage and try to influence the coverage they do receive; and how regularly the press covers what they do.

Second, we sought to explore the specific ways in which the press might affect the policies and processes of decisionmaking: what are

38

the circumstances under which the press sets the agenda and frames the issues for the policymakers? Under what conditions can the press impact be expected to be substantial?

Third, we examined how officials deal with the media to see whether there are differences which produce differences in coverage and in press impact. We wanted to understand when and how officials take press considerations into account in making policy, when and how they leak information to the press and aggressively try to manage their press relations, and with what results.

What we found out about the consequences for government of today's intense struggle between the press and government is in the chapters which follow.

CHAPTER TWO

MOVING AWAY FROM THE ERA OF COOPERATION

THERE WAS A substantial evolution in the press–government relationship during the twenty years between the mid-1960s and the mid-1980s. A spirit of cooperation used to characterize the way the reporters and officials interacted. Reporters relied on officials, and trusted their information. And the reverse was often equally the case. This had been characteristic of the relationship for much of American history. For example, journalists regularly offered advice to presidents, sometimes at the initiative of the White House and sometimes even complimenting them in print if the advice was accepted.[1] News organizations consistently censored themselves to protect what officials termed "national security." Nothing better manifests that practice than the willingness of James Reston of the *New York Times* to ask his editors in New York to modify the story on the government's preparation for what became the ill-fated Bay of Pigs invasion of Cuba in 1961. At the president's request, Reston urged the editors to take the story off the front page and to eliminate any references which would suggest that the invasion was imminent. They complied, and the rest is history.

Presidents still ask newspapers and television networks not to run stories, and often the news organizations still agree. But they do so now only after great internal angst and after making an independent judgment that lives are threatened or the national security is at stake or some other equally compelling rationale exists. In two Middle East hostage takings, at the US embassy in Iran in 1979 and 1980 and the

TWA plane at the Beruit airport in 1985, news organizations knew information which they did not publish or broadcast, sometimes after a request of the government and sometimes on their own initiative. Even so, the administrations of Jimmy Carter and Ronald Reagan criticized the coverage in both those cases, suggesting that journalists were making news rather than reporting it, practicing diplomacy, playing into the hands of the hostage takers, and the like. Reporters and their bosses responded by arguing that they were responsible to their viewers and readers, not to the government, and that their jobs required them to judge what is the news.

While the relationship between the government and the news organizations obviously was different in the hostage crises from the way it was at the time of the Bay of Pigs, such celebrated examples do not adequately capture the change in the day-to-day interaction which this research has identified. We found from the survey, the interviews, and the cases that the spirit of cooperation which exemplified the way reporters and officials dealt with one another and understood one another twenty years ago has been replaced in large part by a spirit of competition between them which often produces tension and struggle.

How Has the Relationship Changed?

Nearly all the journalists and federal officials with whom we spoke at length and whose involvement stretches back to the sixties shared the view that there has been a considerable evolution in their relationship, although they did not necessarily agree on the nature of the change and the reasons for it. The most compelling evidence, however, comes not from the specific answers to the question about change, but from a broader sense of the differences which are evident in the recollections of those whose service was primarily in the sixties or earlier, versus those whose major public responsibilities came afterwards.

There may have been some selective recollections at work here. Time is said to heal all wounds, even those suffered in the interactions between reporters and officials. Nevertheless, there is some remarkable consistency among officials who served twenty years ago. Talking with Robert Ball, Dean Rusk, John Gardner, Wilbur Cohen, or Richard Bolling about the role of the press simply elicits a very different picture than talking with Henry Kissinger, Elliot Richardson, Peter Peterson, or Zbigniew Brzezinski. Rusk, for instance, who was secretary of state from 1961 to 1969, recounted his Friday afternoon confidential gatherings with thirty-five members of the press corps. "We'd have drinks. And the purpose of those . . . meetings was to sort of wrap up the present week and look ahead to the next week. The ground rule was that these things were not off the record, but they were not attributable. If they wanted to take what was said there into account in the way they thought about their stories or prepared for the stories next week, okay. We'd have a pretty frank discussion."

At one point the *Washington Post* threatened to boycott the sessions unless they were on the record; Rusk said fine, no sessions, if that's the way the press preferred it. The other reporters wanted to continue the chats and the *Post* backed off. At least until the dark days of the Vietnam War when relations deteriorated, it was a society of gentlemen, both figuratively and literally.

Rusk was under no illusions about the kind of news the press was interested in. He talked of his frustration at not being able to get the *New York Times* to publish a list of ongoing multilateral international conferences, but there was a decorum and a personal intimacy to the relationship that made it very different from the one described by Rusk's successors. Cyrus Vance was a post–1970 secretary of state (1977–80), but one who was not known for the kind of aggressive press relations that characterized the tenure of others, such as Henry Kissinger. There was no sense from Vance of personal intimacy with reporters, and no sense that from his perspective they were waiting for his wisdom. Vance talked about the press as "playing a critically important role. The press can either make or break a policy initiative." He talked in general about the difficulty of catching up with a bad story; he recalled the impact of the press having characterized his first trip to Moscow as a disaster because the Russians had not accepted the US proposal for deep arms cuts: "It took many weeks and months to counter the sting of those articles and the effect they gave."

Similarly, there is a tremendous difference in tone and sensibility between the recollections of Theodore Sorensen and of Stuart Eizenstat, both of whom served in key White House staff roles and both of whom are regarded with great respect by the press. Sorensen, who was special counsel to the president from 1961 to 1964 under both John Kennedy and Lyndon Johnson, did not remember dealing with the press as an independent force, only as a means for reaching out: "I doubt that I spent very much time thinking about the press as distinguished from the general public and the Congress." Sorensen doesn't think there are many ways the press can be improved. His chief complaint was simply that the press did not take a long enough view of public affairs. Eizenstat, who served as assistant to the president for domestic affairs and policy for President Jimmy Carter from 1977 to 1981, saw the press as an independent force with which he had to contend. He complained that the press focused on "anything that shows a problem for a president, a disagreement by a cabinet officer, a criticism by a member of Congress." Eizenstat saw the press not as a means of communicating the president's policy, but as a "useful testing device, sort of a litmus test" for policy. If they couldn't be convinced that something was a good idea, then maybe it wasn't such a good idea and certainly the administration was going to have a tough time convincing the public. He characterized the press as a "another actor," a complicating factor, a "part of the policymaking process."

The contrast between Wilbur Cohen and Joseph Califano, two cabinet members responsible for human services who served in different eras, reinforces this difference. Cohen, secretary of health, education and welfare in 1968 and 1969 with more than three decades of federal service behind him, emphasizes his "rather close relationships" with a number of reporters similar to the way that Rusk described his press connections. Cohen attributed this to the fact that he had been around Washington and in the government for a long time before he came into a visible policymaking role, but his characterizations of those friendships is still very different from the way his successors, including Richardson as well as Califano, talked about them. Cohen noted that there were only four or five reporters assigned to HEW on a regular basis. He felt himself to be very accessible to them. He could not remember a single instance of initiating a story with the press or of the press pressing him for information he had but did not want to give them. On leaks, he said that when he was called by a reporter with information that had probably been leaked from HEW, he would offer to check it out but presumed it was accurate. He talked about his own mistakes at not having completely thought through public relations strategies, but believed that the mistakes caused him personal embarrassment more than any policy problem. His general idea, he said, "was not to use the press as part of legislative strategy."

Not so for Califano, who was secretary of health, education and welfare from 1977 to 1979 and had served as special assistant to the president from 1965 to 1969 in Lyndon Johnson's White House. He characterized the press that he had to deal with in HEW, as distinguished from the press during his tour of duty on Johnson's staff, as "aggressive." And he was equally aggressive in using the media to sell his policies, whether it was anti-smoking to the general public, or hospital cost containment to the Congress. He did not dwell on the personal friendships he has with members of the press as elements of his professional relationship with them. He was a policymaker with a conscious and deliberate plan for dealing with an important and difficult force that was both hard to control and able to be useful. Richardson, who served as undersecretary of state, secretary of health, education and welfare, secretary of defense, attorney general, and secretary of commerce between 1969 and 1977, took a much more hard-nosed view. He did not establish or try to rely on personal relationships with reporters. It was strictly business: "I dealt with the press on the assumption that they also had a job to do."

James Schlesinger, who served as chairman of the Atomic Energy Commission, director of the Central Intelligence Agency, and secretary of defense between 1971 and 1975, and then returned to the government in 1977 for two years as secretary of the Department of Energy, spoke about the evolution in a way that captured much of what others had to say as well. "Relations between the press and government have changed. We have an early period which ended with the Vietnam War in which basically the press took government handouts and reprinted them. I can well recall . . . watching Sherman Adams . . . guide the press during the Little Rock crisis. What he told the *New York Times* faithfully appeared the next day. . . . That period ended sometime at the beginning of the Vietnam War, when the press became skeptical, not cynical but skeptical. For a period there of three to five years, it was inclined to take what the government handed out and sprinkle it with salt as it were, and not try to demonstrate that the government was wrong but on the other hand not accept its handouts. . . . Then we had another period, which started basically with Watergate and ended only about 1980, in which the press took great delight in demonstrating that the government was wrong.''

This is not to say that before Vietnam relations were always smooth, just more often that way. Schlesinger adds the insight that the interaction between the press and government depends to a considerable degree upon the mood of society in general, lending credence to the notion that the Vietnam / Watergate era was one which coincided with a transition in that relationship. Schlesinger believes that the pendulum has started to swing back toward the skeptical from the cynical mode.

Note that Schlesinger, like Califano and others, describe the relationship of reporters and officials in terms of the attitude of the press toward policymakers. That seems to be the factor that has most obviously changed from the viewpoint of the policymakers, and to a considerable degree it is the variable that the journalists identify as well. Distinguished reporters with long-time Washington experience are even stronger on this point than their counterparts in government. For them, the Watergate / Vietnam period represented what Albert Hunt, a member of the advisory group for this study and the Washington bureau chief for the *Wall Street Journal,* called a ''sea change.'' He measured the change along the same lines as Schlesinger used, from healthy skepticism to unhealthy cynicism on the part of the press. Jack Nelson, Washington bureau chief for the *Los Angeles Times,* pointed out that this breakdown in trust had two parallel but very different consequences for the conduct of officials. In some instances, ''a lot of people within government became leery of the press. On the other hand, there were other people in government who maybe counterbalanced that, who saw [from Vietnam and Watergate] that the press could do a really good job of getting information out that those other people thought ought to get out.''

The argument then is that the performance of government in Vietnam and Watergate contributed toward a cynicism on the part of the press which manifested itself in the attitude and actions of reporters toward government. The more cynical were the reporters, the more wary and secretive were the policymakers. The change in the behavior of the press had consequences for the way public officials conducted their business as well.

There were some significant differences in our survey between the policymakers who had left government by 1973 and those who served after that which reflected this change.[2] Officials who served in the sixties and early seventies spent much less time with the press and thinking about press matters than did their successors. Seventy-two percent of them spent five hours or less a week on the press, compared to 53 percent of the rest. The more current policymakers were twice as likely to have spent more than ten hours a week on the press as were their predecessors. Second, those who were in government after 1973 were much more likely than their predecessors to see the press as having had a negative impact on policymaking. They were more likely to believe that the press had decreased the chances for their attaining their policy goals and made action on issues more difficult, and that negative press had had long term affects on their careers and had affected their credibility. They were much more likely to worry about leaks, evidence of both the lessening of trust and the impact of a more aggressive posture on the part of both the press and the officials.

Finally, the longer out of government, the less likely the policymaker believed the press had a dominant effect on policymaking, and the more likely it was that the policymaker would characterize the relationship with the press as friendly rather than hostile.

Only one of the policymaking stories we examined in detail, the fight to pass legislation to reorganize the Post Office into a government corporation in 1969 and 1970, occurred place before this change took hold. In that case, Postmaster General Winton Blount and his associates in the government used a sophisticated marketing and promotional campaign to gain broad press attention and support for a particular reform plan, with the expectation that the coverage would be a catalyst for popular pressure on the Congress to enact the bill. It was a bald effort to manipulate the press and on the whole it was very successful. After six months or so, the postal unions, which steadfastly opposed the bill, finally realized how well orchestrated the reorganization campaign had been. Union leaders tried to get the media to make an issue of how the press had been manipulated, but by then there was too much momentum behind the administration's postal reform. Union complaints fed into the media's sense, by then shared among the public, that the unions were selfishly standing in the way of progress.

In our research we found another example of a public policy marketing campaign in the 1960s which was remarkably similar to Blount's effort and just as successful. Elliot Richardson recalled his own strategy for getting the state legislature to enact a sales tax when he was lieutenant governor of Massachusetts in 1965 and 1966. ''I created a statewide organization called Citizens for Fair Taxes,'' Richardson said, ''and we set about developing public support. We created chapters in all the principal municipalities in Massachusetts. We got favorable editorials, I think, in all the dailies in the state, or all but one. We generated a letter-writing campaign. We had people phone in on talk shows, and things like that. And, eventually we got the sales tax through over the united opposition of the Democratic leadership in both branches [of the legislature] and the state AFL-CIO, even though the Democratic majority in the legislature was two-to-one against us.''

Except in elections, it is hard to imagine in the 1980s the kind of open, stark, and explicit marketing campaign on behalf of a policy, like that developed by Blount and Richardson in the 1960s. But it is the starkness and the explicitness that has changed, not the willingness of some public officials to try to control or shape what images the public receives or, in some cases, their success in doing so. Policymakers now are in general no less interested in getting favorable coverage for themselves and their programs, but the press is less of a static force upon which the policymaker can exercise his or her will. Jimmy Carter's campaign to build support for returning the Panama Canal to Panama or Ronald Reagan's effort in behalf of his 1981 tax cut were just as concerted as the Blount Post Office reorganization, but the techniques had to be more subtle. The change in attitude in the press identified by officials and journalists alike affects the tactics that officials can use to get their messages to the people.

A bald marketing campaign would have a more difficult time succeeding now than it did in the 1960s. For one thing, the press is much more likely to question any initiative on the part of policymakers before accepting the official rationale. They share their skepticism with their readers and viewers. One way of doing this, for example, is by the use of what Adam Clymer of the *New York Times* once called the "smart-aleck close"[3] He was referring to the television correspondents' practice of finishing their pieces with a remark which signals their viewers that they are not buying into the government's position as they have just reported it. For another, the media nowadays are much more likely themselves to try to make an issue about such obvious efforts at managing the news without waiting for a policy opponent to raise it first. Exposing the strategies of policymakers to control the message may not be a convincing reason to readers and viewers for opposing the policy, but it helps to ensure that the press fraternity will be on their guard not to be taken in.

If the attitude of reporters has changed the climate of the press–government relationship over the last twenty years, the emergence of television as the central medium of public affairs has had just as significant an impact on the techniques and the routines of the way they do their business with one another. Television has become so much of a presence that it is easy to forget how relatively recently it has become a force in policymaking. It was only in 1962 that CBS and NBC went to half-hour nightly news programs. (ABC did not follow until several years after that.) In those early years of the nightly network news, what was in the morning newspapers would determine what stories the networks would set out to cover for the evening program. As the size of the audience, staff and budget grew, so did the influence and role of television news. Now, programming innovations and technological advances have changed the relationship between print and electronic journalism. Morning news programs on all three networks often make news or advance stories, thereby providing the framework for the rest of the media, including the newspapers, to pursue during the day. Technological advances such as the use of tape, minicams, and live feeds have enabled the networks to break stories and beat the newspapers to the news, so that they are now doing their own share of agenda setting for officials as well as for other journalists. Policymakers have noticed the change. One vivid example is the Reagan administration's responses to the criticisms of the accelerated eligibility reviews of Social Security disability recipients from 1982 through 1984. The story illustrates just how important an influence television has become.

Television and the Social Security Reviews

It is mid-May, 1983. A crew from the NBC show *Real People* is in El Campo, Texas, to shoot some film for a segment on Master Sergeant Roy Benavidez, the last Medal of Honor recipient from the war in Vietnam. Benavidez had received the award from President Reagan himself at a special and very emotional ceremony at the Pentagon two years before. After reading the long citation recounting Benevidez's exploits and hanging the medal around his neck, the president had embraced the Hispanic war hero. Tears welled in their eyes.

The *Real People* segment was not due to run until Veterans' Day in November, but the crew was in Texas in May to get some footage of a parade honoring Benavidez. While in El Campo, *Real People* was doing an interview in Benavidez's house. In the midst of the shooting, a cameraman noticed a letter from the Social Security Administration on a desk and asked Benavidez about it. The letter, Benavidez explained, had just arrived and informed him that he was being dropped from the disability rolls.

The *Real People* profile of a national folk figure had suddenly and accidentally become an investigatory piece about how the country turns its back on its heroes.

Benavidez had been dropped as part of a comprehensive review of the disability rolls, referred to as the CDI (Continuing Disability Investigation). The review had been mandated by Congress during the presidential election year of 1980; program costs had more than quadrupled during the Nixon and Ford administrations. When enacted in 1956, the disability program was to provide benefits only to those who were "unable to engage in any substantial gainful activity" for a period of at least twelve consecutive months. Over the years elaborate procedural safeguards added to ensure due process for the applicant increased the flexibility of that rigid test. For example, the initial determination of eligibility was made by the state, but the most significant level of appeal was to federal Administrative Law Judges (ALJs), who performed a de novo review and used different interpretations of eligibility. Thus it was possible for the disability examiner and the ALJ to come to opposite conclusions in the same case and both be "right."

The rate of ALJ reversals of state eligibility denials had reached 59 percent.

At the end of 1980, a random review of 3,000 disability cases indicated that the rate of ineligibles on the rolls might be as high as 20 percent. That meant that as much as $2 billion a year might be involved. Both the General Accounting Office (GAO) and the Office of Management and Budget (OMB) recommended that the CDIs be accelerated, and in February 1981 the target for reviews scheduled to be completed that year was doubled by the newly inaugurated Reagan administration, to a total of 275,000.

Most of whatever coverage of the reviews there was in the early fall of 1981 was in local media. The stories mostly were of a single genre: a report about a person who was cut off the disability rolls while clearly still unable to work or unable to get hired if willing to work. It made for particularly good television, with pictures of obviously disabled persons who had been declared ineligible and of desperate teary-eyed families providing a suitable backdrop for criticizing the policy. Even in cases where there were no obvious mistakes, the process sometimes produced cruel results. Recipients who were terminated lost their benefits after sixty days and were ordered to repay any payments received after the date of their medical recovery. Appeals took so long that sometimes serious financial hardship was endured even if eventually the applicant was reinstated.

In November, television coverage of the CDIs came to Washington. WRC-TV, the NBC affiliate in the District of Columbia, broadcast a story that the president saw when it was repeated the next morning as part of the local news segment within the *Today* program. The president was upset and asked for some answers. The answers suggested that the individual in question did not qualify for disability, and that he had been working while receiving benefits. The president used the incident often to illustrate unfairness by the media and to reinforce the idea that weeding out the ineligibles was a worthwhile pursuit.

CBS news ran the first network CDI story in December, adding a new element which became part of the standard fare: a quick word from one of the public officials who was responsible for the policy. Here it was an SSA associate commissioner saying that he believed SSA "had a responsibility to the American tax-paying public, as well as to the people who are dependent upon the Social Security system for benefits, to be sure that people who are no longer eligible for benefits do not get benefits.'' Then the official was asked how he felt about the suicide of a man who left a note blaming Social Security for ''playing God.'' ''What do you want me to say about that?'' the official responded.[4]

By early 1982, the CDI process was becoming a national issue with coverage in the *Washington Post* and the *New York Times*. Pressure for reform was beginning to build in Congress, but it took two television events, one in March and the other in April, to begin to make the CDIs a policy under re-examination by the administration.

In March, columnist George Will resurrected the old WRC-TV story. On ABC's *This Week With David Brinkley*, Will recounted that the president had told him about a Washington TV station that reported a man had been cut off the disability rolls under the Reagan administration when the truth was that the man had been cut off in 1980 under Jimmy Carter and had been cut off because he had held a full-time job. The Will story was the opening shot in a ten-day administration barrage designed, as White House Director of Communications David Gergen recalled later, to show that the problems with the disability reviews weren't ''as bad as was being painted.''[5] A few days later, in a long interview in the *Daily Oklahoman*, the president himself used the WRC-TV story as an example of how the administration's efforts were being treated unfairly.

The president's criticism made the nightly news on CBS and NBC, but it turned out that the man in question had been cut off during the Reagan years, that there was no hard evidence that he had held a full-time job while collecting disability, and that, even worse, he had just been reinstated on the rolls and awarded $2,324 in back payments. The president's inaccuracies were reported across the country. The White House began a quick retreat. The president departed from his prepared text at the next available opportunity and apologized to the press. The apology was covered on all three networks.

The issue of press fairness was temporarily put to rest, but not the issue of administration fairness. The WRC-TV story aftermath reinforced growing concern about the CDI process, and the trickle of local stories became a deluge.

Congressman Jake Pickle (D-TX), chair of the subcommittee on Social Security of the House Ways and Means Committee, still supported the process, but began to acknowledge the problems: "Some harshness has occurred . . . that was not the intent. But when we call in that large a number of people, it is inevitable that that kind of result will happen."[6]

SSA Commissioner John Svahn and his deputy Paul Simmons began to take steps to control the damage. They decided to try to prevent the stories by catching them before they could happen and to defend the program head-on against its critics. First, they exempted 125,000 recipients slated for review by moving them into the permanently disabled category. Then they sent out a program circular to the regional offices to assist them in explaining the CDI process to the local press. They met with national reporters who were following the story and had a session with the editorial board of the *Times*. None of this seemed to help much.

As Svahn and Simmons were trying to stem the tide, the administration learned that Bill Moyers was going to do a documentary on the impact of Reagan social welfare policies. The White House swung into action; again it was television that had provided the motivation.

Several days before the April 21 broadcast date, David Gergen learned that the program, to be called *People Like Us*, was going to display three case histories of recipients who had suffered from Reagan's budget cuts. When advance reviews of the documentary appeared on the morning of the twenty-first. Gergen directed HHS to begin working up profiles of the three cases. He called CBS to ask that the administration be allowed both to screen the documentary before it was televised (as the TV reviewers had been able to do) and to have time for an administration response. The requests were turned down. Gergen asked for a transcript in advance of the show, and was turned down again. CBS News issued a statement rejecting the requests "based on long-standing CBS News policy."[7]

The program opened with Moyers contrasting Reagan's pledge to protect the truly needy with Moyers's contention that "some helpless people are getting hurt." The three hardship portraits followed, one involving a cerebral palsy victim who had been cut off under the CDI process, after which Moyers concluded that the administration's budget cuts were "pulling the plug" on "many" poor people.[8]

At the White House senior staff meeting the next morning, the president said that "there's a lot in there that we can come back on." They agreed to counterattack. At a breakfast with reporters that morning, Reagan's domestic policy adviser, Edwin Harper, criticized the accuracy of the program: "It would be totally without justification, totally unreasonable to characterize this administration's policies as a war on the disabled. There are people who are cheating the taxpayers out of $2 billion a year. How do you root out the $2 billion cheaters?"[9]

Gergen held a contentious thirty-minute press briefing around noon, challenging CBS's fairness and methods. At HHS, Dr. Robert Rubin, the assistant secretary for planning and evaluation, followed with his own contentious briefing on the accuracy of the program. CBS rejected a White House request for rebuttal time, and was the only network to cover the administration's attack. The next day, CBS issued a statement standing by the facts of the stories and the documentary as a whole.[10] Whether or not *People Like Us* and its aftermath helped make the press more sensitive on the question of Reagan's fairness, there is little doubt that it made the administration more sensitive to the seriousness of the problems in the CDI reviews.

Gergen immediately began pressing HHS to support continuation of benefits through appeal. On April 28, seven days after the Moyers program and only a month after Svahn had testified against the idea to the Congress, Svahn and HHS Secretary Richard Schweiker dutifully issued a statement saying that they would support legislation for continuation of benefits. "The Reagan Administration," the press release explained, "wishes to be fair to those persons whose cases are being reviewed."[11]

Through the summer and fall of 1982, SSA officials followed their about face on continuation of benefits with four additional significant reforms, all designed to slow the pace of the CDIs and curb abuses of the process. These steps took place against a backdrop of voluminous print coverage which fueled a burgeoning Congressional interest in doing something about the problem. By December, a modest reform package was moving through the Congress. In the midst of hearings on the legislation, CBS ran another CDI segment. Ed Rabel was the correspondent. After the inevitable case histories, Rabel noted that former recipients were dying from the disabilities that SSA said were not serious enough to keep them on the rolls. The camera then focused on SSA's Simmons, who said "We are not out to kill people, we are not out to have a—we're not out to support a system that—that is harsh, cruel, or otherwise unfair to people." Simmons says that Rabel asked the question, "Are you trying to kill people?" but only his answer was aired.[12] The impression, of course, was either that Simmons was indifferent to the deaths or that he agreed with the critics of the program. In either event, the viewer was left with no reason why the CDIs should be continued.

A watered-down version of the CDI reforms was passed and signed into law by the president on January 12, 1983, the same day that he swore in Margaret Heckler to succeed Schweiker as HHS secretary. Heckler had lost her seat in Congress in the 1982 elections, but had called for reform of the CDIs during her campaign. The new law was a stop-gap measure, enacted to buy time until a more comprehensive legislative package could be produced. Later that month, the Administrative Law Judges sued HHS, alleging that they were under the threat of reeducation, discipline, or even dismissal if they allowed too many appeals. The judges eventually lost their suit, but the publicity surrounding it in early 1983, including depositions made public and testimony before Congress, undoubtedly added to the public impression that the problems with the CDIs were real and they were due at least in part to the pressure within the administration to save money and cut costs, even at the expense of fairness to some recipients.

One of the subordinate issues which began to emerge as Heckler was quietly negotiating a new legislative package with Pickle was the impact of the reviews on those recipients who were disabled because of mental impairment. Since there seemed to be so much room for discretion about whether such recipients were capable of "substantial gainful activity," critics charged that there was a pattern developing where mentally disabled beneficiaries would be thrown off the rolls but were nowhere near able to work. In April, the GAO issued a report, hotly contested by SSA officials, which said that over 90 percent of the mental impairment cases were being reversed by the ALJs because SSA was taking such a hard line.[13] Strong support was being expressed in both the House and Senate for a moratorium. The administration continued to oppose it. It was then that the *Real People* crew discovered the plight of Roy Benavidez and television brought the White House back into the arena again.

Armed with the information in the letter found on Benavidez's desk, Robert Wynn, the producer of the *Real People* segment, contacted a friend at the National Security Council and was put in touch with Simmons. Wynn and Simmons recall their conversation differently. Wynn says he was looking for help for Benavidez and that Simmons's response was to stonewall and suggest that the case ought to go through the regular process, since it was already before an ALJ. Simmons says that Wynn tried to get him to appear on the program and that he declined because he knew there was no way he could explain the CDIs in the context of defending dropping the last Vietnam War Medal of Honor recipient from the rolls. [14]

Wynn's friend at the National Security Council then put him in touch with Mike Baroody, Gergen's deputy in the White House. Baroody was immediately concerned. As Gergen said later, "An Hispanic war hero who had been honored and then mistreated by the administration was one of the worst stories we could imagine from a communication standpoint." [15] Baroody encouraged Wynn to come in and talk about the case, but made sure that he got a rundown on the situation from HHS before the meeting. The information provided by HHS suggested that it was not at all clear that a mistake had been made in cutting Benavidez off.

According to Benavidez, his war wounds had left him with two pieces of shrapnel lodged in his heart, bayonet wounds in both arms, severely impaired functions in his arms and legs, a punctured lung, restricted pulmonary function, and back pain that prevented him from sitting or standing for more than forty-five minutes at a time. In 1976, eight years after receiving his wounds in Vietnam, Benavidez retired from the military with an 80 percent disability rating and opted for Social Security disability insurance as well. In the intervening years, he remained quite active; he attended junior college for two years, was involved in politics, and gave frequent speeches to local high schools, veterans' groups, and the like. He was proud that he lifted weights and jogged to stay in shape. There was clearly some doubt as to whether he was "unable to engage in any substantial gainful activity" for the past year due to his impairments. There was, however, one way to keep him on the rolls, one which neither the administration nor Benavidez himself wanted to talk about: mental impairment. At his ALJ hearing on May 16, a psychiatrist had suggested that Benavidez's war injuries had wrought such an emotional toll on the man that he was incapable of holding a job. The ALJ had directed Benavidez to see another psychiatrist, and there was an examination scheduled for early June.

At the White House meeting, Baroody told Wynn that there was nothing he could do since the case was before an ALJ, but that the administration would like to help Benavidez find a job if he lost his appeal. Wynn asked if he could bring Benavidez to the White House the following weekend. Baroody agreed. On the Thursday before the weekend meeting, Benavidez turned down two offers of White House help in finding a job.[16] Spencer Rich of the *Washington Post* got the story and he immediately began calling the White House and HHS for information and comment. On Friday, Rich's piece made page one, accompanied by a photo showing Reagan embracing Benavidez after presenting him with the Medal of Honor. CBS Morning News mentioned it briefly. Wynn's interest in Benavidez began to be complicated by his interest in the *Real People* story; he called Baroody to ask whether the weekend meeting could be filmed and to inform him that in any event Benavidez would be giving interviews at the Washington Monument afterwards.

All day Friday, HHS received inquiries about the case. Simmons was the designated responder. In interviews with UPI and NBC, Simmons sought to shift the focus away from the question of whether the administration had deserted Benavidez to the question of whether Benavidez qualified for benefits. None of the stories mentioned that Benavidez was still receiving benefits pending the outcome of the appeal.

While Simmons was making the case that Benavidez's heroism and connection to the president had nothing to do with his eligibility, Baroody recommended to Gergen that they allow the meeting with Benavidez to be filmed. "We did not want to be or to appear to be disinterested in this man and his problems, and for that reason it was better to go on camera," Baroody said. If they hadn't agreed, they expected *Real People* would have filmed Benavidez outside the locked White House gates. Gergen also said that he hoped that the White

House meeting would spur the HHS bureaucrats to "make sure things run better."[17]

To make that message clear, White House spokesman Larry Speakes told D'Vera Cohn of UPI on Friday that the president was not only "personally concerned" about Benavidez, but that he was also "sympathetic to the plight of . . . all the other unfortunate victims of the squeeze created by the [1980] law. We recognize it as a problem that affects many Americans. The president has asked [HHS] to seek some way we can be helpful." Cohn noted that Speakes's comments represented a "sharp break with those of other administration officials who staunchly defended the reviews, although conceding some mistakes are made."[18] The White House ducked the issue of Benavidez's eligibility; Gergen reasoned that the possibility that the White House would have supported someone who didn't deserve to be on the rolls was not as bad as the likelihood that if they didn't talk to him sympathetically on Saturday he would leave as a "very bitter man doing interviews all weekend. Anyway," he added, "the country owes more to a war hero. You just can't turn your back on them."[19]

Baroody called Wynn on Friday and agreed to the cameras. It was not a comfortable meeting. Baroody went through all his points, but none made the *Real People* segment in November except Baroody again offering to help Benavidez get a job, followed by Benavidez turning down the offer. ("I will never work anywhere else," he later told a Congressional committee, "unless I am in the military. . . . All I know is how to jump out of airplanes and run with a rifle and kill an enemy and have men follow me and give orders.")[20] Benavidez left and gave his interviews at the Washington Monument. Few of the follow-up stories mentioned that Benavidez was still receiving benefits, and only UPI discussed the difficult eligibility requirements. There was no network coverage at all. The print stories continued, emphasizing the deserted war hero slant. There were editorials the following week citing the Benavidez case as evidence of the need to reform the CDI process without reference to administration efforts in that direction.

It is unclear how much impact the stories were having inside the administration. Just before the Benavidez case became public, Heckler had approved a reform package which included a moratorium on almost all mental impairment cases. The proposal was scheduled for consideration at a June 1 Cabinet meeting, four days after the Benavidez story broke. OMB opposed the package because of the estimated $200–300 million in savings which would be lost. On the surface it appeared that when the Cabinet gave its approval, the Benavidez case had produced the reforms. It is more likely that the brouhaha simply wiped out any chance OMB had of scuttling them. In any event, after the Cabinet meeting, SSA officials began to leak the information that broad reforms would be forthcoming in a few weeks. On June 7, Robert Pear wrote a page one story in the *New York Times* which provided the details of the package, which Heckler then released herself in a press conference later that day. Pear's story tied the reforms directly to the Benavidez case, a connection which Heckler denied explicitly at the press conference, although Pear's account found its way into most of the stories.

Heckler's announcement was on all the networks and received broad print coverage, but it was not universally applauded. Advocates for the disabled saw it as an attempt to stave off more sweeping reforms in the Congress, and Congressman Pickle, who thought he had been negotiating a legislative package with Heckler, was taken by surprise. In her effort to stay on top of the story which Pear had broken in the *Times,* Heckler had failed to touch all the Congressional bases. Pickle's response was essentially to abandon the negotiations and begin to work with disability advocates on the more sweeping proposals.

The Benavidez case had made the disability reviews big news again. The ALJs kept the momentum going with testimony before Congress about what they believed to be ''improper pressure'' which had been put on them by HHS. On June 20, PBS aired a *Frontline* program on the CDIs. Judges were furious with the number of cases stemming from the CDI process. By early 1984, there were forty-three thousand cases pending in the district courts, with the backlog growing by two thousand a month. There were more than one hundred disability class actions pending, and several hundred motions or threats to hold Heckler in contempt. By March of 1984, fifteen governors had pulled out of the program completely and fourteen states were under court orders to show that there had been medical improvement before anyone could be dropped from the rolls. Other states had made significant modifications. Courts had ordered over one hundred thousand former recipients retroactively reinstated, pending review of their medical improvement.

With all of this momentum, the White House still wanted to deal with the problems administratively and opposed legislative reform. Four days before the vote in the House in a last ditch effort to stave off Congressional action, officials leaked the news that Heckler was prepared to announce an eighteen-month moratorium on the CDIs. However, at that point dangling the moratorium made no difference; on March 27, 1984, the House approved Pickle's broad reforms by a vote of 410–1. In April, Heckler announced that she was suspending the CDIs until legislation could be enacted to restore "order and consensus in the disability program." She said it was "the only fair thing to do."[21] The Senate unanimously passed a bill on May 22 which was substantially weaker than the House version and it appeared for a while that reform was going to be stalled in the conference committee. This was due at least in part to the moratorium, which stopped the flow both of stories in the press and constituent complaints to the Congress. Finally, in September, with the elections approaching, a bill emerged out of the conference committee and was passed unanimously by both houses.

From early 1981 when the acceleration decision was made until the fall of 1984, this was primarily a story of HHS against the world. The opponents included the Congress, the courts, the press, the states, and the ALJs, and even the White House. Three times during those forty-five months HHS's handling of the issue was interrupted by White House intervention. Each time it was television that had triggered the White House involvement. And in two of those three instances, White House involvement marked a turning point in overall administration policy toward the disability reviews. If these events had been taking place twenty years before, it is extremely unlikely that it would have happened the same way, because television would not have been there as a catalyst. Because of its wider reach and emotional impact, the intervention of television was different from print. In conversations with distinguished present and former government officials, the presence of television was cited frequently as having made a significant change in the relationship between the press and government over the last two decades. It is perhaps the most important factor in the way in which the relationship has changed over time.

The Presence of Television

Policymakers believe that television has not only emerged as a medium central to the policymaking process, but also that its presence has had consequences for the way government works. Television adds momentum to the movement away from the spirit of cooperation and toward the era of struggle between reporters and officials. Some policymakers have resisted and resented this trend; others have seen television as a resource and taken advantage of it.

Television has provided government officials with an unprecedented opportunity to reach millions of people at one time with the same message. The *New York Times* is read by about a million people a day, but fifteen times as many people are watching any one of the three network news programs each night. Elected officials, understandably sensitive to the need to develop broad public support for themselves and their policies, generally recognized the value of television and incorporated it into their regular routines earlier than did their appointed colleagues in government. Yet sophisticated nonelected public officials have instinctively understood the impact of television for a long time.

Back in 1962, Robert McNamara, then the secretary of defense, used television at a crucial moment in the midst of a serious policy debate to win the public to the administration's position. It was shortly after the Cuban Missile Crisis. The administration was under fire in the Congress, with Senator Kenneth Keating (R-NY) leading those charging that all the missiles were not out of Cuba and the US had been duped into believing they were gone. According to McNamara, "The president was very much concerned about it and I said to him. I thought we could probably convince the public that we were right and our critics were wrong in the charge that we had been duped. He said, how can you do it? I said I think we can present our case on TV. To do so, we'll have to release some classified material but . . . if it's agreeable to you, I think we can do it. He said OK. So I asked John

Hughes, who was the senior analyst in the Defense Intelligence Agency and a very articulate individual, to join me. We had a live TV conference that lasted about an hour and a half. . . . We showed the photographs of the missiles coming into the sites and the missiles going out. Then I opened the conference to questions. All this was on live TV. It was very convincing, very powerful, and I think very effective. It was effective because it was presenting the truth and the facts in a very vivid way. It was a very powerful counter to the criticism and, I think, effectively stopped them.

From the policymaker's perspective, television is an important addition to the process because it is a way of getting directly to huge numbers of people, including the millions of Americans who do not pore over the fine print in the news columns of daily newspapers every day. Henry Kissinger, assistant to the president for national security affairs (1969–75) and secretary of state (1973–77), said that television is "the most important" medium for a policymaker interested in seeing that the policies are correctly interpreted by the public. In Califano's view, television is "much more important for educating the public" than print. The *Post* and the *Times,* he said, "are methods of communicating with other policymakers. . . . Without television, we would not have had the sort of mini-revolution in values on the issue of smoking."

Policymakers take note of what is said on the network news, not as much for the content itself as the way of finding out what the people are learning. As Kissinger said, "I almost never watch the evening news . . . because the things I am interested in are covered in too superficial a way. I was only interested in what they covered and for what length of time to learn what the country was getting."

As Kissinger suggests, television is not only more efficient if the goal is to communicate with vast segments of the public, but it is also a different kind of communication. It is on one level, as he argues, more superficial because there is so little air time available. Yet television, unlike print, requires visual images in order to work. The pictures add depth to the stories as well as complications in communicating them. Television is also a more intense and emotional medium than print.

Generally speaking, government officials have not had vast experience with television before they assume senior policymaking positions. Whether they have come up through the bureaucracy or from the private sector, they usually have not had to worry much about how they come across electronically, about reducing what they had to say to seventy seconds, or about providing an exciting visual to help tell their story. Elected officials, on the other hand, come into office already having had to reach large numbers of people with brief but intense and memorable messages. It is not surprising that television seems to have a greater presence in Congress than in the executive branch. Richard Bolling, congressman from Missouri from 1949 to 1983, says it is the "key change" in press–government relationships in the Congress in the past twenty years. He believes that the independence of current congressmen is attributable in large part to their ability to maintain an image through television which is separate from their role in the actual lawmaking process. Melvin Laird was a congressman from Wisconsin from 1953 to 1969, chairman of the Republican Conference, and later secretary of defense (1969–72). He says that the growth and active role of television has changed the press–Congress relationship so that now there is much more individual scrambling for coverage than there used to be. Wilbur Mills, member of Congress from Arkansas from 1939 to 1977 and chairman of the House Ways and Means Committee from 1957 to 1974, said that if he were back in public life and had a message to get out to the people, he would use TV because "it's much more effective than any other means." Mills argued that the dominance of television on the thinking of the American people has given the medium "a lot more influence now than it used to have" in setting the agenda of government. Califano says that he, too, can notice the difference: "When you go up on the Hill now, for the first time in the last couple of years and you really hear the guys talk, they'll talk about did they make page one of the Post above or below the fold, *and* talk about whether they got thirty seconds on the evening news. . . . All you have to do is look at the Congressional Record in the House on any significant debate and you can find fifty good quotes because they're all fighting to be one of those guys who gets into the Rather coverage."

While television has created the opportunity for direct communication between the policymaker and a wider public, it has also created new challenges. One is the overall challenge of communicating well in a new medium with new constraints and requirements. As Rusk said, "It takes a while for people to accustom themselves. It is a special experience being in front of that television camera, where you can't scratch your nose, you can't pull on your ear, you can't cough or say 'er-er.' There's a certain tension or strain." Bolling thought that the inability or unwillingness of leaders to come to grips with the medium and master it was a very serious problem for the Republic: "The major disaster in this country is that the society and the politicians have not yet become at ease with television."

Television demands succinctness in a complex world. John Gardner, who was secretary of HEW from 1965–1968, but who since that time has had substantial television experience as founder of Common Cause, is still struck by the difficulty: "It's astonishing how compact you must make your message if you're going to have a pretty good batting average in getting it across." Another aspect of the challenge of television is the difficulty of controlling what will get on the air. Kissinger called it "the most elusive" medium because so much discretion is exercised by so many people between the hour-long interview and the minute or two that the viewers may see.

Some officials seemed to have an instinctive understanding of how to make the medium of television work in their favor. McNamara's live press conference after the Cuban Missile Crisis is one example. As secretary of commerce from February 1972 to December 1973, Peter Peterson also took enormous pride in his selective and sophisticated use of the medium. He stressed the need for a visual image to convey policy to the public through television. He recounted his campaign to deal with flammable fabrics and children's clothes. The Department of Commerce research operation had developed a substance which could make the fabrics flame-proof. To dramatize this breakthrough and to give the administration some time for further development, Peterson called a press conference and had his six-year-old daughter set a match to her favorite doll's clothes. As Peterson says, "Anyone who had a daughter would understand that even the secretary of commerce, even as callous as he was, wouldn't take a risk like that'' without knowing that it was going to work. It did work, the clothes did not burn, and the pictures were flashed on television screens all over the country.

Stuart Eizenstat, who served well into the television era, pointed out that the advantages of television to the policymaker are minimized because as officials master the use of the medium, others do as well. Looking back, for example, he thought that President Carter had made a mistake in inviting so many groups into the White House because they would so regularly walk out the door after the meeting, face the cameras on the White House lawn, and take the opportunity to criticize the president because he did not give them everything they asked for. Television is ''a great bully pulpit,'' Eizenstat said, ''not only for the president, but for whoever can get in and get back out.''

Fundamentally, then, television presents the opportunity for the policymaker to reach a vast audience with a crisp, easy-to-understand message. Television journalists are forced by the constraints of the medium and the conventions of the news programs to present information in very tight packages. As Eizenstat said, ''They are under enormous pressure to get stories into a twenty-two-minute evening news segment. They've got to sell their story to the producer, it's got to be interesting, and it forces them to come at the story from the standpoint of its entertainment and sales value.'' Vance added that television stories had to be more ''juicy'' or ''sensational'' to get on the air.

There is a question lurking here which none of these comments directly addresses. It is whether the emergence of television as a powerful force in public affairs costs something in terms of the quality of governance. Dean Rusk, for example, believes that television has diminished the value of the dialogue between the executive and legislative branches in Congressional hearings. Attendance may be up, but the conversation has been altered. ''When the television cameras are there . . . half of the [Senators] had pancake makeup on, all ready for the show. And that kind of a scene is not a real exchange between Senators and the witness. They're talking over each other's heads to a wider audience. And my judgment is that the quality of discussion under those circumstances suffers a great deal.''

To Eizenstat, the conventions of television more than those of print force reporters to ''focus on conflict, on personality, on the veneer of the story rather than the substance of it." In 1980, during the time he was in the White House, the Carter administration was faced with a decision about whether or not to relocate 710 families who were living close to an abandoned toxic waste dump called Love Canal located near Niagara Falls, New York. An unvalidated study was made public that indicated a surprisingly high rate of chromosomal damage among some residents. Television coverage helped to turn what was essentially a local story into one in which the whole country was involved, or at least watching. Policies in which there is a high level of public interest and, better yet, a high level of public support, are easy policies to pursue. Television creates the interest, and sometimes, as in the Love Canal case, it generates sympathy and support as well. The relocation decision that seemed so far away at one point was much easier to make a couple of days later after the steady drumbeat on the nightly news. Television also moves the issue dramatically up the bureaucracy. It was television, more than any other single factor, that brought the White House into the policymaking process when the Social Security disability reviews were coming under fire. Because the whole country is watching, the president must get involved or otherwise he would be perceived as not caring about the problem.

This suggests another impact of television. In both the Love Canal and the Social Security review cases the press seemed to generate a very quick response from the administrations involved. Television in particular seems to produce this effect, almost forcing a one-day response so that the follow-up story will not be that there was none. A follow-up in print is a very different matter. There's no print analog to the reporter standing on the White House lawn live at 7:00 P.M. telling fifteen million people that the president has no response to the crisis the reporter reported the night before. That "news" would not be a front-page story in the *New York Times;* it would not be a story at all. Vance talked about the pressure to respond on TV while he was Jimmy Carter's secretary of state: "The president would want me to trot down to the news room and put something on the news before the 6:00 news so as to counter a story that had come out of Bonn or some other place. I felt it was a waste of time. And unless it was something of really critical importance, I did not do it. . . . I had more important things to do, which used to irritate the president. . . . You could spend all your time running down and putting out snippets that the White House would like to have you put out. And if the secretary of defense or of state goes down and does it, then you're probably going to get on the evening news, and that's what they would like.''

Lloyd Cutler, who was White House Counsel from 1979 to 1980, wrote about precisely this point.[22] He argued, based on both his experience and his observation, that TV presented a kind of doomsday clock to the administration. ''Even before the advent of TV news, print articles about troubling events created a political need for prompt presidential responses. Because TV news accelerates public awareness,'' he wrote, ''the time for response is now even briefer. If an ominous foreign event is featured on TV news, the president and his advisers feel bound to make a response in time for the next evening news broadcast.'' The timing affects the quality and deliberativeness of the response to a crisis. It takes items which otherwise would get attention and puts them on the back burner, setting the agenda for the president and therefore the nation. Cutler believes that the pressure on the process thereby affects the substance of policy, making some options more likely to be chosen than others. As in the Love Canal case, TV coverage might have the effect of making an otherwise difficult decision easier to make because it can ''speed the coalescence of public backing for an initiative.'' By making some policy considerations more likely than others, TV has an impact on content as well as process.

Five separate and potentially troubling impacts of television have been suggested here by these policymakers: television diminishes the quality of communication among officials in public settings such as congressional hearings; forces oversimplification of the issues; nationalizes a story and puts it on the policymakers' agenda; creates a supportive environment for certain options; and accelerates the policymaking process. There is a tension between the need for policymakers in the 1980s to master television in order to be good and successful policymakers, and what they perceive to be the costs of being subservient to its demands. Only twenty years ago, television and the pressures it brings simply were not important. Wilbur Cohen said that reading the *Washington Post* and the *New York Times* first thing in the morning became part of his job at HEW, in part because both President Kennedy and President Johnson did so, and were likely to call him very early to discuss something they had read. When asked whether watching the evening news was similarly part of his job, he answered that he didn't recall a single instance in which a story on the evening news had not been in the paper that morning. That is very different from the world that Cutler described, and the difference cannot be explained by the difference between domestic and foreign policy. Television has become an enormous factor in the relationship between officials and the press. It has provided policymakers with a new and powerful resource for communicating with the public and for building understanding and support for policy initiatives. It has also presented a complicated challenge for them because it is a medium which requires special skills to use effectively, skills which most officials have not tested and developed. Finally, television's reach puts pressure on the policymaker not only to master it, but also not to be controlled by it. If television demands a response, there are felt pressures to make one, ready or not. If television demands a policy that is easy to explain and possible to visualize, then perhaps those policies that do not fit those constraints are less likely to be adopted.

The danger from television does not arise from bad reporters or bad journalism; it is a risk from the power and the characteristics of the medium itself. The qualities of the medium are different than print; thus, television news has different impacts on policymaking. Those five worrisome impacts of television do not inherently lead to bad policymaking. They create the opportunity for it, just as they create the opportunity for improved policymaking. In the Love Canal story, there is a strong sense that the policymakers allowed themselves to be pushed by television, and the public response that television can generate, into making a relocation decision that they could not then justify by their own standards on either procedural or substantive grounds, although it was a decision they most likely would have come to eventually anyway. In the CDI reviews, the White House felt forced by television to deal with an issue it had previously ignored, and to initiate and support changes in a policy that had produced unintended problems. Television is notable in these situations for its presence and its influence on policymakers and their priorities. Officials think of television as a force that cannot be brushed aside.

The pressure officials feel from television has been a major contributor to an overall sense on their part that the press–government relationship has changed. The central consequence of this change has been to challenge the existing convention that the job of the press was more or less to report what officials said and did, and the job of officials was simply to run the government. Reporters were on the whole less willing to challenge the government. Most journalists covering Washington today are professionaly skeptical if not cynical, about what policymakers say and do, and current policymakers, particularly those who seem to be the most successful in achieving their policy goals, look at their professional responsibilities in such a way as to include dealing with the press. The roles of reporters and officials increasingly seem inextricably intertwined, like different colored strands in a single ball of thread.

CHAPTER THREE

CONSEQUENCES OF A PERVASIVE PRESS

E VERYWHERE WE TURNED in our research—the cases, the survey, and the interviews—we found evidence of how central the press is to the decisionmaking process in government. As Robert McNamara said, before his government experience he believed that "all you had to do was figure out the right thing." He learned, however, that "you also have to figure out how to explain it to the public." Over 96 percent of the senior federal policymakers we surveyed said that the press had an impact on federal policy, and over half of them considered the impact substantial.

Part of the explanation for this is that everywhere policymakers turn in Washington there are reporters to deal with. Journalists are there, doing their jobs, asking questions, looking for information. The dramatic increase in the number of Washington-based journalists has extended the reach of the press deeper into the bureaucracy and added to the number of reporters covering those policymakers who were already well-covered. Policymakers simply cannot avoid the media; as a result of the sheer presence of the press, policymakers' jobs are different than they otherwise would be. Because the press is such a presence, policymakers spend a lot of time thinking about and dealing with press matters. They use the press to explain themselves to colleagues and constituencies, and to learn what other officials and groups are thinking about them and their programs. They understand that what the press covers and how it covers the news can affect their policies, the way they do their jobs, and their careers. As a consequence, for many policymakers managing the press has become an integral part of their professional routine.

Sometimes, press considerations are so much a part of policy-making as to be indistinguishable from it. That was true at several points during the ten months President Carter took to make his decision on the neutron bomb. Yet, the neutron bomb story is not a typical case of federal policymaking or of press–government interaction. Granted, no one policymaking story can be expected to represent them all; but this one is just especially out of the mainstream. It featured a single reporter with unique background and interests working for a newspaper with a special role in Washington, initiating the story with enterprise journalism, and setting the tone for all the coverage to come.

Of course, Walter Pincus is no ordinary reporter. Pincus knew a lot about the subject. He had been a co-author of a major study in the Congress of US nuclear commitments overseas. He had very strong opinions about the merits of the weapon which, by his own admission, influenced his coverage. He is unusual among news reporters for daily newspapers in that he is willing to acknowledge purposefulness in his work. Long after the neutron bomb decision had been made, Pincus expressed his surprise at what had happened because, he said, "All I really wanted to do was raise the debate about short-range nuclear weapons, because they're idiotic." Pincus's explicit interest in the policy was abetted by another special advantage he had: he was working not only for a powerful newspaper, but for a television network as well.

'And the *Washington Post* is no ordinary newspaper. The *Post* is the hometown paper for the national capital, the paper of record for the activities of the federal government, the paper most federal officials read first in the morning. To government insiders, the news in Washington means to a considerable degree what appears in the *Washington Post*. As former Secretary of State Henry Kissinger said, "the one thing that is read by everybody in Washington that matters is the editorial and op-ed page of the *Washington Post*." Or, as Phillip "Sam" Hughes, who has held several major policy positions, put it, "The best way to find out what's going in this town at any given moment is to read the goddamn paper, the *Post* notably." John Gardner said that he "fairly often" learned about his own department by reading the *Post*.

Nevertheless, the unique qualities of the press–government connection in the neutron bomb decision do not fully explain the enormous impact of the press on what happened there. We also looked at another decision of the Carter administration, the 1980 relocation of the 710 families at Love Canal. The routines of the interaction between reporters and officials in that case were much more typical of day-to-day press–government relationships. There the decisionmakers moved more decisively than they did with neutron bomb deployment, and the reporters who covered Love Canal had no special expertise in the subject. Yet the press played no less important a part of the story.

The Love Canal Relocation

Love Canal has become a catchword, one that symbolizes fears people have about health risks from environmental dangers and about the inability or unwillingness of government to deal with the problems. But back in the late 1970s, concern over toxic wastes was just beginning to build and Love Canal was familiar only to a handful of environmentalists and the people who lived in the area around Niagara Falls in upper New York State. Senior officials at the Environmental Protection Agency were concerned about public perceptions that the government was not acting decisively about the problems of hazardous waste and, late in 1979, decided to do something about it.

A Hazardous Waste Enforcement Task Force was formed. The mission, according to Jeffrey Miller, then acting head of the EPA's Enforcement Division, was "to affect legislation, and to try to turn the press around from criticism of the agency's handling of the hazardous waste problem to acceptance that the agency was doing what it could, but lacked all the tools it needed."[1] Influencing the coverage was at the heart of the policy.

One of the first products of the work of the Task Force was a lawsuit filed on December 20, 1979, by the Department of Justice on behalf of the EPA against Hooker Chemical, the city of Niagara Falls, the Niagara County Health Department, and the Board of Education of the city of Niagara Falls. The suit asked for $124.5 million, for an end to the discharge of toxic chemicals in the area surrounding Love Canal, plus clean-up of the site and relocation of residents if necessary.

71

The crisis at Love Canal had developed slowly. Hooker had dumped 21,000 tons of chemical wastes in the abandoned canal site between 1942 and 1952. Unbearable smells, dead grass, paint peeling off the backs of houses, and other problems were reported by residents living near the site as early as 1943. In 1958 some children had been burned by debris on the property. Street construction crews complained of itchy skin and blisters. By 1959, black sludge was seeping into basement walls. Sump pumps had to be regularly replaced. Chemical odors could be noticed after every heavy rain. Backyards were becoming unusable. Holes opened up on the baseball diamond. Trees and shrubbery that backed up to the Canal were dying. Residents complained in vain to the city of Niagara Falls, which by then owned the site. Finally, in late 1976, tests were done which proved that the sludge in the cellars was toxic and that Hooker was the source.

Neither Hooker nor the city was willing to address the problem as its own. The congressman from the area, John LaFalce, made his first visit to the site in September 1977, and brought in the EPA. There were more tests of the air, water, and soil. In the spring of 1978, alarming results began to come in, and the state took action.

On August 2, the New York health commissioner announced that ten carcinogenic compounds had been found in vapors in homes around Love Canal, that there existed a "great and imminent peril" to the health of the people living there, and that residents should not eat food from their gardens or use their basements. Pregnant women and children under two years old living at the southern end of the area were urged to relocate.[2] On August 7, New York Governor Hugh Carey toured the area for the first time, and promised the crowd that the 239 families living in the so-called inner ring of homes on the Love Canal site would be moved.

Between August of 1978 and the filing of the EPA suit in December of 1979, a $9.1 million state-financed construction program to secure the site by diverting the leaching and placing a cap on the canal was undertaken, but there was sharp disagreement among scientists involved about the continuing health risk for nearby residents.

In January 1980, the lawyers at Justice and the EPA agreed to do a quick "pilot study" among Love Canal residents to look for chromosomal damage, which would be evidence of exposure to toxic chemicals. They chose people who would be most likely to show damage, people who had already exhibited some possible manifestations, such as cancer or children with birth defects. There would be no control group, but if the results looked "promising" they planned to go ahead with a full-blown rigorous scientific investigation which could be used in court. None of the senior administrators at the EPA were aware of the pilot study; the political, legislative, and public information arms of the agency were uninvolved.

Around the first of May, the consultant doing the study phoned the EPA to report that he had found chromosomal aberrations in twelve of the thirty-six people tested. In a confirming letter sent shortly thereafter, he noted that the findings were "believed to be significant deviations from normal, but in the absence of a control population, prudence must be exerted in the interpretation of such results." He recommended that the larger study be undertaken.

Miller recalls that there was a lot of activity at the EPA after the phone call: "The thought process that we went through was that if we have a scientific piece of information which indicates dangers to people living in that area, it is the responsibility of the agency to make that information known to those people. Otherwise, you may well be adding to the medical difficulties in the area, which would be irresponsible. Well, at that point, you have to ask two questions. One, is this scientifically OK or not? And second, what kind of response should the government itself make, or should it make a response?"[3]

At the same time, the White House independently had become involved in Love Canal. The mayor of Niagara Falls had requested the use for Love Canal residents of apartments in the area, owned but no longer needed by the Air Force. Jane Hansen, an aide to Jack Watson, who was secretary to the Cabinet and assistant to the president for intergovernmental affairs (and in the process of becoming chief of staff in the White House), began to put together a compendium of all the health studies of Love Canal residents. In the course of that work she learned of the Justice/EPA pilot study.

This was a difficult time to have a new crisis facing the Carter administration. The president was beating back a time-consuming and expensive intraparty challenge from Senator Edward M. Kennedy (D-MA). The economy was not in good shape. American hostages were still in Iran. Fidel Castro was allowing some Cubans to leave the island and seek refuge in other countries, principally the United States. On April 24, the president's secret hostage rescue mission stalled on an Iranian desert, causing tragedy, embarrassment, and the resignation of the secretary of state. The trickle of Cuban refugees became a flood; by May 15, over 46,000 Cubans had arrived in the US, all needing housing, food, relocation assistance, and jobs.

Finally, if there were going to be another crisis, it was double trouble that it was going to be in New York. For two years Governor Carey had been pushing hard but unsuccessfully for federal help with Love Canal. The governor was personally close to Kennedy, although he never endorsed the insurgency. The week before Love Canal was to become a major issue again, Carey announced that he was urging both Kennedy and Carter to release their delegates so that there could be, in his word, an "open" convention. It was hardly an idea designed to win over the hearts and minds of Carter and his staff.

On Thursday, May 8, Hansen met with LaFalce, who briefed her on the history of Love Canal. The following day, she was briefed by the EPA on the pilot study. Although only the phone call had been received, it was assumed that whether to make public the results was not an issue, only when and how to do so. Notes taken at the meeting quote a Justice Department lawyer saying the EPA was "leaky," and that the study would not stay out of the press for long.

Hansen and two members of the Council on Environmental Quality (CEQ) told Watson about the study on Monday evening, May 12. Watson directed Hansen "to pull together the pieces for the federal response." There were many people in and out of the government who knew something about the study and at least one of them had tipped off the press. By Thursday, May 15, a few reporters were making general inquiries at the EPA which suggested that they knew something about the study, if not anything more than its existence.

On Thursday, Hansen wrote a long memo to Watson in which she said that she was concerned that "momentarily the press / media will have the results" of the study. She outlined an "action plan" which recommended that the Administration "take the offensive *quickly* in announcing the results of the studies ourselves." She urged that they say that officials would verify the data within a week, which would "provide us with some flexibility and give us a week to answer some important questions and determine our course of action." She said that "Carey will probably blast us for whatever we decide to do . . . [so] . . . we might as well get on the offensive, express our concern by releasing the results of the study, and announce some positive steps."

The decisionmaking was already being driven to a significant degree by press concerns. The fear that the results of the study would leak was affecting both the process and the policy options. A plan for packaging the government's position was needed in order to frame the story positively, as well as to provide a week's breathing room to make a more deliberate decision. The policymakers were acting in anticipation of the likelihood that they could not control the information for long, and that once it was out they would have to deal with a barrage of criticism from Carey.

The memo had the desired effect. Watson called a meeting for Friday "to get to the bottom of the situation." He was concerned, he recalled recently, "with the public's perception, not so much the public at large, but the public that was directly affected. . . . I was very concerned about wrong, rumor-filled, distorted information getting to them through the press."[4]

The meeting was held at 11:00 A.M. on Friday, May 16, in Room 248 of the Old Executive Office Building. Senior administrators from all the agencies involved were invited. Notes from the meeting indicate that the decision was made to inform the study subjects immediately and to hold a press conference the next day, Saturday, to release the study results and announce the federal response. Representatives of the Justice Department argued for a Friday press conference, but the need first to inform the study participants what their own tests showed was deemed to be an overriding consideration. They agreed on a complex series of events for the next day, Saturday: a Washington press conference, an individual briefing by EPA officials for each of the study subjects to be held at the Love Canal Homeowners Association office, a briefing for local officials, a press conference for local press in LaFalce's Niagara Falls office, and late morning calls to inform Governor Carey and the two US senators from New York. Wednesday was set as the day for making the next decision.

Then, someone leaked. That afternoon, the *New York Times* called the EPA looking for comment to include in the story it was running on Saturday about the pilot study. The government had lost the initiative, but for the moment at least, it was still only an EPA story about a regional problem.

The Saturday morning news included most of the information that the government was planning to release at the press conferences. Irwin Molotsky's story, on page one of the *Times,* attributed the results of the study to "federal officials" who "asked not to be identified."[5] The story strongly suggests that the leak did not come from the EPA, but did originate with someone who knew of the press conference plans. The article quoted a Hooker spokesman criticizing the release of the study, emphasizing the preliminary nature of the findings, and expressing concern that the publicity would cause panic among Love Canal residents. The article mistakenly reported that the federal officials had only been made aware of the conclusions on Thursday, lending further credence to the sense that all this was being done in haste because of the seriousness of what was discovered.

The government was in a difficult position, trying to disseminate pretty horrible-sounding results while stressing their tentative nature and the need for verification. The situation was further complicated by the leak. By the time of the press conference, the government's chief news—the study itself—was already old news for the reporters, and they used the conference to try to advance the story. The new news was made in response to questions at the Washington press conference, not in the government's prepared statement releasing the findings of the study. On the question of relocation, EPA Deputy Administrator Blum said that a decision would be made "probably by Wednesday." On the question of who would pay for relocation, she was quoted as saying that "We certainly can't let money stand in the way."[6] She characterized the results of the study as "alarming." Despite some words of caution, the overall thrust of the day's activities was that something of enormous import had taken place. As LaFalce recalls, "EPA handled it with such immediacy and such alarm and sense of urgency, that it created an aura that was impossible to cope with rationally."[7]

The administration had held the information for some two weeks. When they released it they did so in a way so as to signal a national audience that this was a very big deal. Since the study was the Saturday pre–press conference story, the press conference story turned out to be primarily about the possibility of relocation. Had there been no leak and the study was the story, perhaps the tentativeness of the findings would not have been lost. The officials involved expected to be able to control events, even after they had lost the initiative. Instead, the leaked stories plus their own elaborate plan for Saturday helped set the stage for an escalation of the demand for relocation from Love Canal families whose anxieties, in turn, would be fed by a national sense of compassion and fear of toxic waste, stoked by enormous press coverage.

The press conference in Washington made the CBS and NBC nightly news. In the Sunday *New York Times* there were four Love Canal related stories, including two on page 1. By then, it was a national story. The networks had given it coverage, and the primary regional newspaper, the *Times,* has a national readership. It quickly became a national story not only because it was covered by national media, but also because it tapped into anxieties shared by people everywhere. The coverage continued, with the networks devoting a substantial amount of time to reporting every twist and turn in the Love Canal story for the next few days. The ongoing interest from the networks and the *New York Times* helped to ensure that the White House would be increasingly involved.

Watson had informed the president about the Love Canal press conference in a memo which seemed to anticipate that events were already moving ahead of the policymaking:

> . . . it appears that the residents face an immediate health hazard that demands speedier response than litigation. . . . Justice and I did not feel that we could conceal the information until [Wednesday, when the study would have been evaluated] . . . people will have to be moved when validation is in. The state has been characteristically uncooperative . . . I . . . will attempt to avoid a lengthy public battle resulting in no action and growing hysteria among Love Canal residents.[8]

It did not take long for the hysteria to manifest itself. The residents of Love Canal were fanning the flames, in part for the benefit of the attendant press. On Monday, they engaged in a little friendly hostage taking, holding two EPA officials for several hours. Carey was doing his part, publicly criticizing the federal government's handling of the situation and calling for a fully federally funded relocation.

By early Tuesday it became clear to Watson and Hansen that whether or not there was legal authority, available money, a Carey agreement, or a study validation, this boil had to be lanced. They remember stopping to talk between the White House and the Old Executive Office Building. Watson said something like "I think these people have been jerked around enough . . . we'll just have to go ahead." The decision was made.

At a Tuesday White House meeting, the government scientists argued in vain for more time to assess the relationship between the chemicals and the health risk, an attitude Watson characterized as "writing a scientific treatise on the head of a pin."[9] It was too late. The discussion turned to what needed to be done to prepare for a relocation announcement the next day, Wednesday.

One of the sticking points was the agreement with Carey or, more precisely, the lack of one. There was a big gap between what he wanted and what the White House was willing to commit. They agreed to say they would "share" the costs, language which each side could interpret in its own way. Carey promptly went to the press, characterizing the agreement in the light most favorable to the state. So when Barbara Blum faced the press on Wednesday to announce the relocation, she once again was dealing with a story which had already been published, and published with a spin which did not make her, or the federal government, very happy.

After the press conference there was relief among the residents of Love Canal, continued determination in Albany to increase the federal contribution, and frustration in Washington that things are not often as they appear to be. The review of the pilot study was completed that day, concluding, as have other studies since then, that there was "inadequate basis for any scientific or medical inferences from the data (even of a tentative or preliminary nature) concerning exposure to mutogenic substances because of residence in Love Canal."[10]

The Press Is Central to the Job

By its sheer presence, the press was an integral element in the judgment to go ahead with the Love Canal relocation by way of a process which Barbara Blum characterized years later as "the worst public policy decision during my four years with the government."[11] The media were a continuing factor in the story simply as a function of their performing the basic responsibilities of journalism: finding out what was going on and reporting it. One of the primary consequences of the pervasiveness of the press is that on a big policy decision the media will be central to the policymaking and inevitably play some role in the process if not the result, just because they are there, reporting what happened, generating and maintaining public interest.

In the Love Canal case, there was no reporter-protagonist who had an investment in the story, the way Walter Pincus did with the neutron bomb. There was just a horde of reporters in and around the government, covering the news, looking for stories, asking questions, seeking leads, doing their jobs. They were sophisticated and solid, but had no unusual expertise.

The techniques of press–government interaction were conventional: press conferences and leaks. The *New York Times* and the *Washington Post* did run some pieces inside the paper on the scientific aspects of the story, but the main stories were written by reporters who could not be expected to have understood in scientific detail what was involved in demonstrating a connection between a particular health defect in a certain percentage of the population and the presence of toxic chemicals in the neighborhood. There were no international elements here, and policymakers were willing to make decisions.

The content of the decision was dramatically different in the two cases. Neutron bomb production was an issue in which every citizen had an equal stake, but the consequences were in dispute and in any case remote. The Love Canal relocation affected only a handful of families, but their health appeared to be in immediate danger and their problem tapped widely held fears about unforeseen and uncontrollable environmental hazards. Even though Love Canal was a more routine example of press–government interaction than the neutron bomb story, the press was just as pervasive and the impacts just as substantial.

The media augmented if not supplanted normal channels of communication. For Watson, Hansen, and the others, the pressure they were getting to act was the result of messages being conveyed to them through the media from Carey, from the residents of Love Canal, and sometimes from the press itself. The government officials used the press to send messages back, although they tried to deal directly as well. They preferred to talk in person to those most centrally involved, but they found themselves unable to do so to their satisfaction, in part because Carey and the residents found it more powerful to speak to the administration through the press.

Some measure of the force that the media added in the Love Canal decision can be seen simply in the volume of coverage. Granted that for the *New York Times* it was both a local and a national story, it is still remarkable that in the ten days up to the immediate aftermath of the relocation press conference, there were thirty-one separate articles in the *Times,* including eight front page stories and three editorials. The network news programs devoted thirty-one and a half minutes to the story during that period, a substantial amount of time for them. In the neutron bomb case, there was a similar intensity of coverage, but since the decisionmaking process stretched out over nearly a year, the heavy press interest was clumped at the beginning and at the end of the story.

The leaked Friday story on the pilot study also had an impact. It threw the government's game plan out the window, and significantly affected both the substance and the speed of the policymaking from that point forward. The leak was a much less dramatic intervention than the original Pincus story in the neutron bomb case, but still very important. The purpose of the press conference changed. What had been designed to announce the study became, in Barbara Blum's words, an effort at "mitigating the damage" by showing that the federal government was in control and taking steps that were both responsive and responsible. Blum remembers the situation from Saturday forward as being like "two people standing in a field and being pelted with five hundred balls."[12] Most of the balls were being lobbed by the press.

In both the neutron bomb production and the Love Canal relocation decisions, the press was very much a part of what happened. Each would have been a different story had the press not been there, or had the press acted in a different way. Take Walter Pincus out of the neutron bomb story and there probably would have been no story. Take the press out of the Love Canal relocation decision and at the very least the step to relocate would have been taken more deliberatively; perhaps it would not have been taken at all.

In both cases, the officials involved had to think about and deal with the press. That sounds like a simple and obvious point, but it is important in understanding press impact. In both of these stories the policy choices became major issues for the government. Sometimes the press plays a significant role in determining what becomes a major issue. But even if the press does not figure prominently in putting the decision high up on the agenda, once it is there the press is part of the story. Everything the media do has an impact on what happens next.

It is a characteristic of significant policy decisions that officials will have to deal with the press, whether or not press strategy has been a part of the decisionmaking process. It was true in the neutron bomb production and the Love Canal relocation. It was also the case in the other policymaking decisions which we examined in depth.

Press Time

Officials spend a lot of time thinking about and dealing with the media. That in itself is both a significant impact of the press on policymaking and one good indication of the extent to which the press is an integral part of the policymaker's job. The results of the survey of senior federal policymakers from the last twenty years and the long conversations with some of the most respected policymakers from that period confirm that the press takes a lot of their time.

Nearly 50 percent of all the senior federal officials who responded to the questionnaire said they spent over five hours a week thinking about or dealing with press matters. In the case of the neutron bomb decision, almost all the major policymakers in the White House, the Department of Defense, and the Department of State were involved in developing or implementing the press strategy. That was, as we have seen, a somewhat unusual case because in a partial sense the policy itself was framed as a strategy for the media. Even in the Love Canal relocation, however, planning the press component of the policy was a matter that engaged the energies of Jack Watson and senior White House staff, as well as top officials at the EPA, Justice, and other federal agencies. At the Love Canal press conferences themselves, the EPA had the lead role but people from Justice at the first conference and FEMA at the second were also spokespersons.

This is not unusual. Whether senior federal officials like it or not, dealing with the press has become a significant part of the time they spend in their jobs. This is so almost without regard to policy area, although among those who responded to the survey, officials in foreign policy were somewhat more likely than the rest to have spent more than ten hours a week with the press and those who worked in human services somewhat less likely to have done so. Members of Congress spend more time with the press than those in the executive branch. Among those in the executive branch, the longer they served and the more recently they served, the more likely it is that they spent over ten hours a week with the press.

Overall, about half of the survey respondents spent between zero and five hours a week dealing with the press, over a quarter spent between five and ten hours, one out of seven spent between ten and forty hours.

John Gardner made a distinction between time actually preparing for interviews or press conferences, which was only a "tiny fraction" of his day, and the general "awareness of the role of the press" as an "instrument" of leadership, which affected much of what he did and would account for "a very substantial percentage" of his time. In the same sense, McNamara told us that he spent a "tremendous amount of time" trying to influence coverage. Theodore Sorensen said that he spent "some time with the press almost every working day." For Richardson it was a "significant" amount of time in any of his Cabinet jobs and for Brzezinski it was an "extensive" amount of time.

When these policymakers talk about time with the press, they do not see the press as an intrusion into their lives, but as a resource for them in doing their jobs. Policymakers who spend a lot of time dealing with press matters do so in part because they see the press as an opportunity for them to explain their programs and build support for their initiatives. There is a connection between time spent with the press and an effort to generate coverage rather than just respond to it. The more hours officials spent with the press, the more likely it was that they actively sought coverage.

To a less significant degree, the more hours they spent, the more likely they were successful in getting that coverage, and the more of the stories written about them they initiated. Over a third of those who spent more than ten press hours a week thought they initiated at least 50 percent of the stories done about them or their programs, whereas less than a quarter of those who spent less than five press hours felt that way. The more time officials spent with the press, the more likely they were to believe that good press makes the policy process easier, that negative press makes the policy process harder, and that positive press would help their careers.

The picture here is clear. According to the survey, nearly half of all senior federal officials spend a significant amount of time, over five hours a week, dealing with the press. Those who spend more time with the press tend to be more aggressive about it and more successful in achieving the coverage they desire. The longer officials spend in government, the more time they spend with the press. (Is working the press a key to longevity?) Over the past twenty years, there is a clear trend toward officials spending more of their time on press matters.

It is a related consequence of the pervasiveness of the press that the overwhelming majority of senior federal officials are actively engaged in press relations. Over 75 percent of them try to seek or influence news coverage regarding their office or agency, a figure that holds up pretty much across the board. Three quarters of all senior federal officials sought coverage no matter when they served, how long they served, in which branch they served, or whether they were liberals, conservatives, or moderates. They were somewhat more likely to have sought coverage if they were in foreign policy, and somewhat less if they were in commerce and agriculture.

While there still are senior federal policymakers who do not deal very much with the press or press issues, there are very few officials at the highest levels who are not actively engaged at all in press matters. Time with the press is both a result and a cause of the centrality of the press to the job of making policy. It is a reflection of the reality that another consequence of the pervasiveness of the press is that policymakers use the press and rely on the media for a variety of purposes. Seven out of ten senior federal officials use the mass media and the trade press for information about their own policy areas. Eighty-five percent of those officials say they use the mass media to find out what is going on in the rest of government. Nearly seven out of ten officials found informal and unofficial communication with the press useful in their jobs.

Perceptions of Press Impact

The significance of the impact of the media in the neutron bomb and Love Canal policymaking reflects the general experience of senior federal officials. There was a strong consensus among the policy-makers we surveyed that the press has a substantial influence on federal policy. They make it very clear that in their experience the media were a critical element of their jobs. Overall, over 56 percent of the senior federal officials from the last twenty years believe that the press had a substantial effect on federal policy. In fact, over 10 percent of that group say that the press had a dominant effect! Only 3 percent of all officials say that the press had little or no effect on policy in their experience.

Over and over again, policymakers reiterated an awareness of the impact that the press had on what they did. Califano talked about the regularity with which "high policy officials say, 'What will that look like on the evening news or on the front page?' " Sorensen said the press was a central vehicle for making policy acceptable to Congress and to the public. To Sam Hughes, the evidence of the scope of the press impact was that "you make your decisions, by God, with one eye on what the press is going to say."

The bigger the impact of the press, the more the policymakers are involved in dealing with press. This is one of the most important consequences of press impact for government. Those officials who believed that the press had only a modest impact on policy in their experience[13] tended to a disproportionate degree to work in areas which are less glamorous, less political, and less well covered by the press, such as commerce, agriculture, and human services. Peter Peterson and Elliot Richardson both commented that the press was less of a factor at the Department of Commerce. As Richardson said, "It's very hard to get good copy'' at that department. John Gardner and Wilbur Cohen said the same thing about human services. Members of Congress were much more likely than officials in the executive branch to believe that the press had a substantial impact. Within the executive branch, those who worked in foreign policy were somewhat more likely than the rest to believe that the press had a big impact. Understandably, public affairs officers were much more inclined than officials as a whole to believe that the press was very influential.

There was no correlation between ideology and press impact. Officials who described themselves as conservatives were just as likely as liberals to believe that the press has a substantial impact. This finding is particularly interesting in the light of the ongoing debate about the ideological bias of the Washington press corps and whether coverage tends to favor one point of view or another.

Officials who believed the press had a significant impact understandably dealt with the press differently than those who thought it was not as important. For example, policymakers who thought the press had only a modest impact were significantly more likely than the rest to have spent only five hours or less a week with the press or thinking about press matters. And they were less likely than the others to have actively tried to seek or influence coverage about themselves or their programs.

The nearly six out of ten officials who said the press had a substantial impact were much more likely than the others to spend more time with the press. (Over 70 percent of those who spent more than ten hours with the press and over 60 percent of those who spent five to ten hours a week with the press thought the press had a substantial impact overall.) They were more likely to have sought coverage, although no more likely to have been successful when they did. And they were much more likely (59 percent to 46 percent) to have initiated over one out of every four stories done on them or their agencies. Another salient indication of the active engagement with the press of those who thought the press had a substantial impact on policy is that they were twice as likely (40 percent to 20 percent) as their colleagues to have found informal communications with the press very useful.

There are two important points to be made about the overall impact of the press. First, officials overwhelmingly believe that the press plays a major role in the policymaking process. This is a case of what they say goes, because if the policymakers themselves believe the press is influential then by definition, it is. Second, the chief consequence of the substantial impact of the press is that officials are more actively and aggressively involved in dealing with the press. They relate to the press in many ways, they spend a lot of time on press matters, and they actively seek coverage for themselves and their programs. As a result of the presence of the media and their effect on what they do, most officials find themselves personally involved in the management of their press relations. it is simply part of the job.

CHAPTER FOUR

SIGNIFICANT IMPACTS OF THE PRESS

T HE STORIES OF the particular policy decisions around the neutron bomb, the Social Security disability reviews, and the Love Canal relocation make plain what should not be surprising, namely that the press has a huge and identifiable impact.

Policymakers generally share the view that among the most significant impacts of the press occur early on the policymaking process, when it is not yet clear which issues will be addressed and what questions will be decided. Officials believe that the media do a lot to set the policy agenda and to influence how an issue is understood by policymakers, interest groups, and the public.

Policymakers also agree that the press affects the process of policymaking, although there is far less consensus among them about precisely how that impact is felt. The coverage of the media tends to have two specific impacts. First, the press speeds up the decision-making process. Second, coverage, particularly negative coverage, tends to push the decision making up the bureaucracy to a higher level of officials.

Finally, policymakers do not say that the press has had an impact on their own policy choices. That is no surprise. Officials cannot be expected to identify instances when they altered their own best judgment about a policy option because of influence they felt from newspapers and television. To try to understand how the press affects policies themselves, it is necessary to look beyond the testimony of decision makers and see what happened in particular cases. From that perspective, it appears that the press can have a substantial effect on the policy choice, as well as on the policymaking process.

Who Sets the Agenda and Frames the Issue?

Both policymakers and reporters have professional interests in which policies are on the political and public policy agenda. Policymakers believe that they have the responsibility to establish priorities; reporters think they have the responsibility to focus attention on important issues officials are not addressing. Each is concerned about the other having too much influence.

Officials express frustration at having their priorities affected by what the press decides to cover. Policymakers want to control the flow of information, at least to the degree that they determine what are the issues being addressed in the policy area they are responsible for. Journalists express their frustration when they believe that the policymakers are unduly controlling the flow of information and deciding what will be news. This has been particularly characteristic of the relations between the White House press corps and the White House of Ronald Reagan, but it has been so before and undoubtedly will be so again.[1]

The efforts of journalists, officials, and outside groups all affect what is on the public policy agenda. Sometimes it is impossible to look back at a particular governmental policy decision and sort out with any degree of certainty just exactly how the issue came to center stage, whether it was primarily an individual initiative or the result of interaction among the various interests and players. The Post Office reorganization in 1969 is an unusually clear example of the capacity of policymakers to influence the agenda, although it was not an issue which had universal interest among the public. Officials in the Post Office Department were able both to focus public and congressional attention on their issue and to control the language of the debate. To accomplish that, they borrowed techniques which had been tested and proven on Madison Avenue and in the heat of political campaigns.

Officials at the Department of Defense barely got their perspective on the neutron bomb into the debate. For openers, they hardly tried. The response to the original June 6, 1977, Walter Pincus story in the *Washington Post* was a terse statement simply confirming that the weapon was being developed, followed three days later by a page and a half explanation of the bomb. At that point Pincus and Donald Cotter, the nuclear weapons expert who ended up with the responsibility for dealing with the press on the issue, started meeting, on a background basis, at Cotter's initiative. It was based on Cotter's advice, that the Department made no comment at all on Pincus's second big story, the June 24 article reporting that the neutron bomb was part of a plan to shift most nuclear artillery to an enhanced radiation basis. Then, near the end of the month, Cotter began getting more and more annoyed at the coverage and, over the objections of Tom Ross (the assistant secretary of defense for public affairs), began his frontal attack on the *Post*.[2] It was not until July that the department finally began a modest but coordinated campaign to get its point of view across to the press. And it was not until July 12, the day before the vote in the Senate on Hatfield's amendment to kill the bomb, that President Carter spoke out in favor of continued funding. According to Hatfield, Carter's intervention saved the bomb. The day after the Senate vote, the White House released the only educational material on the bomb formally provided and distributed during all of 1977 and the first half of 1978. It was a three-page release, sent to editors and news directors around the country.[3] By then, it was a case of too little, too late, and the wrong address, since the continuing battle for the weapon was to be fought abroad.

The process of agenda setting is not subject to rigid rules or formulae. It is the result of the interplay of various currents, including but not limited to the intent of both journalists and officials. Journalists can set the agenda without trying, just by doing their jobs. Many senior officials acknowledge and concede a major agenda-setting role to the press. Sorensen said that at the White House, the press setting the agenda was part of the routine: "Those [issues] that were highlighted in the press and those that came up repeatedly at press conferences were bound to get into the White House and get Presidential attention." Elmer Staats, whose more than forty years in the federal government included service as US comptroller general from 1966 to 1981, tells a story of reading an article about the ownership of farm land by foreign interests while he was at the General Accounting Office. He asked someone to look into it. "We began to check to see if the Agriculture Department had any information, and they said 'No, we don't have any. We don't think it's very much but we don't know.' So we proceeded further and went out to the state capitals of the farm states and found out that they didn't know it either. So we put together an interesting report which resulted in some legislation which required the Department of Agriculture to get reports through the states as to changes of land ownership where you could identify a foreign owner. . . . We picked that idea right from the press.''

To some extent, agenda setting is accepted by officials because what becomes a high priority issue for the media may be a reflection of what the people are thinking about. As John Gardner said, ''Editors have a very keen sense of what their readers are concerned about, and readers read what their editors are concerned about. The press and public opinion are pretty closely linked; sometimes you understand the ups and downs and sometimes you don't. Nobody really knows all the reasons for the ebb and flow of interest in a subject. The press isn't just sitting there saying 'We will not sensationalize this issue.' There are currents in the public and events that they're linked to that affect the press.''

Trying to control the agenda when the press is looking in another direction is not easy. Clark Clifford, secretary of defense from 1968 to 1969 at the end of the Johnson administration, talked about the difficulty of controlling the agenda at a press conference: ''The press and I would go into a press conference each with our own motives. My motives would be to get out to the public certain decisions that had been made, or certain attitudes or certain stories that I thought it would be useful if the public had. . . . Now, individual members of the press would go into a press conference with exactly the same notion. They would have particular questions and areas that they wished to cover and I could not control that. . . . In a number of instances, something would have happened that I thought should have received widespread coverage in the press, and the press would have differed on the newsworthiness of it.''

But officials try to control what is covered, and many of them believe that they have had some success. Cyrus Vance said that he could influence the agenda, although not control it, by not answering questions on subjects that he wanted to keep as far out of the public debate as possible. He saw a great difference between affecting *what* was discussed, which he thought he could do pretty well, and controlling *how* issues were discussed, which he thought was much more difficult. Foreign policy officials have more latitude not to answer questions for reasons of national security. Zbigniew Brzezinski shared this view, suggesting that an administration with an "activist" foreign policy could determine an agenda for the press, except for events which transpired over which the administration had no control. One of the reasons that it might be particularly difficult to affect how the foreign affairs story is covered is that journalists reporting on foreign policy tend to be among the most knowledgeable and sophisticated about their area of any group in Washington. They tend to stay with the subject for a long time. Henry Kissinger said he thought of the reporters covering the State Department as experts, who had spent a lot of time "developing a pretty good sixth sense" sometimes to the point where they were "better at the nuances of the game" of diplomacy than the diplomats themselves.

In the administration in which Vance and Brzezinski served, there was a dramatic example of controlling the agenda by using Vance's technique. During the spring of 1980, after the failure of the Iranian hostage rescue mission, the White House decided that what was needed was a period of quiet diplomacy during which the hostage crisis was not the lead news item day after day. To try to accomplish this, the administration consciously avoided commenting on the situation and tried to generate interest in other issues. To a considerable degree, they were successful. The networks and leading newspapers found themselves with much less to report with the government quiet. As a result, for a long period of time the coverage, particularly on the front pages and as the lead news items, virtually disappeared.[4]

"Pete" Peterson noted how a sophisticated understanding of the way the press works can help to control what is on the news: "One of the things Chuck Colson used to say and a thing John Connolly for example, did very well, was visualize that Walter Cronkite story, visualize what that twenty-second one-liner is that captures whatever it is that you're talking about. It has to be sufficiently memorable that the editors will say, 'well, that captures the point.' . . . In limited space, whether it is the newspaper or television, they tend to resort to selectively using that material which is memorable or quotable. . . . You use that both negatively and positively. For example, if there's a subject that you're very ambivalent about, or haven't yet arrived at a policy, or you don't want a certain story to be published, you can be verbose, circuitous, ambiguous, dull, or turgid so that the editor won't know what to take.''

Schlesinger said that he had success in influencing what the press was covering by focusing his attention and his comments on issues which he wanted to spotlight to the exclusion of others, some of which might have been more important to him but were already in the news.

While other officials we talked with offered similar suggestions for trying to influence what is covered, there was an overall sense that in general the press, or perhaps the public through the press, was the dominant force in controlling the agenda. This conclusion is confirmed by the views of senior officials as a whole.

Most of the officials responding to the survey felt unable to control the agenda by initiating stories on their own. Nearly half, 46 percent, felt that they initiated less than a quarter of the stories about their office or agency. Nearly two thirds of them, 63 percent, said that over half of the stories written about them were initiated by the press. Only 26 percent believed that they initiated over half of the coverage about themselves or their agencies. Who were those officials who were able to control the agenda more than half the time, and what can we say about them in comparison to their colleagues who were less successful at doing so?

Liberals and members of Congress were much more likely to have initiated over 50 percent of the stories about themselves than were moderates, conservatives, or persons who had served only in the executive branch. Within the executive branch, officials whose primary policy area was commerce, agriculture, trade, or economics were most successful at initiating the stories written about them. This is probably a function the difficulty of getting any coverage at all, mentioned earlier by Richardson and Peterson in reflecting on their time at the Department of Commerce. By a substantial margin, those who worked in foreign policy were least likely among all the policy areas to have initiated over 50 percent of the stories about their agencies. At first glance, this seems to run counter to the view suggested earlier by Brzezinski and Vance that they had some success in controlling the agenda in foreign policy. But in foreign policy, there are events occurring all over the world which become part of the agenda. Thus, even though senior officials in foreign affairs feel that they can influence what is at the top of the foreign policy agenda at any single point in time, almost every substantial international event is a news story of some kind with implications for US foreign policy, and officials can do little to affect the sheer quantity of news in this area.

Those officials who said they initiated over half of the stories about them or their agencies seemed to be more comfortable with the press than their colleagues. They were much more likely to have spent more than ten hours a week on press matters, and they saw themselves as much more successful in getting coverage. Not surprisingly, those officials who initiated less than 25 percent of the stories about themselves or their agencies were also least likely to have sought coverage. Officials who initiated more than 50 percent of the stories about them were somewhat more concerned than the others about the bad effects of negative press. They were much more likely to believe that negative press slows the process and affects careers. They were somewhat more likely to have leaked. They were more likely than the rest to believe that the press has a substantial overall effect on policy. They were much more likely to describe their relations with the press as friendly. The more stories senior federal officials initiated, the more likely they were to believe that the press more frequently relies for new on formal channels, such as press releases and press conferences.

Those senior federal officials who did best at setting the agenda were, in short, realists about the press. They did not operate under illusions about how the relationship between the press and officials ought to be in some perfect world. They figured out more or less correctly how it worked, and made it work for them. They did not necessarily like the idea that personality stories and negative press had significant impact, but they accepted it. They seemed to be able to distinguish between the romantic Woodward–Bernstein image of how the press operates and the more mundane day-to-day routines. What we know about the relationship between the press and officials seems to square with their view: the press has a big impact on policymaking, spending time and working with the press helps with coverage, and much of what becomes news is transmitted to the press by policymakers themselves. The Post Office reorganization is the most dramatic, but not the only example of this we found. Throughout all the cases and in the interviews with successful policymakers as well, there was a strong sense that working hard at press relations produced more success than just letting coverage happen.

Setting the agenda is no mean feat. As former Secretary of Defense Robert McNamara said, ''One has to work at introducing to the press, drawing the attention of the press, obtaining the coverage in the press of what one thinks is important . . . it was very, very difficult.'' It may be worth the effort. Most officials believe that the press controls the agenda much more than they can or do. The evidence suggests that officials can influence coverage and control the agenda to a substantial degree, very often more than they think they can.

Vance made the distinction between influencing what was reported and influencing how it was reported. The way the press frames the issue is as important as whether or not it is covered at all. If the press characterizes a policy option one way early on in the decision-making process, it is very difficult for officials to turn that image around to their preferred perspective. Policymakers are often faced with the nearly impossible task of catching up with the first story. One of the most graphic examples of that problem for officials came in the neutron bomb production and deployment decision.

The characterization of the weapon as a bomb that ''kills people and leaves buildings standing'' appeared in the first article by Walter Pincus and was with the story until it was over. It is difficult to overstate the frequency with which neutron warheads were described in the media in those terms. During June and July of 1979, that language was used regularly by AP and UPI and appeared in fifty of the sixty news articles in major newspapers we surveyed. Among the broadcasters who used it were Bruce Morton, John Chancellor, David Brinkley, Floyd Kalber, Walter Cronkite, Dan Rather, David Hartman, Tom Brokaw, Phil Jones, and Bettina Gregory. A few conservative columnists and some newspaper editorials during those months reflected something closer to the Pentagon's view of the weapon, but the overwhelming weight of the coverage, news and commentary alike, reinforced the initial framing.

Officials also had problems with the framing of the issue in the Social Security disability reviews. The new comprehensive review process had been instituted by the Carter administration and a Democratic Congress because of anecdotal evidence that there were many recipients receiving benefits who were not entitled to be on the rolls. It was generally believed that the Social Security Administration's existing procedures were not adequate to the task of weeding them out. When a preliminary study suggested that the number of ineligibles might be much higher than assumed, the Reagan administration, under prodding from the General Accounting Office, decided to accelerate the reviews dramatically.

For months, officials understandably continued to think about the accelerated reviews as a policy for saving taxpayers' money by catching cheaters; but the press increasingly was reporting on it as the government "purging" the rolls and causing terrible hardship to many deserving people along the way. By the time Social Security Administration officials realized that the press and public had a view of the program that was very different from their own it was too late to do anything about it, and the new review process eventually collapsed.

In a similar way, the Reagan administration struggled unsuccessfully to overcome the way the press framed the issue in another visible initiative, the administration's decision to reverse the IRS policy of denying tax exemptions to schools that discriminated based on race.

Framing the Bob Jones Tax Exemption

Back in 1970 the Internal Revenue Service (IRS), under pressure from Congress and with the support of President Richard Nixon, decided to take away tax exemptions from segregated schools. There was no explicit authority to do this, no statute passed by Congress giving the IRS the power to deny exemptions to schools which would qualify except that they discriminated based on race. The IRS theory was that all organizations which had been specifically enumerated in the Internal Revenue Code as tax exempt, such as churches, charities, and educational institutions, had to be charitable to be eligible for the exemption, and that organizations which did not conform to "public policy," such as the policy against discrimination based on race, could not be considered "charitable" in the common-law sense of that term.

For the next ten years, that policy remained more or less untouched. The Congress never explicitly endorsed it, but acquiesced in it at several opportunities. In 1978, the IRS proposed new and tougher regulations which, in effect, required private schools to meet racial quotas or lose their tax-exempt status even if they certified that they had nondiscriminatory admission policies and had tried to recruit black students. The proposed regulation proved very unpopular; the IRS received 150,000 protest letters about it in six months. The Congress intervened to block implementation of the regulation, but during the congressional debate even the most ardent opponents of the new IRS test affirmed their support for the underlying 1970 ruling.

While the congressional debate over the test did nothing directly to undermine the 1970 policy, it had at least two important indirect effects. First, it alerted a large number of organizations and institutions to the potential trouble which an aggressive IRS could cause using the "public policy" rationale as a basis for denial of tax exemptions. Orthodox Jews, for example, were worried about whether their tax exemption was at risk because sexes were seated separately in their synagogues. Second, it awakened political conservatives, particularly in the Republican Party, who believed that government should not interfere in such private associations. The 1980 GOP platform promised to "halt the unconstitutional regulatory vendetta by Mr. Carter's IRS commissioner against independent schools," and candidate Reagan made similar pitches to religious audiences,[5] including one at Bob Jones University (BJU).

BJU is a fundamentalist religious school, founded in 1927 in Greenville, South Carolina, with a kindergarten to graduate school student body of six thousand. Until 1971, BJU did not admit blacks, on the grounds that the Scriptures allegedly proscribed a separation of the races and expressly forbade interracial dating and marriage. Between 1971 and 1975, BJU did admit blacks, but only those who were already married to blacks. In 1975, the university went so far as to begin admitting unmarried blacks, as long as they agreed not to date or marry outside their own race or encourage others to do so. For nearly a decade, BJU had been in the courts, fighting the 1970 IRS ruling. The university won in the district court, but lost on appeal, with both courts using strong language in their decisions.

In September 1981, the Treasury Department began its routine review to determine what position the government should take on the request by BJU for certiorari to the Supreme Court. The senior Justice and Treasury Department officials who would be expected to be involved (not including those at the very top of either Department), agreed that the government should urge the Court to hear the case and should defend the 1970 IRS ruling as it had done up through the judicial process. (At this point there were actually two cases, because the case involving BJU had been joined with a similar case brought by Goldsboro Christian School, an institution that did not admit any blacks.) Justice filed a brief to that effect and the Supreme Court granted certiorari in October. Lawyers in the Tax Division at Justice then began work on the main brief, anticipating a mid-December filing. It was not until December, when the draft brief began to be circulated within the highest levels of the Justice Department, that the position began to be questioned.

William Bradford Reynolds, assistant attorney general for civil rights, read the brief and raised concerns about it with Deputy Attorney General Edward Schmults. With the filing date only a week off, Schmults reluctantly encouraged Reynolds to prepare a response to the brief. At the same time, Bruce Fein, an associate deputy attorney general in Schmults's office, prepared a memo for Schmults laying out the history and the arguments on each side. After hearing out Reynolds and Fein, Schmults was sufficiently disturbed that he decided to call Timothy McNamar, the deputy secretary of the treasury. That was on December 8, and at a series of meetings during the next three weeks, those men plus Treasury General Counsel Peter Wallison went back over the cases and thrashed out the issues. Doubts began to grow about the 1970 ruling, but the discussion focused on the legal issues, not on the political or public relations aspects of where they were headed. As Wallison remembers, "There was a kind of ivory tower quality about it all. It was a lot of lawyers . . . articulating pros and cons, but articulating them as you would before a court, instead of thinking about how you would articulate it to the public."

Their discussions were beginning to move toward a consensus that the public policy rationale for denial of tax exemptions was not specifically authorized by the Congress and that it could not distinguish in its application from a ruling against Bob Jones University because it violated public policy against racial discrimination and a ruling, say, against Wellesley College because it violated public policy against sex discrimination by not admitting men.

They had been able to get the filing deadline extended to January 8, but they had still not decided what to do. During this time, there was talk of proposing legislation to enact the policy contained in the 1970 ruling, but that avenue was not pursued as the pressure of the approaching filing date concentrated their attention on the case. The group had some awareness of the potential political fallout from a reversal; back in mid-December Wallison had written to his boss, Treasury Secretary Donald Regan, apprising him of the review that was taking place and suggesting that the issues involved were "significant enough to raise at the White House level."

Unbeknownst to the officials at Treasury and Justice, the White House was already involved. Congressman Trent Lott (R-MS), the minority whip in the House, had written to the president in early December, urging that the White House intervene on behalf on BJU in the Supreme Court. In the margin of the log of congressional mail next to the summary of the Lott letter, the president wrote, "I think we should."[6]

While the Lott letter never received a formal reply, one copy of the president's notation made its way to Lott and another to T. Kenneth Cribb, Jr., a devout conservative on the White House staff. Cribb wrote to his boss, Edwin Meese, counselor to the president and the senior White House staff person responsible for legal issues with policy implications. Cribb reviewed the case and added dire warnings about the "enormous" ramifications of supporting the 1970 ruling, stressing the interference with religion.[7] Cribb proposed to Meese not that the White House try to change the prevailing view at Justice, but that they make an end run on Justice by persuading the Treasury Department to grant the tax exemptions to Bob Jones University and Goldsboro Christian College, thereby mooting the case.

Meese talked to the president, and the president talked to Treasury Secretary Regan. "Thinking of it as a procedural matter," the president later said, "I just simply told the secretary of the treasury what was going on, and called his attention to it."[8] Regan, however, did not talk to anyone in his department about the brief conversation.

The copy of the president's log notation that found its way to Congressman Lott was also making its presence felt. Lott quickly sent copies of it along to Schmults and Regan, urging that in light of the log the plan to file a brief supporting the IRS ruling "undercuts" the president's position and should not be undertaken without his review. Schmults remembers being surprised at receiving a copy of the president's log from Lott, but since "the president's position was pretty clearly staked out from the campaign,"[9] he was not surprised at the content and didn't bother to show it to anyone else at the department. At this point those favoring reversing the position at Justice and Treasury were looking at it as a legal necessity with cloudy awareness that it would be unpopular politically because of the civil rights consequences. The president and Lott were looking at it as a matter of principle and policy which they supported and which would be enormously popular politically because of its religious freedom and nongovernment interference aspects.

The White House got another chance to send a clear message. On December 22, McNamar and Wallison met with Fred Fielding, the White House counsel. In preparation for the meeting, Wallison had sent along a three-page memorandum which, among other items, raised the political implications by noting that a reversal would be "read as a statement by the Administration that overtly discriminatory practices are not objectionable."[10] In that meeting, Wallison and McNamar told Fielding that Justice and Treasury were going to decide the issue on the legal merits, thereby leaving Fielding and the White House with the opportunity either to get involved or steer clear. Fielding asked a few questions and requested that he be kept informed, but did not pick up on the political considerations.

The next day was spent reviewing the revised and narrowed brief in support of the 1970 ruling. McNamar was still not convinced. Neither were Schmults and Reynolds. On December 28, McNamar made the case for reversal to Treasury Secretary Regan, who approved the policy change and told McNamar to check it out with Meese. McNamar called Meese and told him that he was prepared to go ahead with the reversal, but that it would be "politically very unpopular." He says that Meese responded by asking if McNamar was sure he was comfortable with the legal side of the issue.[11] It was apparently the first time that Meese had discussed the case with a top official at Treasury or Justice.

On December 29, Schmults and McNamar read the next draft of the brief and were still unconvinced. They agreed to recommend a reversal. Schmults wanted to convince himself that the White House knew what it was getting itself into, so he asked for and got another meeting, this one at Fielding's office with himself, Reynolds, and McNamar. Once again, the discussion focused on the law. Fielding says that he did talk with Meese, that they discussed the political impact of the decision, that they did not talk about ways of reducing the fallout or presenting the decision so that it might be best understood, and that Meese said that he knew it would be controversial but that it was the right thing to do. Schmults then re-covered the bases, raising the reversal at the end of a conversation with Meese about another matter, and raising it with White House Chief of Staff James Baker as well. At this point, Schmults and McNamar asked for and received another extension, this one to January 11, in order to be able to fully brief the attorney general and the assistant secretary for tax policy at Treasury, both of whom were away for the holidays.

The return of the attorney general from vacation provided the opportunity for one final review of what was to take place. The review was scheduled for January 6, in the attorney general's office. Again, the discussion was largely a legal debate; the politics surfaced but only briefly and secondarily. Smith decided immediately after the two-and-a-half-hour session to recommend reversal. The Justice Department had undertaken a very comprehensive *legal* review, but no blacks had been involved, no one with primary concern for the public relations aspects of such a policy change were included, and the lawyers from the department's Civil Rights Division were not a part of the process.

After making the decision, Smith called Baker in the White House. Baker, who knew little about the case, went to see Meese, and after hearing more of the details asked for the issue to be discussed at the senior staff meeting the next morning, Thursday, January 7. What went on at that meeting is not clear. About the only thing that everyone agrees upon is that the Bob Jones case was not a major item for discussion.[12] Fielding and Meese were doing the briefing. Fielding remembers that he raised the political risks question, but the conversation quickly returned to whether the legal arguments were sound.

A key decision that came out of that meeting was that the announcement should be treated quietly. The government would file a memorandum with the Supreme Court the next day, Friday, January 8, informing the court that the administration was granting the tax exemptions to the two schools, thus making the cases moot. A press release would be issued late in the day to be followed by Treasury officials holding a briefing for selected reporters, invited because they might be oriented to the legal, rather than to the political or civil rights sides of the issue. Shortly after the staff meeting broke up, Meese and Baker went to brief the president. There was no discussion with him of the political implications of the decision.

The late Friday afternoon press briefing was scheduled at Treasury. Wallison had the lead and he remembers being handed an AP dispatch on the way to the briefing room which began: "The Internal Revenue Service plans to allow tax exempt status to private schools that discriminate against blacks."[13] The briefing had not even begun, and the issue had been framed by the wire service in just the way the administration hoped to avoid. Before he began to speak, Wallison was already in the position of digging himself and the administration out of a hole. It didn't get any better. As Wallison kept emphasizing separation of powers and the like, the reporters kept asking whether the administration's action had the effect of strengthening segregated schools.

The initial press coverage was straightforward, reporting the news although generally unclear on why the policy had been changed. The reporters had understandable difficulty grappling over one weekend with legal technicalities that had been consuming a cadre of lawyers in Justice and the Treasury for months. Quickly, however, the editorial writers and commentators waded in. NAACP President Benjamin Hooks said the decision was "nothing short of criminal." The Americans for Democratic Action called it "obscene." Sen. Daniel Moynihan (D-NY), who had a hand in the 1970 ruling while he was employed in the

Nixon administration, warned that "a quarter century's achievement [in race relations] could unravel in months." On the other side, Connaught Marshner, chairman of the National Pro-Family Coalition, termed it "a real victory," and Bob Jones III said that "we rejoice that God in His own way has allowed this to happen and He gets all the glory for it."[14]

Not surprisingly, these reactions fed on the news stories and vice versa so that the political side of the policy completely overwhelmed the legal. Editorial writers and columnists generally adopted the tax-exemption-equals-federal-subsidy theme and condemned the action in strong language. The administration was portrayed as insensitive at best and sympathetic to racism at worst, and the legal arguments for the change were generally dismissed rather than rebutted when they were mentioned at all. It was assumed that the change had more to do with political debts to the religious right than with the legal and social policy arguments offered by the administration. There were a few very rough days of coverage, and the White House felt the heat.

Finally, and most belatedly, the issue began to receive the kind of political scrutiny at the highest levels that had been lacking until then. The decision and the coverage were the topic of conversation at the Monday, January 11, 7:30 A.M. daily meeting of Michael Deaver, Edwin Meese, and James Baker, the White House management trioka, and at the 8:00 A.M. senior staff meeting which followed. Director of Communications David Gergen recalls that "there was a general sentiment at the meeting . . . that we'd have to deal with this and somehow get the understanding of this turned around. Deaver felt the press coverage was horrible, that Reagan is not a racist, and that "we were not going to be accused of that."[15] The strategy was to issue a statement from the president clarifying his position, and to throw back to the Congress the question of legislation to authorize the 1970 policy. Gergen drafted a statement, later worked on by Baker and the president himself, in which the president emphasized his opposition to racial discrimination and that the decision had been made in a legal rather than racial context.[16]

Before the presidential statement was issued, the heat was already being turned up several notches. Democratic senators were preparing legislation. Some black Reagan appointees were threatening to resign.

And the commentary in the press was scathing, unrelenting, and virtually unanimous in condemnation. Of the 16 major daily newspapers that had editorialized by Tuesday, only one (the *Atlanta Journal*) supported the decision, while only two others even acknowledged that the administration's position had some merit *(Dallas Times Herald* and *Christian Science Monitor)*. The *New York Times* called the decision "tax exempt hate."[17] At the Tuesday 8:00 A.M. senior staff meeting, Bob Jones was again the topic of conversation. It was agreed that a fact sheet was necessary to clarify misunderstandings, and interested staff were invited to attend an 8:45 A.M. meeting with the attorney general for a further briefing. Most of the time at the eight o'clock meeting was spent discussing how the White House should counter the growing perception that the president was either racist or indifferent to bigotry. There was a consensus that something had to be done, but not about what had to be done. As Deaver remembers, "Some of us were concerned with perceptions, with the public view of how our actions were seen; it's not how they were necessarily. And there were others on the White House staff who felt very strongly about philosophical commitments; in their terms, you should do what is right regardless of what the perceptions were. . . . I argued that . . . once the public perception turned sour and the president was being hurt by it, we had to address that instead of going over the hill with the flag flying."[18]

After that meeting, Deaver and Meese took two black White House aides in to see the president, so that the president could hear the reactions of the black community first hand. He was stunned by what they said, "astounded," in Deaver's words. Soon after that meeting, he had the draft statement changed to include language committing himself to proposing legislation. Senator Robert Dole (R-KS) agreed to sponsor it, and the President asked both Senator Strom Thurmond (R-SC) and Congressman Carroll Campbell (R-SC), whose district includes Bob Jones University, for their support.

The new position was not directly inconsistent with the January 8 decision. The president was still saying that the IRS did not have the power to deny the tax exemptions, but now adding that they should have it. It was confusing. The administration was not going to grant any new tax exemptions while the legislation was pending, thus having the effect of reinstituting the 1970 policy, except with respect to BJU

103

and Goldsboro. The administration could not go back and take away the exemptions from those two schools without directly contradicting the January 8 memorandum to the Supreme Court making the cases moot. Everyone pitched in to try to get this across. Gergen issued the president's statement proposing the legislation on the afternoon of Tuesday, January 12, and followed that with a fifty-minute briefing during which he repeatedly stressed that the president had agreed with the January 8 decision only because he did not believe the Congress had granted the IRS the authority to take away the exemption (mentioned eight times), that the president was firmly opposed to racial discrimination (six times), and that the January 8 announcement had been misinterpreted (five times). One-on-one backgrounders were given to leading print and electronic news organizations by Gergen, Baker, Meese, and Deaver.[19]

All of the effort barely made a dent. The political critics continued as if nothing had happened, and the press greeted it as only making partial amends for deplorable conduct. Of the forty editorials on the subject between January 12 and January 18 compiled by the IRS, five supported the administration. Many of the editorials even opposed the legislation, suggesting that the only honorable course to follow was to admit error, roll back the January 8 decision, and withdraw the legal opinion that the IRS did not have the authority to act. To make matters worse, not only was the legislative proposal greeted with lukewarm interest, but it was overwhelmingly characterized not as a clarification of the administration's position, but as a reversal or, more commonly, a "flip-flop." Under the flip-flop view, by filing the legislation the administration acknowledged that the January 8 policy had been racist or insensitive, without actually doing anything about it.

The administration's strategy for communicating the original policy decision was to sneak it out as an issue of tax policy late on a Friday afternoon. In doing so, they encouraged the suspicions of the press, and enabled the perspective of those who saw the new policy as racist to frame the way the public understood the issue. The result was a series of embarrassing steps to try to rectify the perception, leaving the policy in shambles and neither its supporters or its opponents, inside or outside of the administration, satisfied with the result.

The Policymakers Frame an Issue

The advantages to policymakers of being able to frame the issue, rather than having it framed for them in the press, are enormous. The Post Office reorganization fight provides a good illustration. By the end of the summer of 1969, the *New York Times,* the Associated Press, and Postmaster General Blount all believed that the House Post Office Committee (HPOC) was closely divided on postal reform. The first big test would be whether HPOC would vote to use the administration bill, H.R. 11750, or the bill of Chairman Thaddeus Dulski (D-NY), H.R. 4, written with the help and advice of the postal unions, as the basis for the legislation to be reported to the full House.

The administration's proposal was to create an independent government corporation called the Postal Service to be administered by a nine-member Board of Directors. The board would select one of its own as chief executive, and the chief executive would select another board member as chief operating officer. Postal rates would be set by a panel of experts, reviewed and modified by the board to take effect unless vetoed by the House and Senate within sixty days. Wages, job classifications, and benefits would be determined through collective bargaining. The Dulski bill rejected the government corporation solution and essentially maintained congressional control over Post Office operations. Under Dulski's plan, the Post Office Department would stay as a Cabinet-level agency but include a Postal Modernization Authority to finance and manage capital improvements. Every four years, postal rates would be recommended to the president by a Postal Finance Commission, with rates promulgated by the president unless vetoed by Congress. The postmaster general would remain a political appointee, and wages and benefits would be set by Congress.

The initial effect of the agenda-setting efforts of the so-called front organization, the Citizens Committee on Postal Reforms (CCPR), had peaked by Labor Day, having made postal reform a national issue aided and abetted by enormous coverage and editorial support from many of the nation's newspapers. The unions were optimistic that they had weathered the worst of it, and there was still a comfortable majority on the committee to beat back H.R. 11750 in favor of the chairman's bill.

CCPR and the Post Office Department (POD) then narrowed their focus, concentrating on convincing the public and the ten or so still uncommitted members of the HPOC of the great stakes in the choice between the two bills, and that H.R. 11750 was both bipartisan and the only real reform. Press releases were sent out by CCPR objecting to the use of the word "reform" to describe the Dulski bill.[20] White House communications chief Herb Klein staged a media event at the Western White House in San Clemente, flying former Democratic Party national chairman and Postmaster General Larry O'Brien and his Republican co-chairman of CCPR, Thruston Morton, out there for a briefing of the president to be followed by a Nixon–O'Brien–Morton press conference. Press coverage of the extravaganza was as planned, with stories on CBS News, ABC News, and page one of the *New York Times* stressing bipartisanship and emphasizing the choice between the two bills. A week later, on September 9, CCPR staged another piece of theater for the media, this time at the annual meeting in Washington of the National Postal Forum, a group of 2,400 business and government leaders who met to discuss postal problems of concern to the business community. CCPR and the POD were again satisfied with the results: the press covered the convention's close with everyone standing up chanting "H.R. 11750, H.R. 11750."

To direct the effort aimed at specific congressmen, CCPR hired a legendary political operative, Jerry Bruno. Bruno had gained fame as an advance man for John and Robert Kennedy. O'Brien recruited him to form local CCPR chapters in the districts of the ten HPOC members who were thought to be wavering. Bruno had only about six weeks to get the job done before the committee vote.

A typical example of the way Bruno worked was in the Syracuse district of Congressman James Hanley (D-NY). On August 25, a senior POD official flew to Syracuse to give a speech touting H.R. 11750 that had been requested by the local manager of communication and community relations at General Electric, one of the key corporate sponsors of CCPR. The speech received broad press coverage, but of special note was the *Syracuse Herald-Journal*, the larger of the two daily newspapers in the city, which urged "all residents to write Congressman James Hanley in support of this bipartisan effort."[21] The publisher of the paper had just agreed to chair the local CCPR chapter, which also included the mayor and the president of the Syracuse Federation of Women's Clubs among its members, and the Chamber of Commerce, the Junior Chamber of Commerce, and the local Sears store among its supporters. By September 5, Hanley had received over five hundred letters in favor of H.R. 11750. Full-page ads appeared in both the daily newspapers, urging him to support the bill.

A month later, on October 8, the HPOC finally voted on which bill to use as the basis for legislation to be reported to the full House. Enough Democrats voted with the Republicans to create a tie between the two bills; since the motion was to substitute the administration's bill for Chairman Dulski's, a tie meant that the motion failed and the Dulski bill would be the primary legislative vehicle for postal reform. On the surface it appeared to be a setback for the administration, but there was still a long way to go in the process and the tie vote on a committee with a substantial Democratic majority was a sure sign that the administration's message of bipartisan reform had begun to take hold. Months later, when the administration's government corporation bill finally was enacted, the effort at making it understood as the only real reform appeared to have been a crucial step in the process.

Framing the issue is similar to agenda setting. Our data show that the press can and often does have a great influence on how the issue is characterized. For policymakers, framing the issue is not easy, but catching up with the first story is even more difficult. Like setting the agenda, it can be done, and can be done more often than many policymakers think possible.

Impact on Process

Press coverage has a tendency to speed up the policymaking process and to move the decision-making up the bureaucratic ladder. The decision to relocate the families at Love Canal was a dramatic illustration of how the media can affect the timetable policymakers establish for choosing a policy option.

Remember that for a period of about ten days in early May 1980, only a few people in the EPA knew about the results of the pilot study of possible chromosomal damage among Love Canal residents that had been undertaken as part of the lawsuit brought by the government against

Hooker Chemical Company. Then, at a large meeting chaired by Jack Watson in the Old Executive Office Building on Friday, May 16, the policy was set. It was decided to inform immediately the residents who had been tested of their individual results, then to hold press conferences in Washington and in Niagara Falls the next day, and finally to take five days to validate the test to ensure that the preliminary findings hold up and to assess their implications. It was at the heart of that plan to make a thoughtful, well-planned decision about what further steps to take. This involved not only validating the study, but also ensuring that legal authority and adequate financing were available should it be decided to undertake the relocation that the government had resisted to that point.

The Saturday press conference set off a chain reaction, aided and abetted by the leak of the study almost immediately after the Friday meeting which made the study itself old news by Saturday. There was enormous press coverage for the next few days. It was fueled in part by hard news such as the friendly taking of two federal officials as hostages by the residents of Love Canal and the continuing public pronouncements on federal inaction by New York's Governor Carey, and in part by the intrinsic press and public interest in the drama. The pressure brought to bear on the administration by the coverage itself, and by others through the coverage, threw the policymakers out of their program almost as fast as they had agreed upon it.

By Monday, the die was cast. None of the stated preconditions for a decision existed: there was no validation of the study, no clear legal support for a federally funded relocation, no federal funds allocated, and no agreement with Carey on the sharing of costs and responsibilities. But there was a decision to go ahead anyway. The media reported every move of all of those involved, commented on it with editorials and background pieces, and thereby helped make the policymakers feel as if they had to decide, whether or not they were ready to do so.

This was also an element in what happened in the case of the Social Security reviews. For well over a year, the Reagan administration had been subjected to press criticism, essentially from the print media, about the impact of the review of all Social Security disability recipients which had been mandated by the Congress and accelerated

by pressure from the GAO and from OMB. In response to the legitimate concerns, the Social Security Administration instituted several
important changes in the review process designed to mitigate the
unfairness and build in greater sensitivity to individual hardships.

SSA officials say that those reforms were initiated by the agency
based on their own analysis of the problems. However, the administration reforms were always announced following a period of particularly
intense press coverage. This suggests that if the administration were
considering the changes, the press coverage made them move from
consideration to adoption in a hurry, more of a hurry than they would
have done without it.

Policymakers understand that press coverage affects the speed of
the decision-making process. A substantial percentage of those senior
federal officials who responded to the survey cited the effect on the
speed of the process as one of the most important impacts of the press.
Thirty-nine percent of them said that positive press increased the speed
with which an issue was considered or acted upon, and 36 percent said
that negative coverage did the same. (As many officials said that negative coverage *slowed* the process as said speeded it up, suggesting
that negative coverage is a more volatile commodity than positive coverage.)

A similar and related effect of the press on the policy process is
to move issues up the ladder in the government. The more intense—
and the more critical—the press coverage, the higher the level of the
government that deals with the issue.

Once again, the cases illustrate the phenomenon and the federal
officials corroborate the reality of the press impact. In the Social Security disability reviews, Social Security Administration and Health and
Human Services (HHS) officials spent the first year dealing with the
pressure of the accelerated review process on their own. Conversations
with some of them suggest some bitterness that the White House was
not more responsive to the difficulties they faced, both in making the
acceleration work and in responding to the criticism generated by the
reporting of individual cases of unfairness or hardship. The reporting
was being done mostly out in the field by local and regional news
organizations and mostly by print media. For six months, between the
summer and late fall of 1981, the coverage continued in this fashion.

SSA officials Svahn and Simmons reaffirmed their commitment to the program through comments in newspapers and testimony before Congress. Near the end of that year, coverage began to move to Washington, and to television, and suddenly the White House became involved.

One of the first signs that the handling of this issue was no longer for SSA administrators Svahn and Simmons alone came in mid-November when the local Washington, D.C., NBC affiliate aired the segment about the financial and emotional toll that losing disability benefits had wrought on one Stuart Kindrick and his family.[22] The piece was very tough, reporting that Kindrick was kicked off the disability rolls even though the state rehabilitation agency said that he was so severely disabled that they could not help him get a job. Kindrick and his family were in the process of being evicted from their home. When the segment was repeated as part of the local news insert on NBC's *Today* show the next morning, there was one particularly incensed viewer: President Ronald Reagan. Reagan says that he stormed into the office and demanded to know what was going on.[23] The program had suggested, mistakenly, that Reagan budget cuts rather than the accelerated reviews were responsible for Kindrick's plight. Administration officials called the local news director to complain about several alleged errors, although it later turned out that most of their complaints were unfounded. The Kindrick story became something of a cause celebre, being a prime example of press misconduct used in the George Will commentary on ABC's *This Week With David Brinkley,* by high administration officials, and by the president himself. For the first time in the controversy over the accelerated disability reviews, handling the story became a White House project with HHS and SSA doing the staff work for the response, rather than making the response themselves. The more the coverage was on network television and national newspapers, the more the White House became involved.

In a much shorter time frame, the same impact occurred in the Bob Jones case. There, the policy was developed by the Treasury and Justice Departments with White House acquiescence but not assistance. Once announced, the policy almost immediately involved the White House because of the way the story was treated. In retrospect, it is obvious that White House officials completely misread the likelihood that the decision to restore the tax exemptions to Bob Jones and

Goldsboro Christian would create a firestorm, but they did so in part because the technicians, primarily lawyers, who had been working on the issue had focused on the legal merits almost to the complete exclusion of the political and public opinion implications.

The policy was announced on a Friday afternoon. By Monday morning, the White House senior staff knew there was a problem and they were discussing it. The president issued a terse statement saying that he really was "unalterably opposed to racial discrimination in any form."[24] The White House was still hoping it might all just go away. By Tuesday, the editorial writers and the administration critics had not only made the decision into a major issue, but had concentrated their firepower on the fundamental attitude on racial issues of the administration in general and the president in particular. The Monday afternoon statement not only failed to quell the uprising, but it may well have contributed to focusing the issue on both the principle and the principal, rather than the narrow issue of the Bob Jones case and the senior officials in Treasury and Defense who had cooked the whole thing up. There was a revolution in Congress, a budding revolution by blacks and civil rights lawyers in the administration, and a full-scale attack from the press. And, as in the Social Security disability reviews, to the extent that the bureaucrats and senior political appointees in the departments were still involved in this policy, it was to staff the presidential response and no longer to make policy on their own.

In the neutron bomb case, there was an explicit decision to keep the White House at some distance from the issue to give the president all the time he wanted or needed to decide what position to take. Yet even then, it was not long before the issue was not able to be contained any longer and the spotlight was on the White House exclusively.

It was primarily through the efforts of Walter Pincus and the *Washington Post* that the story was kept alive for a month or so after it first broke. The vote in the Senate on the Hatfield amendment to delete funds for the neutron bomb provided another hard news story, but more important it put the question into the White House. The press had fueled the debate enough so that Carter and his senior staff genuinely feared that if he did not come out against the amendment he could find the decision on the bomb made for him by the Senate.

This was not as clear an instance as the others of the press coverage in and of itself moving the issue up the ladder. The continuing attention did, however, substantially increase the risk to the White House of staying uninvolved. The president tried to oppose the Hatfield amendment without declaring himself on the bomb, and to some extent he ended up with the worst of all possible worlds. He received credit—or blame—for the defeat of the Hatfield amendment, but he and the White House could not go out and sell the bomb because he was still leaving his options open on production and deployment. As a result, he left himself in an even more vulnerable position when the issue broke wide open in Europe than he had been at home.

In the Bob Jones, Social Security reviews, and neutron bomb cases, the coverage which pushed the issue up the ladder was largely negative in tone. In the Post Office case, where the administration was benefitting from essentially positive coverage, the president was not forced to do anything. He more or less stayed out of the limelight and the decision-making process; he was able to choose his opportunities, getting involved when the White House could make a crucial difference rather than have the taking over the whole policymaking enterprise. Senior federal officials agree that whether the coverage is positive or negative has a substantial effect on whether or not the issue moves up. Only 10 percent believe that positive coverage moves responsibility to more senior officials, whereas 43 percent believe that negative coverage does.

Impact on Policy

In the decision of the Reagan administration to abandon the accelerated Social Security disability reviews, the press not only speeded up the process but probably, despite the protests of officials to the contrary, affected the content of the policies as well. Officials seemed not only to make policy quickly in response to press coverage, but to change and reverse their policy positions abruptly when adverse publicity peaked.

For example, in March 1982 Svahn testified to Congress that he opposed continuing benefits up to the appeal to the ALJs of a state denial of eligibility. A month later, he issued a press release reversing himself. The two most visible intervening events were a *Newsweek* cover story entitled "Reagan's America: And the Poor Get Poorer," and that devastating Bill Moyers documentary on CBS entitled *People Like Us*. Both featured the familiar—to print readers—stories of individuals who had suffered difficulties as a result of being removed from the disability rolls, in some cases unjustifiably.

That policy reversal was the first of a series of reforms that were instituted over the next few months, many of which had been previously explicitly and publicly opposed by the administration. The changes were prospective and therefore did not affect the people already being processed under the accelerated reviews. Officials knew that those cases in the pipeline would produce their share of "horror stories" and they were right. The problems received more coverage than the changes, and the administration continued in early 1983 to consider ideas for more reforms in the review process.

Then the pattern of publicity to reversal repeated itself. In April 1983, deputy SSA administrator Simmons testified in opposition to legislation imposing a moratorium on cutting mental impairment cases from the disability rolls. Then, in May, came the story about Roy Benavidez, the last man to receive a Congressional Medal of Honor from the Vietnam War. Benavidez had just been dropped from the disability rolls, although he was still receiving benefits pending his appeal, and he was receiving his military pension as well. For several days at the end of May, Benavidez was big news while at the same time, the HHS package of reforms was making its way to the Cabinet Council in the White House for approval. The reforms were endorsed, including the moratorium on mental impairment cases which Simmons had testified against in April. At the very least, the coverage and the Benavidez story put the CDI issues on the top of the agenda, grabbing the interest of the White House, making OMB opposition ineffective, and the policy testified to a month before inoperative.

Even more dramatically, in the brouhaha over the Bob Jones tax exemption policy the overwhelming and overwhelmingly negative coverage made it extremely difficult for the administration to make the policy stick. There the press played a particularly powerful role. At the time of the policy announcement, the senior policymakers involved, whether at Treasury, Justice, or the White House and whatever their individual rationales and levels of information, all favored restoring the tax exemptions. The intense hostility which characterized the coverage, aided and abetted by the intensity and hostility of many of those outside the press whose views were being reported, turned the situation on its head. On Friday, when the granting of the tax exemptions was announced, officials expected trouble but not the possibility of a reversal of the policy. By Tuesday, it was clear in the White House that the only way to salvage the situation was to get as close as possible back to the status quo ante with the minimum embarrassment. Here the press affected the likelihood of success of the policy almost to the point of making it impossible to keep it in place. Still, the effect was to make it extremely difficult for the policymakers to do what they wanted to do, to raise their agony level to the point where it was clear to those involved that gracefully backing away would be the easiest way to go.

The press had characterized the issue as whether the president was sensitive to racial matters or even willing to condone some forms of race discrimination. Given the difficulty of the task and the likelihood of success, the administration chose not to try to argue about the president's values or reframe the debate. They changed the policy. In both of these cases, as in the neutron bomb case, had their been no press or had the press been of a significantly different slant, there would probably have been a different policy outcome.

There is little doubt that press coverage affects the capacity of policymakers to get their policies successfully adopted and implemented, and that whether the thrust of the stories is negative or positive is an important factor in determining the effect of the coverage. As Clifford put it, ''If the president made a decision and the press generally favored it, then . . . you'd get it rolling. If he made a decision in some matter, or had a policy on a matter, and the press was generally against it, it added a good deal to the difficulty.''

Clifford represents the view of most of the senior federal officials who responded to the questionnaire. Over three quarters of them believe that positive press increased their chances for attaining their policy goals. More than 70 percent of them said that negative coverage decreased their chances for achieving their policy goals. Very few said that positive press hurt (5 percent) or that negative press helped (6 percent). Note that what we are talking about here is not the press changing policy, as if it were the major actor and determinative force. We are talking about the press having an influence on the capacity of policymakers to turn their ideas into policies that are adopted and implemented. We are talking about the press changing the odds.

In the Post Office reorganization, for example, positive news stories and favorable editorials were very important, although not the only, elements contributing to the eventual passage of the administration's proposal. They helped to create an environment in which a reluctant Congress could be moved. But it is not at all clear that there would have been a reorganization if there had not been a strike, and if the administration had not made a major concession in agreeing to tie together postal pay raises and the reorganization.

The press in the neutron bomb deployment and production case had a similar effect, but going in the opposite direction. In the year-long debate over the bomb, an essentially unfavorable press made it extremely difficult for those in the administration who favored the weapon, including the national security adviser and the secretary of defense, to convince the president to move ahead. But the president probably still could have sold a decision to go ahead right up until the time he decided not to do so. Public opinion polls said the people favored production, most of his key advisers were supportive, there was a clear majority in the Congress, and the allies in Europe had been prepared to defend deployment. What the press did was change the odds, making it much less likely that Carter would approve the bomb than would otherwise have been the case.

In both the Bob Jones case and the neutron bomb case, where the coverage was essentially negative, the press had the effect of stopping the process and providing the opportunity for—or forcing—officials to stand back, look at the policy, and rethink it all over again. Senior decision makers—Gergen, Baker, Deaver, and Reagan in Bob Jones; Carter and Powell in the neutron bomb—acted as if they were not responsible for a policy that had already been made and was supported by senior executive branch officials in charge of the policy area. They went through the policymaking process almost as if they were considering it in the first instance. In Bob Jones the reassessment was done very quickly and in neutron bomb it took a year, but in both cases the president started over from the beginning, exploring the options and reviewing the merits of each. This pattern is a characteristic effect of negative coverage. Half of the respondents to the questionnaire said that negative press causes policy reassessment.

In both of those cases, the result of the reassessment amounted to a policy reversal, although the policymakers involved would not characterize it that way. Policymakers do not like to think of themselves as being inconsistent and do not like to be seen as inconsistent, as having made a mistake, or as having changed their minds. In both cases, the new policy was not announced as a direct reversal, but was framed as a new option, one that had not been fleshed out before and one which provided the policymakers with the possibility of saying that there had not been a reversal at all. Yet, we know that when a barrage of negative coverage intrudes into the policymaking process or follows a policy announcement, there is a tendency to reassess the decision and then to find another option that can be characterized as something other than a reversal. Forty percent of our respondents said that negative coverage causes them to reshape their policy options. Press coverage, particularly negative coverage, affects the number of options considered, often in both directions.

In these cases one effect was to create new options. But in the Bob Jones case, there was also a narrowing of the options which could be considered. No option would be viable which failed to protect the president's racial sensitivity flank, and that limitation obviously affected the possibilities. That is also what happened in the Love Canal relocation. Options that might have been considered had there not been so much pressure to act, and act fast, were simply not available. Coverage that affects policy narrows the options in the direction of the coverage and provides an incentive for creating new options, some which might be more cosmetic than real. In the survey, a fourth of the respondents said that negative coverage caused them to increase the number of policy options considered and an equal number said that it caused them to decrease the number. Both seem to be true, sometimes simultaneously. Even positive coverage has an impact on options, according to some of our senior federal officials. About one in six said that positive coverage increased options and almost as many reported that in their experience positive coverage decreased the number.

We realized from the outset that it would not be easy to find instances where the press changed the content of policy. Establishing a causal relationship is always difficult when there are so many factors involved. The policymakers responsible for the policies are not likely to acknowledge that they adopted a particular policy because of pressure from the media rather than considerations of the public interest. Policy advocates both inside and outside of government are likely to overstate their own impact, even when it is felt through the press. The assessment of participants in the policymaking process of the role of the press is likely to be affected by the limits of their own self-awareness and by their views of the policy outcome.

With that caveat, we looked for cases where we had reason to believe the press played a significant role, but in only three of the six we explored in depth—the Post Office reorganization, the neutron bomb production and deployment, and the Bob Jones tax exemption—does it appear that there was a significant impact on the heart of the policy content. In all six of the cases there was an impact on the process of policymaking. Joseph Califano has said that the impact of the press was one of the biggest differences between his two tours of duty in government, first in the White House under Lyndon Johnson and then as secretary of HEW under Jimmy Carter. The impact of a more aggressive press in his experience was that he put less in writing, involved fewer people in decision making, and made decisions more quickly than he otherwise would have done. Yet when we interviewed him for this research, the only instances in which he said that the press had an impact on the content of policy were those in which he had been using the press to further his own policy goals.

Califano's response was typical of what we found in our interviews. Senior policymakers could easily find instances where they had used the press to their advantage, or where the press had made life difficult for them to do the people's business, or even where the press had caused other policymakers to change policies, but they were hard put to identify cases where the press had changed *their* policies. As James Schlesinger said, ''While I will adjust the way I present things based on the mood of the press, I am not going to change the substance of what I am attempting to accomplish. I will just bull ahead for better or for worse. But I don't think that all people in public office, wisely or unwisely, take that position. Many of them will skitter off in one direction or another, depending on what the press has to say.''

Policymakers do differ in this regard. Henry Kissinger acknowl-

edged that there were instances where the press was the dominant factor in changing policy when he was in office, although he, too, could
not come up with a specific case.

In general and over time, the press has more substantial and significant an impact on the process of policymaking than on the content
of the policies themselves. Yet the press does have some very clear
impacts on policy, including affecting the likelihood of adoption and
implementation, and the nature and number of the options considered.
Beyond that, there are some instances where it is clear that the press
itself was the dominant factor in determining the policy itself. Or, to
state it the other way, in a small but significant number of policy decisions the outcome would clearly have been different if the press had
not been there.

CHAPTER FIVE

THE
CONDITIONS FOR
BIG PRESS IMPACT

S OMETIMES THE EFFECT of the press on the processes and products of federal policymaking is more substantial than at other times. That suggests that there might be certain conditions under which the press impact can be expected to be considerable.

We looked at several factors that might make a difference: who was involved in the decision making; which department was making the policy; at what stage of the process the coverage occurred; whether the stories were focused on personalities, issues, or process; and whether the coverage had a generally positive or negative cast to it. But the most important variables for big press impact were whether the government's press and public relations people had been a part of the decision making early on in the policymaking process, whether elected officials were involved, and whether the coverage was negative. The story of the Reagan administration's effort to restore tax exemptions to Bob Jones University and other private schools which racially discriminate was a dramatic illustration of policymaking in an environment in which a big press impact is a likely result.

What happened there? Why was the administration unable to get its message out? Why did everything it did or said become interpreted as a smokescreen for bigotry?

Officials who dealt with the media during this crisis believe that the coverage was a product of the conflicting strategies with which they approached the press and the press's own prejudices. David Gergen, who probably did more press briefing than anyone on this subject, believes that it was a combination of two assumptions on the part of the press. The media believed that the administration was soft on civil rights and strong on the religious right, so that the policy was consistent ideologically; and that the administration was extremely competent, especially in its dealings with the press, so that officials must have known how it was going to play and have intended it that way. Treasury General Counsel Peter Wallison's view is that there was a kind of pack journalism at work. "I was overwhelmed by reporters; they were coming in through the windows and doors, over the phone, and through the transom. I was terribly frustrated throughout this whole period because I said the same thing to every reporter who called: that we had done this out of concern over granting power to administrative authorities that didn't have a legislative basis. Not once could I get a reporter to focus on that, and there was barely ever anything in their stories that reflected Treasury's viewpoint, because they did not think our concern was responsive to what they felt the story was."

Wallison added that the media were "entangled by their own framing of the issue." They would have had to change the whole direction of their stories in order to take seriously the administration's defense. Over at Justice, William Bradford Reynolds was Wallison's counterpart in dealing with the press. He has a less charitable perception of what happened: "Once the press saw the hue and cry, saw this had gone down as anticivil rights, none of them were willing to stick their heads above the bunker to get shot at . . . they were not going to take on the civil rights people, or print anything that might be perceived as anti-civil rights."[1]

Even if in the administration's view the media went astray, the administration's press strategy, or lack of it, enabled it to go that way. There was no press strategy, there was no attention at all to handling the public relations side of the issue until the ball was thrown at the eleventh hour to Assistant Treasury Secretary for Public Affairs Anne McLaughlin. It was on Monday, January 4, four days before the announcement of the policy reversal that Deputy Treasury Secretary McNamar called McLaughlin to alert her that the reversal was imminent. It was apparently the first time in the weeks of discussion that a person with special responsibilities for the public relations aspects of policymaking had been involved. And it was presented to her as a fait accompli, not a decision in the making for which her advice was being solicited.

She recommended the details of the plan: file the motions mooting the case at 4:00 P.M. on Friday, release a statement at the same time under McNamar's name which included a chronology of the legal history of the cases and selected press clippings, and provide a background briefing for the national press. The late Friday afternoon release was designed both to deemphasize the decision and to ensure that the administration's perspective would dominate the evening news; with an earlier release the interest groups would all have been contacted by the press and their reactions would have been part of the initial story. The release plus briefing was to provide the fullest possible explanation without having a full-scale press conference, which would have been an exception to routine policy for the Justice Department in a pending case and would have given the whole business more attention than they wanted. The statement was from McNamar and the briefing at Treasury so that it would have the best chance as being seen as a tax story, not a civil rights story. To emphasize that, the legal reporters, not the civil rights reporters or the political reporters were invited. The press release was reviewed on Friday in Regan's office by senior officials from both Treasury and Justice, including the two Cabinet officials. Those gathered took great pains to ensure that the administration's reversal of position was carefully explained; no one present suggested adding language directly addressing the civil rights issue. No one involved expected the issue to disappear. They just hoped that, in the words of Deputy Attorney General Edward Schmults, "some people would appreciate that we had legitimate concerns that weren't racially motivated."[2]

Following the announcement, no background material was released, no formal briefings were provided by the legal experts, neither the attorney general nor the secretary of the treasury made public pronouncements or provided their own background sessions, and no official appeared on a network news program to provide the administration's rationale. There was no campaign at all. They had acted as if the press would have no impact on their policy, and for a good while they continued to act that way.

Wallison says "we were retreating so fast we never had an opportunity to marshal our forces and set up a line of defense.'' McLaughlin recalls no push from above to mount an educational effort, so she passed all the press inquiries on to Wallison until the issue escalated off her desk up to the White House. At Justice, the strategy was to hunker down, in part because everyone wanted to see the issue portrayed as a tax matter, not a civil rights one, and in part because Justice does not normally comment on pending litigation. The only time in the month of January that Attorney General Smith mentioned the issue to the press corps covering the department, he said that he would not comment on it because the case was still pending; later he said he believed that ''what the administration could certainly have done much better would have been to more effectively explain their position.''[3] There were obviously other reasons for the reticence at Justice than the fact that the cases were still before the Supreme Court. Schmults commented, ''What happened is that the press framed the issue as race and we were bathed in the heat. . . . Everyone dove to the bottom of the foxhole; no one wanted to be personally identified with this disaster . . . because they were afraid they would be called racist. . . . No one explained why we had mooted the case.''[4]

There was another complication for both Treasury and Justice. Very quickly, the White House took over the management of the issue, including management of the press. The attitude was that the whole decision-making process had been badly handled; if the departments then started their own counteroffensives to explain the administration's position, they would have run head-on into the White House efforts to change or modify the decision. Besides, the White House people did not believe it possible to educate the press corps on an issue this complicated in a matter of days when they already had a view of what it involved. The decision to propose legislation to give the IRS explicit statutory authority to do what it had already been doing for a decade, even if it complicated the overall posture of defending the January 8 decision, was made to provide tangible evidence of where the president stood on the issue of racial discrimination. But as Wallison noted, the White House, obsessed with jettisoning the racist tag, was not predisposed to explain why the January 8 policy change made sense and why the proposing of legislation was consistent with it. To the White House, trying to explain and defend the policy change was a naive pursuit. And if the January 8 policy was seen as racist, then having the January 12 legislative proposal seen as inconsistent with and a reversal of the January 8 policy was not such a bad idea.

The White House strategy was essentially reactive, to absorb the criticism of the January 8 decision as being insensitive and incompetent, but to attack the idea that the president, or the administration, was racist. To some extent it worked as planned. Here is what *New York Times* columnist Tom Wicker had to say on January 18:

> All right, Ronald Reagan is not a racist. The White House tells us that, instead, he's an uninformed and uninvolved president who on an important question of domestic policy didn't know what he was doing. Neither did his senior staff.[5]

Wicker went on to emphasize that this was not his view of the situation, but the official White House view being disseminated by Meese and Deaver.

The White House effort to undermine the racist tag in part by asserting that the January 8 decision had not been handled well, led the press naturally to look for who it was that had messed up. That became the theme of the stories during the second week, with most of the finger pointing being done at Edwin Meese, and being attributed in the press to the ubiquitous anonymous White House "sources." Understandably, the criticism of Meese provoked a counterattack from him and the Bob Jones decision had turned into a story about in-fighting among the senior White House staff. There was only one way to put a stop to that story: have the president take responsibility for the January 8 decision, thereby making irrelevant whether one or another of the staff had been the cause of the mess.

The president did just that at a press conference on January 19. He might have been moved to take that position in part by the realization that his log notation on the Trent Lott letter was about to be made public. In any event, his acknowledging that the mistake was his own changed the story once again, this time back to Ronald Reagan's depth of involvement and sensitivity to minorities. The president's press conference put the Bob Jones story more or less to rest for good. The buck stopped there.

In retrospect, the testimony of the participants is consistent. All assume that wherever the responsibility lies, more attention to the potential press reaction early on would have given the story a far different ending. If the press impact had been taken into due consideration at the beginning, the policy reversal might never have been made or, more difficult perhaps, it would have been done in a context which might have mitigated the reaction.

The power of the press to affect the policy was inordinately enhanced, if not actually created, by the failure of the policymakers to give the same thoughtful attention to the communication aspects of the policy as they had to the legal merits while the policymaking was under way. The policymaking process focused hard on the potential consequences of the decision for the separation of powers between the executive and legislative branches, and for the tax liability of other institutions in society. The policymakers explored alternative legal strategies in great detail. But the potential consequences for the policy and for the policymakers of the way the policy would be communicated and understood were all but ignored. Options of a press strategy which might involve the public in the policymaking earlier on were never raised.

Assessing the impact of the press in any particular case means taking into account not only what actually happened but also what might have happened had there been a different plan for dealing with the press or, in the Bob Jones case, had there been any thoughtful plan at all. What was striking here was the absence of deliberation about how and when to go public and how to take into account the possible press responses, once the reversal was being considered.

Given the policymakers' failure to think hard about the communication aspects of the policy during the decisionmaking process, it is not surprising that the press had a great impact once the policy was announced.

The Role of the Public Affairs Staff

If there is a single dominant message about the conditions for press impact from the Bob Jones case, it is a notion about the role of public affairs staff, and public affairs thinking, initially identified for this project by Eileen Shanahan and reinforced over and over again in this research. Shanahan, herself both a respected journalist and a former assistant secretary for public affairs at the Department of Health, Education, and Welfare, pressed the idea that senior federal officials as a whole wait too long before involving their public affairs people in the policymaking process. As a result, policymaking is done without adequate attention to the way the policy will be received and the way it ought to be presented.

The policymaking stories we researched for this project support Shanahan's contention. Forgetting about the communications aspects of policy options is no accident. Policymakers too often believe that because they have held press conferences, given interviews, written a couple of op-ed pieces, and read the *Post* every morning, they are experts on the press, as well as on the policies. Not only do they underestimate the difficulty of dealing with the press, they also are particularly ill suited to thinking about it and doing that job themselves when they have been involved as advocates and / or as specialists in the policy development itself.

From the policymakers' perspective, there are reasons not to involve their own public affairs people or not to dwell on the public relations implications of the policy options. To the extent that the public affairs people are bridges to the press they also are sources and resources for the press. Policymakers sometimes prefer to keep information from them on the theory that what the public affairs people don't know can't be provided to a reporter. The public affairs staff traditionally are not regarded as substantive in the professional executive branch culture, they are often not up to speed on the technical aspects of the issues, and they are therefore sometimes seen as a drag on policymaking rather than as an asset.[6] In addition, the content of public affairs work— assessing the press response, packaging and communicating the message—may be seen as interfering with the consideration of a policy on its merits. Rejecting a policy choice because it would not be explainable to the people or the Congress appears to some policymakers as compromising their responsibility.

Yet, research and experience strongly suggest that the absence of public affairs professionals, or at least of careful consideration of the communications aspects of policy choices as a part of the policy process, is a central factor contributing to the press having a considerable (and, from the policymakers' point of view, sometimes disruptive) impact on the process and the policies. Compared to the other policymakers, the public affairs people are professionally disinterested in the substance of the policy, except with regard to its communications aspects. That gives them some degree of distance in looking at the implications of what is being proposed. Part of their job is to perceive what the public reaction will be.

Anne McLaughlin, the assistant secretary for public affairs at the Treasury, said she "blew her stack" at her boss, Deputy Treasury Secretary McNamar, for the inadequate warning she received on the Bob Jones policy reversal.[7] She was not only left out of the decision making, but was then handed the decision and told to prepare it for the press with very little notice. How much difference her input would have made would only be speculation, but it is not hard to imagine that she would have been a forceful voice against the policy on public affairs considerations, and, if she had been involved at an earlier stage, it is more likely that the corrective legislation, or some other component which would have been evidence of the administration's good faith on the discrimination issue, would have been included. If that is true for her, it is much more true for Gergen and Deaver at the White House; they would have been involved in the policy and communications considerations had Meese or Fielding put the issue on the agenda for the senior staff.

There is a pattern here. In the debate over the deployment and production of the neutron bomb, Assistant Secretary of Defense for Public Affairs Thomas Ross knew nothing about the bomb when the story broke. He then acquiesced in the handling of very sensitive press relations by Don Cotter, a policy advocate without professional credentials in dealing with the media. Cotter declined to take the advice offered by Ross, going off on his own crusade to counter the Pincus story.

In the struggle in the Carter administration over whether to relocate the families at Love Canal, the public affairs people at the White House, the EPA, and Justice were almost completely ignored. The press strategy was developed and the press releases were written by policymakers who had no particular experience in dealing with the press and who were burdened by their own vested interest in the substance of the policies.

In the Social Security reviews, for an excruciatingly long period of time the policy experts had primary responsibility for handling the press. They were so confident of their position from the perspective of what we might call the technical face of the issue that they lost sight of the other, very real, if less tangible faces involving the politics and the image. Neither the press nor the Congress nor even the courts could convince the policymakers that the reviews were creating more problems than they were solving. It was their policy, they believed in it, and they too easily discounted the criticism and the motives of the critics without listening to what they were saying. They did not appreciate until well down the road that the public criticism, from the press and in the press, was having consequences for the policy itself.

On the other hand, in the most successful example of policy-making that we studied, the reorganization of the Post Office, the circumstances were vastly different. One fundamentally distinguishing characteristic of the policymaking there is that professional public relations people were involved from the start, both at the Post Office Department and with the outside advocacy organization. The press and the public relations strategy were an integral part of the policymaking process, as the postal unions who opposed the reorganization soon found out.

Beyond the involvement of public affairs people, or public affairs thinking, there are other factors which we examined to try to assess whether there were any other specific conditions under which the press can be expected to have a substantial effect.

We looked next at which government department was making the policy. Then we examined the stage of the policymaking process when the press coverage took place from very early on when the policy problem was just coming to the surface, through the point at which the policy was adopted, and to its implementation. Finally, we looked at the kind of story that was involved: for example, was it a personality story, a process story, or an issue story? Was it a negative story or a positive story?

Where in the Executive Branch?

To try and assess which departments of government might have the potential for particularly high vulnerability to press influence we looked at four characteristics from the questionnaire responses: officials' assessment of the overall impact of the press on policy; the percentage of all the issues in the policy area reported by the press; the percentage of stories about the policy area which were initiated by the official; and success in getting coverage.

The more involvement of the press in a policy area, the higher the potential for substantial press influence on policymaking in the departments responsible for the area.

Senior federal officials whose primary focus was the law were among those least active in dealing with the press. In the Bob Jones case, most of the policymaking centered in the Justice and Treasury Departments; almost all of those involved were lawyers. Lawyers are trained to depend on the power of reasoned argument to persuade; but dealing with the public through the press also requires symbols and emotion. Lawyers are conditioned by training and temperament to deal with the legal issue as the central issue. Thomas DeCair, who was handling public information for the Justice Department at the time, put it this way: "We weren't trying to win the PR battle with the briefing; we were just trying to get across the idea that there were some legitimate legal issues."[8] Among all the policy areas, senior federal officials in law, legal services, and law enforcement spent the least time with the press and were least likely to acknowledge having tried to use the press. The lawyers tended to treat the press formally when they dealt with it at all.

Senior officials in foreign policy were at the high end of press activity. They spent substantially more time with the press and were much more likely to have sought coverage than their counterparts in the rest of the government. These results were revealing. Based on those factors, foreign policy was the area with by far the highest potential for press influence. It was at the top of the policy areas in all four categories. Senior federal officials in foreign policy believe that the press had the biggest overall impact, that more of their issues were reported, that they initiated fewer of the stories about them or their agencies, and that they had the lowest success rate in their press relations.

Two factors may help explain this finding. First, in foreign policy almost everything is news. Officials at senior levels know that almost any issue that comes across the desk is likely to be covered at some point. Second, covering foreign policy tends to be a long-term beat for Washington journalists. Former secretaries of state Rusk, Vance, and Kissinger all made a point of commenting on the sophistication and expertise of the reporters covering the department, and that may also contribute to the greater potential for press influence.

On the low potential impact side were commerce and agriculture, human services, and those dealing with legal issues at Justice and elsewhere. Senior officials in the area of commerce and agriculture were way above the norm in having initiated over 50 percent of the stories about themselves or their agencies (41 percent of them but only 26 percent of officials overall) and below average in estimating overall press impact (51 percent to 57 percent). Those in legal policy were above average in success in obtaining desired coverage and below average in the number of officials reporting that over 60% of all their issues were covered.

The human services policy environment also seems to be anomalous with respect to press coverage. Human services is an area where there are so many policy issues, many of a technical and minor nature, that only those with the most inherent drama and the broadest impact are covered. Former secretaries John Gardner and Joseph Califano both emphasized this point. Gardner said that the department was "not in the line of fire" in the same way as is the secretary of state, where all the issues are controversial and newsworthy. To Califano, "HEW is not well covered, by and large. Part of it is the resources of the press. . . . It's the largest department of government." Compared to foreign affairs, he said, HEW is "simply not news."

The survey responses confirm this view. Only 29 percent of the human service policy officials reported that more than 60 percent of their issues were covered compared to 38 percent overall. And only 49 percent of human services policymakers said that the press had a very substantial impact on policy, compared to 57 percent overall.

There is one place in the executive branch where the level of engagement with the press is extremely high, much higher even than in those departments dealing with foreign policy: the White House.

The White House Environment for Press Impact

In this study we did not focus on the White House. Nevertheless, we were often drawn back to the White House as we followed the press and the policymaking process. The White House is more like the Congress than the rest of the executive branch in its dealings with the media. First, it is full of people, including in particular the president, who have had substantial experience in dealing with the press, obviously with some success. Second, like the Congress, the actions of the White House are subject to the scrutiny of a large and permanent press corps. Third, as an elected official and as the chief executive of the government, the president needs the press more than do senior officials in the departments. He relies on the press in part to get the message out. He has a stake, a political stake as well as a policy stake, in all the important decisions being made in the government. Ex officio, all presidents and all White House staffs are activists in dealing with the press. Theodore Sorensen characterized this well. "It would not have been of any value to think of policy in the abstract," Sorensen recalled. "I had to think of policy in terms of its acceptability to the Congress and the public. That means I had to think of the press, the press being the means by which the public and to some extent the Congress learn about the president's policies."

In each of our case studies, as the decision making became more intense the White House became increasingly involved. What started out as policies for the bureaucracy in the Love Canal relocation, Social Security reviews, and Bob Jones turned into White House concerns as the issues began to get more attention.

Only in one of the cases, the neutron bomb deployment and production, was the decision explicit a presidential one from the outset. In Love Canal, the EPA continued to be the agency out in front as far as the press and the public were concerned, but the decisions were made in the White House and the choreography was done by White House staff. In the Social Security reviews, the policy was largely a departmental matter until the White House became involved after the networks started to cover the issue. In the Bob Jones tax exemption case, the White House gave passive approval to the new policy at the initiative of Treasury and Justice, but once the firestorm broke, the White House took the lead. Only in the Post Office, where the news was mostly good, were the departmental officials who started the process still there in their lead role at the end. Part of the explanation here is that once a story gets big or a policy issue gets hot, the White House has to get involved because of the president's political and policy stake in it. But what makes a story big or a policy issue hot sometimes has a lot to do with the press coverage. Coverage gets attention, particularly from elected officials. And coverage, especially negative coverage but positive coverage as well, increases the visibility of the issue for everyone. If the coverage is good, there will be some interest from the higher-ups in basking in the reflected glory. If the coverage is bad, then the higher-ups will want to help put out the fire, ideally before it arrives at their doorstep. This is essentially what happened in the case of the Social Security disability reviews where the White House intervened to counter the bad coverage well before there was any assumption of the decision-making responsibility.

The survey results tend to confirm the notion that you can't study the press impact in policymaking without encountering the White House. Senior federal officials share the view that coverage increases the importance of the issue and that negative coverage in particular moves the issue up to more senior officials. Their views were similar to that of Sorensen and the other officials interviewed who served in senior White House staff positions.

The intimate relationship between presidential–White House policymaking and the press, as characterized by Sorensen, gives the White House an opportunity denied to other officials to set the agenda. When the president has an affirmative policy in any area, according to President Jimmy Carter's national security adviser Zbigniew Brzezinski, he can determine what is news. "An administration, if it's activist, and ours was in the area of foreign policy, tends to determine an agenda for the press. Not exclusively, and certainly many events transpire over which you have no control, but by and large we set the agenda."

Stuart Eizenstat, assistant to the president for domestic policy in the Carter White House, agreed that the power is there to control the agenda, but argued that it is a short-run advantage. "You can't for any length of time really manage the news. . . . The first day coverage may be exactly what you wanted. Ultimately, someone is going to dig into that proposal, and they are going to find the soft spots."

Even leaks take on a special meaning when it is the White House doing the leaking. Brzezinski argued that there is really no such thing as an unauthorized leak in the White House, since those doing the leaking are the authorities. His own "leaks" were not leaks because they were "deliberate acts designed to promote the policy we were trying to implement." Eizenstat had a different view. He said that it was inevitable that agencies would try to influence presidential decision making through the press, but leaking by members of the White House staff is simply unacceptable. The White House, in his words, "ought to be a place where the president can rely on having people who have no ax to grind other than to protect his own interest."

Eizenstat underscored the power of the White House to influence coverage. "The White House is a very difficult place to cover. It's the *most* difficult place to cover in most respects, because on the Hill everybody wants to talk. It's their job to get into the news and to be quoted. In the executive branch, it's certainly the cabinet secretary's job to make news and to articulate policy. In the subcabinet bureaucracy, even though it may not be their job, there's a symbiotic relationship that exists over time between the reporters who cover it and the bureaucracy as such, so there's going to be plenty of contact there. You can always get a story by walking into someone's office. The White House is a different story. Its access is circumscribed; even when you are in the building, you have to be led by the nose to get to a particular office. It's a very tough place to cover."

Interestingly, Eizenstat was concerned that the power of the White House to control the news could be used to the detriment of the policies being pursued. He suggested the Carter energy plan of 1977 as an example. There the policy was kept secret until it was ready to be announced. The problem was that because the consultation had been so limited, when the program was finally unveiled in an address to the Congress the element of surprise worked to its disadvantage: "In the basic policymaking process, surprise is not to be sought: it's to be avoided. Surprise embarrasses people. It puts their backs up. It makes the Hill suspicious that they haven't been included. It makes agencies less willing to cooperate on policies with which they disagree. If they feel they have been consulted, they feel they have had the opportunity to put their two cents in, which the press can help them do by venting some of these things.''

Another former White House policymaker also criticized the abuse of White House power in dealing with the press. Pete Peterson, who was in the White House as assistant to the president for international economic affairs under President Richard Nixon, said that in times of tension the Nixon White House would pull back from the press, severely restricting access. The result, Peterson believes, was that the journalists would rely even more heavily on critics of the administration for their information, and there would be less opportunity to get a balanced view of the policy, never mind a chance to respond to any distortions. He said that the press was viewed ''as either something to be used or as an enemy.'' Of course, he added, if the administration does not communicate with the enemy, i.e., the press, then there is no way that the reporters will change their minds, or even present the administration's point of view for readers and viewers to consider.

The enormous potential the White House enjoys for controlling the flow of information is unique in government; and the risk of doing so for short-term gain and long-term disaster is always present. Unlike the Congress, there is not the same familiarity between the press and officials at the White House. The engagement is more distant. But like the Congress, because elective office is involved, there is a high potential for being influenced by coverage and a great apparent need to influence coverage as well. What distinguishes the White House from the Congress in terms of the potential for press impact is that the stakes are always high, and the kind of intimacy and regularity of contact that produces a certain cynicism and relaxation of intensity on the Hill does not exist there. As a result the White House pays extraordinary attention to the details of coverage and thus creates perhaps the most volatile environment in the entire government for a substantial press influence.

Potential for Press Influence in the Congress

Not surprisingly, at the other end of Pennsylvania Avenue we found that the environment for press impact among leaders in the Congress is substantially different than that for senior appointed officials in the executive branch and much more like that in the White House. Members of Congress need the press in a more direct sense than do those in the departments and agencies. Members need to let their constituents know what they are doing, need to use the press to learn what opinion is back home, and need the national press if they are considering running for higher office. We surveyed those members of the House and Senate who had been in leadership positions, either in party leadership or as chair or ranking minority on the most powerful committees. Like their executive branch counterparts, they had risen to the top levels in the institution in which they served. Yet there were substantial differences between their two worlds in their dealings with the press.

For one thing, leaders in Congress were way above senior executive branch officials on two of the factors identified as suggesting a high potential press influence, and way below on the other two. They had a much higher estimate of substantial overall press impact (70 percent to 57 percent), and a much higher rate of those who believed that over 60 percent of their issues were covered (45 percent to 35 percent). This would suggest substantial vulnerability to press influence, but leaders in Congress also reported a higher success rate (48 percent to 36 percent), and a much larger percentage who said that they initiated more than 50 percent of the stories about themselves (55 percent to 22 percent). The environment for press influence in the Congress is sui generis, with an extremely high level of interaction, a high degree of intimacy and familiarity, and an acceptance of their mutual dependence and willingness to use each other.

As to the level of interaction, 58 percent of the executive branch people we polled spent five hours a week or less on press matters, whereas only 44 percent of the members of Congress spent that little time. On the high end, 14 percent of the executive branch people spent over ten hours a week, but 27 percent of the members of Congress did so. Still, a quarter of the members in our survey said that they wished they had spent more time with the press, much more than among the bureaucrats, illustrating again that legislators see the press as vitally important in doing their jobs.

Members of Congress look on the press more as a constant presence to be dealt with and used as a resource than as a force outside of their jobs which nevertheless affects their performance. Members of Congress, particularly leaders, do not have to go out and find the reporters; they are there all the time. For many executive branch officials, even at the senior levels, the press do not come around very much unless they have a real problem. Those in Congress were less likely than those in the executive branch to have actively sought coverage (76 percent to 65 percent), even though they spent more time dealing with press matters and the press reported a higher percentage of all the issues they dealt with.

Members of Congress have a more familiar and even intimate view of the press than do their executive branch counterparts. For example, our survey revealed that members of Congress are less worried about negative press than are the bureaucrats. They understand the element of truth in the cliche about yesterday's article being today's fish wrapping. Executive branch officials are more likely than legislative leaders to think that negative press will be believed and will have big impacts, such as moving responsibility to more senior officials or increasing the importance of the issue within the government.

While congressional leaders are less likely to see negative press as a problem, they are more likely to see positive press as an asset. They are more likely than their executive branch counterparts to see positive press affecting careers, as affecting their credibility, as being believed, as increasing the importance of the issue within the government, and as moving the issue to a more senior official. More than legislators, executive branch officials see the press as magnifying the importance of special interest groups, and as raising the level of government which pays attention to the group's concerns. The executive branch people are understandably more sensitive to the power of organized outside groups, such as Lois Gibbs's Love Canal Homeowners' Association, to affect their policymaking; for the Congress all that external noise goes with the territory. In general, then, members of Congress have a more benign view of the press—it can help you more than it can hurt you—than do those in the executive branch.

Other manifestations of the more intimate relationship between the press and officials on the Hill than in the bureaucracy are the use of informal communications with the press, the reliance on the media for information, and the willingness to leak. Forty-five percent of the members of Congress, but only 28.5 percent of the executive branch officials, found informal communications more than somewhat useful. Fifty-seven and a half percent of Congressional leaders but only 25 percent of senior bureaucrats relied on the mass media very much for information about their own policy areas.

While the executive branch worried about leaks much more than the Congress (76 percent to 63 percent), leaders in Congress were much more regular leakers (52 percent to 37 percent). We gave all the respondents who said they leaked fourteen possible reasons for leaking and asked which applied to them; members of Congress were much more likely to have chosen eight of the reasons, for five there was no significant difference, and only on one—leaking to undermine another's position—were the executive branch officials much more likely to have given it as an explanation for their own leaking. One of the most vivid examples we found of this use of leaks in the executive branch came from Zbigniew Brzezinski, who claimed that the State Department used leaks against him. According to Brzezinski, "There were people outside [the White House], particularly in the State Department, who used the press simply as a way of making certain that I did not overshadow the Secretary of State. . . . They were reacting to . . . my greater role . . . by leaks or by suggestions to the press designed to discredit me."

A very clear picture emerges from these responses: in the Congress, or at least among their leaders, the press is a familiar and regular presence, and an important part of their work. For the counterparts in the executive branch, the press is much less known, more to be feared, and its conventions less comfortable and less integrated into policy-making. The result of that is that the Congress is an unusual environment for press influence; there is a very high potential for press impact, and yet also a very high potential for senior members to influence the coverage.

When in the Process?

We have seen that the Bob Jones story was vulnerable to a substantial press impact because the communications aspects of the policy had not been taken into consideration early on. Another factor which made it ripe was that when it did become public, it surfaced as a story at a stage of the policymaking process when press influence appears to be at the maximum.

Consider the policy process as having five not always perfectly distinguishable stages:

1. problem identification—the period during which the issue is making its way on to the agenda for the policymakers;
2. solution formulation—when the policymakers are developing and sorting out the possible responses;
3. policy adoption—the stage when the options are being assessed and a choice is being made and disclosed;
4. implementation—when the policy is being put into effect; and
5. evaluation—the point at which the success or failure of the policy is being assessed.

From the perspective of the bureaucratic participants in the Bob Jones story, the announcement of the policy change and the mooting of the cases before the US Supreme Court put this story into the evaluation stage. The problem had been identified, the solutions had been thrashed out, the policy had been adopted, and had been implemented. From the government's point of view at the time of the announcement, there was nothing left to do but wait to see how the policy was received and go on to the next problem.

In retrospect, those involved say that they did not expect the story to die, but even those like Treasury General Counsel Peter Wallison who predicted the severity of the reaction did not conceive of the possibility that as a result of the coverage they would find themselves reconsidering what they had so painstakingly and deliberately done. The policy evaluation stage is the one at which the policymakers are most exposed and have the least flexibility in dealing with the impact of the press; they have made their contribution and they are now sitting back to see how well it works. Usually evaluation occurs down the road; here the evaluation was instant because the policy involved not a new government service or piece of military hardware, but a philosophic, political, and legal judgment. It was the judgment that was being assessed, and the values which it appeared to represent.

In the Bob Jones case, there was no press coverage until evaluation, but usually the press is involved as the problem is identified and throughout the policymaking process. Even so, senior federal officials believe that it is at the evaluation stage of the process that the press has the greatest potential for a large impact. That is also what happened with the Social Security reviews. Among the officials in our survey, 43 percent said that stories at the evaluation stage had a large or dominant impact on them, higher than at any other stage. There was a pretty clear consensus that stories at the solution formulation stage had the least impact. This notion runs somewhat counter to the findings about the potential for the press to affect the number and shape of options being considered; in the experience of senior federal officials negative coverage in particular seemed to have had a substantial impact on options.

For bureaucrats at the high levels, the solution formulation period is central to their legitimacy. It is the stage of the process when they are doing what they believe they are primarily paid to do; the technical face of the issue is and perhaps ought to be given more weight at this point than at any other. It is not surprising that senior officials would be most sensitive to maintaining their distance from outside pressures during the solution formulation period. It is also true, as suggested earlier, that they are least likely to acknowledge the influence of the press at this stage, even though we have seen in the cases that the press can have an impact on the policies themselves.

Most of the coverage that we examined in the case of the Love Canal relocation took place at the time when the solutions to the policy problem were being considered. The coverage had a substantial impact. The timing for the decision was appreciably shrunk, and the decision was clearly made before all the information was in. Looking back on it, there is a strong sense among those involved that the decision to relocate was inevitable. Whether or not that is true, it seems irrefutable that the coverage kept the pressure on and helped drive them toward relocation. If the press did not make that outcome inevitable, it at least contributed in a major way to making it the most likely result. The coverage was not all or even substantially negative; it was more notable for its quantity and persistence than whether or not it was supportive of the government action.

The last policymaking case which we studied in depth was the Justice Department's handling of the investigation and resignation of then Vice-President Spiro Agnew in 1973. The coverage began when Jerry Landauer of the *Wall Street Journal* obtained a copy of the letter the US attorney had sent to Agnew informing him that he was under investigation.[9] For over two months, the Justice Department pursued the vice-president under the glare of continuing coverage, which often revealed intimate details of the investigation. Leaks of information themselves became an issue.

Coverage in the Agnew story occurred at the solution formulation stage, where the Justice Department was wrestling first with strategic issues in the investigation, and then in the plea bargaining negotiation. From the department's perspective, any coverage was a negative, whether the coverage itself was positive or negative in content. Some of the stories were clearly on the negative side, questioning the Department's professionalism and credibility. Yet it is very difficult to ascribe to the coverage any change in the strategy and policies adopted by the Justice Department. They did change their modus operandi in light of the leaks, in order to try to reduce press access and to control information better. They added a whole new piece of the process with an extensive internal investigation to try to find out whether anyone in the department was the source of the leaks. And Justice Department officials, including the attorney general, had to spend time and effort dealing with the leaks as an issue in themselves. But the heart of the policymaking, the process leading up to the adoption of positions toward the investigation and toward the making of a deal for the vice-president's resignation, seems to have been undertaken well insulated from the press pressure.

There was also a difference between the Congress and the executive branch in officials' assessment of the impact of stories at various stages of the policymaking process. Overwhelmingly, the legislators believed that stories at the problem identification stage had the most impact. These are the stories that put items on the policy agenda, and members of Congress see themselves both being influential by getting the press to cover new issues and reacting directly themselves when a new issue is reported. The neutron bomb case is an example of congressional reaction to agenda-setting coverage. Walter Pincus's initial story put the neutron bomb on the table in a way that it would otherwise never have been. The first dramatic response to his story was in the Congress. Within two days after the article appeared, Senator Hatfield had filed his anti-bomb amendment and the administration was forced to deal with the problem immediately and in that context. For senior officials in the executive branch who responded to the questionnaire, agenda-setting stage stories had the same impact as policy adoption stories, and both had less impact than stories at the evaluation stage. For members of Congress, agenda-setting stories have greater impact than the evaluation stories. While there was a difference in the order of impact, there was a more dramatic difference in the degree of consensus within the groups. Around 40 percent of the executive branch officials said that those three types of stories—problem identification, policy adoption, and evaluation—had a large or dominant effect. Among legislative leaders, however, the consensus for a substantial impact for problem identification and evaluation stories was in the 60 percent range. The dramatically higher degree of consensus in the Congress suggests that the impact of the press on policymaking there is more clear and more uniform than the vast executive branch bureaucracy.

What Kind of Story?

The Bob Jones policymaking occurred with a lack of deliberation about press strategy and at a stage of the process which made it most likely that there would be a big press impact. Was it also the type of story that would produce a substantial impact? There is some suggestion from the results of our survey that policymakers themselves see the story type as a more important variable than stage of the process. Over 80 percent of the respondents said that story type made a difference in impact. There were greater agreement and substantially wider difference from top to bottom among story types than among process stages.

We identified four story categories, based on content:

1. personalities, reputations, hirings and firings;
2. how the organization worked and how policy was made;
3. immediate policy issues; and
4. long-term problems.

At the outset, the Bob Jones story was clearly an immediate policy story. It was not long, however, before it took on aspects of a personality and reputation story. The president's own sensitivity to racial issues and commitment to fighting discrimination quickly became the subject of the coverage. Finally, the story became a policy process story. It was not the typical process story, telling how it happened after the fact. It was more like a whodunit, looking for the senior White House official who would take the responsibility for a decision which soon came to be regretted, at least for the way it was understood.

Immediate policy issues have more direct impact on officials and decisions than any of the other story types. Nearly half of the senior federal officials who responded to the survey said those stories had the greatest impact of the four story types, and another 20 percent picked them second. It is no coincidence that the coverage in each of the six cases we studied in depth was about immediate policy decisions, although we did not consciously take that into account in selecting them. We were looking for stories in which the media seemed in the first instance to have played a role in the policymaking process, to have been part of the story. While in the Bob Jones case and in the Agnew resignation case there were clearly several story types involved, the others were pure immediate policy coverage.

Both the immediacy and the policy orientation are important here: the stories that have the most impact seem to be the ones about *policies* and with an *immediacy* to them. Stories about long-term policy problems were the clear choice for having the least impact of the four, with over 60 percent of our senior federal officials picking them third or fourth. This assessment runs somewhat counter to the studies of press coverage of the civil rights movement and studies of press coverage of the Vietnam War which suggest that the press played a significant role, over time, in affecting the government's policies on those long-term problems. There are studies now underway looking at the impact of the press coverage of nuclear issues on long-term policymaking in this area.[10] Perhaps one reason that policymakers believe that long-term policy stories have the least impact is because they, too, have a short-term perspective, at least about the issues of concern to them while they held high federal office. As John Gardner told us, "Most public officials, including myself when I was in HEW, take a short-term point of view. Long-term planning is like how to get through the weekend. . . . The press fitted that short-term view very well. That was their time span, too."

The Impact of Negative Coverage

In the Bob Jones case, not only the content but also the slant of the coverage were the kinds that have a substantial impact on the people, products, and processes of policymaking. The stories were overwhelmingly negative in tone. Only the very first stories could be considered neutral, and within a day or two the coverage became overwhelmingly critical of the policy.

Policymakers complain that the press looks for bad news to report. In Califano's words, the press is "more interested in illuminating dark places than in saying the sun is shining." Schlesinger says disparagingly that "the press spent a great deal of time looking for the supposed scandal." Journalists respond by arguing that it is not news that people are doing their jobs well, or that government is working, or that most of the houses did not burn to the ground last night. That negative coverage is more likely to become news than the positive has consequences for policymaking.

Not surprisingly, our research showed consistently that negative stories have a substantially bigger impact on policymakers than positive stories. Officials are more likely to react to negative stories, to do something in response to them than they otherwise would have done, than to positive stories. For example, twice as many of the senior officials in our survey believe that positive coverage has no effect as believe that about negative coverage. Positive stories validate action and accelerate existing momentum behind a course of action. Negative stories are arresting. They make policymakers pause, although there is no clear consensus about what happens when they do.

Over a quarter of the policymakers believe that negative coverage *increases* the policy options, the range of choices that the decision maker considers in determining what course to follow. Another quarter of them believe that negative coverage *decreases* policy options! But it is the difference in the reaction to negative and positive stories that most vividly illustrates the powerful impact that negative stories can have on policymaking. Nearly twice as many officials believe that negative coverage will increase the importance of the issue within the government as believe that positive coverage will have the same result, three times as many say that negative coverage slows the process as say that positive coverage slows it down, and *four* times as many officials believe that negative coverage moves responsibility for the issue to a more senior level than believe that positive coverage does the same. Finally, and importantly in terms of how federal officials think about and plan their dealings with the press, significantly more senior federal officials believe that negative coverage hurts their credibility on other issues than believe that positive coverage helps it. Positive stories, or stories without either a negative or positive slant for that matter, do have specific identifiable impacts, but on the whole they tend to reinforce whatever is happening in the policymaking process. On the other hand, from the perspective of the policymaker a negative story almost always disrupts the flow.

One kind of negative story which deserves special mention here is the conflict story. Policymakers often cited two kinds of conflict stories which they believed created especially difficult problems for them. One is the conflict-in-the-administration story, the personalization of a policy debate that is going on within the government. The other is in the international arena, a story focusing on a particular disagreement between the American government and that of another country which by its nature thrusts all the existing areas of agreement into the far background.

During our conversations with policymakers, the conflict article was raised frequently as an example of a negative story which does not serve the public interest. It is really not a negative story in the sense that we have been talking about, because it does not on the face of it involve criticism of the policy or the policymaker. However, those involved usually do not want it to be written and feel adversely affected by its publication. The policymakers argued that the press gravitated toward conflict stories, sometimes even creating them. Former House Ways and Means Chairman Wilbur Mills said, "The press likes feuds." Clark Clifford's view was simply that "The press is looking for some kind of conflict. . . . If there's a small difference that exists within government, it becomes substantially exaggerated when it is presented to the people."

Dean Rusk tells a story which illustrates the premium placed by the press business on the conflict story. According to Rusk, once, at his initiative, a reporter researched and wrote an upbeat story about a successful diplomatic exchange between Averell Harriman and President Sukarno of Indonesia. It was a long feature piece that analyzed the processes of diplomacy. Ten days went by and the article did not appear. Finally, the reporter showed the rejection slip message to Rusk: "Sorry," his editor had written. "No blood. No news."

Rusk bemoaned reporters' thirst for what he called the "Sic 'em, Fido" story. "They love to come in and say, 'You know, Senator So-and-So said this about you.' If you're not careful, you'll say: Did that SOB say that? Well, let me tell you about the senator!' First thing you know, you've got a feud going."

Note two points of reference here. First, executive branch people were much more likely than their Congressional counterparts to have leaked to undermine another's position. One possible explanation was that at the senior levels of the executive branch, where most officials are political appointees, it is not acceptable behavior to knock a colleague in public. Presenting a united front is the expected conduct; arguing out policy options in public violates that norm. They are all supposed to be on the same team. In Congress, arguing out the policy options in public is what the institution is all about. Each member is on his or her own team to a large extent. Thus, bureaucrats are much more disposed to *leak* information in order to strike a blow at a policy protagonist in another department (or within his or her own agency for that matter), than to do it on the record. The information is leaked in order to make the debate public while avoiding responsibility for the conflict story. If there is a practice in the executive branch of leaking personal policy conflict information, it is hardly surprising that the press regularly publishes such stories. Every day on the floor of the

Senate and the House members of Congress readily display their personal policy differences, and that reality is hardly news.

Another point of reference here is the earlier discussion about the impact of different types of stories. The survey finding that personality stories were a pretty distant second to immediate policy stories in terms of impact was somewhat of a surprise, since one of the regular complaints from officials about the press is that there is too much emphasis on personalities and not enough on substance. Our cases do confirm the sense that it is the immediate policy stories that have the greatest impact, but the conventional wisdom that positive personal stories about individuals are to be coveted, critical ones to be feared, and that there are too many of both of them, should not be discounted so easily. Officials are probably somewhat reluctant to acknowledge that they are so affected by their own personal coverage. What we discovered about the pervasive concern over stories covering the personalization of policy conflicts may be evidence that they are affected whenever their names are in the paper more than they care to admit.

More important than the criticism of conflict stories is the question of whether they have an impact. The policymakers who complained about these stories from the vantage point of international affairs felt strongly that they do. James Schlesinger tells a story about a trip to Germany he took as secretary of defense which was designed to build support for the continuing American role in the defense of Europe. He remembers that his speeches about the policy issues were not treated as news, but there was a spate of articles comparing unfavorably his personal style in visiting American soldiers stationed in Germany with that of his predecessor, Melvin Laird. In his view, the interest in conflict, negative stories, and personality worked in this case to bury the substantive purpose of the trip.

Vance cited the coverage of his first trip to Moscow as an example of how reporters' taste for conflict can undermine policymaking. The Russians turned down his proposal for deep military cuts, and the response by the press was that it was a disasterous turning point, and that US–USSR relations were at a dangerously low ebb. Vance said that nothing of the kind was true, and that the turndown was part of the negotiating process. The press obsession with the conflict "colored people's thinking about the Soviet Union and about the state of our affairs in a very negative way that hurt us both at home and abroad.'' And Vance argued further that stories about conflict between individuals created ''internal tensions.''

A story portraying a conflict between two officials has a tendency to create its own reality, generating a conflict if none existed or, as is more often the case, making a real conflict out of a difference of opinion or a potential conflict. For Dean Rusk, the emphasis on conflict in the press undermines the practice of diplomacy. ''Diplomacy is committed to a measure of optimism. Diplomacy must always proceed on the basis that something constructive can be done. Otherwise, we'd turn it all over to the soldiers and we'd all burn up. . . . Sometimes that measure of hope, as you try to reflect it, translates into a Pollyannaish approach. . . . It's unreasonable not to expect officials in government to be advocates of the policies they are representing. . . . But the critical approach, the critical gauntlet that public officials run through . . . [and] . . . present-day standards of something called credibility . . . try to deprive the public official of his role as advocate.''

Perhaps the strongest statement on this issue came from Brzezinski, who was both a source of information for the press about what the government was doing and an advocate for certain policies. The press focused on the policy disagreements, he said, usually personalizing them. That, he argued, ''has institutional consequences for relations between the branches of government, and even some personal consequences.'' When his major responsibility was to explain and implement policy decisions, his press was good and so were his press relations; when he became a public advocate for policy which was being hotly debated within the administration, his relationship with the press became ''a vehicle of the policy contest.''

Finally, there is a sense from the policymakers that the press attention to the conflict has a negative impact on public attitude toward the government. Eizenstat thought it made government trivial because it led to coverage that focused on ''the veneer of the story rather than the substance of it.'' Whatever the speculation about the impact of the conflict story on policymaking, it is clear to us that those stories bother the policymakers a lot. Personalizing the conflict within the administration cannot help but strain relations and impede communication.

Emphasizing the areas of conflict over the areas of agreement in international affairs has to affect, at the least, how the people view the situation, if not how the diplomats view it as well. The conflict story is an especially sensitive setting for press coverage of policymaking.

CHAPTER SIX

HOW POLICYMAKERS DEAL WITH THE PRESS

OLICYMAKERS HAVE TWO basic approaches in dealing with the press: active and reactive. The activists see their jobs as including the development of strategies for dealing with the public relations aspects of policymaking. As a consequence, their work often involves going out and selling themselves and their programs. Reactivists see their jobs as dealing with the press only when the press comes to them—or when they are by their own accounts making news. Cyrus Vance stands out as one of the senior policymakers from recent years who most clearly took the reactivist approach.

Vance was unenthusiastic about dealing with the press. In the ten months between Walter Pincus's article on the neutron bomb and President Carter's decision to defer production, Vance as secretary of state was almost invisible on the issue. Vance said he spent "more time than I liked" on press matters. While he recognized that the press played a "critically important role" and can "either make or break a foreign policy initiative," he said that he would deal with the press on background whenever possible, rather than in a press conference or other formal setting. Managing the press was a burden to him: "I did what I had to. But I had a great deal of confidence in Hodding [Carter, his assistant secretary of state for public affairs]. And whenever I could get Hodding to handle something, I would turn it over . . . so that I could wrestle with substantive problems."

Vance distinguished between what he called the "substantive problems" and dealing with the press. In retrospect, this put him at a

disadvantage in achieving his policy goals when his views were competing with those of the national security adviser, Zbigniew Brzezinski. Brzezinski talks about his role with the press as changing from an
"expeditor" of the administration's policy to a "protagonist in policy
disagreements." As a protagonist, although he says he was assuming
that responsibility at the encouragement of the president, he was more
aggressive in dealing with the press, and in initiating coverage for his
policy ideas. As an example, he cited the period when the US government was becoming increasingly concerned with Soviet activity in
Ethiopia. He says he "began to insert into the press that this is an issue
they should play out, and began to give them information on the subject, and have the CIA also disseminate information abroad on the
same subject." Brzezinski alleges that during this time "people at the
State Department at the highest level would give off-the-record briefings saying that I am shooting myself in the foot" in using the press
to advance policy positions and goals. He believes that the perception
that he was trying to undermine Vance, which he says was fomented
by officials at State, hurt his relations with the press. However, it was
Vance the reactivist and not Brzezinski the activist who left the government because of policy disagreements after the failure of the Iranian
hostage rescue mission.

James Schlesinger was an activist in his thinking about the press,
but often became reactivist in his approach. He was thoughtful and
deliberate in his press relations. He saw the press in strategic terms,
but frequently came down on the side of not initiating coverage and
now, to some extent, questions his own tactics. He practiced openness
in his dealing with the press, primarily because he believed it led to
good relations and that a positive relationship enables a policymaker
to get the benefit of doubt from journalists in difficult situations. He
was conscious of the impact of the press in affecting the processes of
policymaking, and acknowledged that as soon as press attention was
focused on an issue within his purview at the Defense Department, he
"got right on it, even to the detriment of such things as forces, funding
program, alliance relations, and so on." Even the most minor items
got his active engagement once they became news because he began
to believe that all the department's programs were affected by any
publicity. This is very different from Vance, who took pride in dele-

gating everything possible to Hodding Carter. Schlesinger recalls at least one instance of pushing himself into a more active role in trying to manage an apparently relatively small issue. A *Washington Post* reporter, he remembers "had discovered that one of our nuclear subs had had this stripper on board who had done some dancing on the top of the submarine and downstairs . . . and was not fully clad at the time she was doing it. And the Navy went right after the skipper. The *Post,* and the rest of the country, of course, picked up this kind of case. And you would think that the Navy would have a reasonably favorable press under those circumstances, but, no, it wasn't that. It was 'our boys are having good clean fun, or not so clean but it's fun, and they need some relaxation, and here is this fuddy-duddy Navy trying to discipline a commander.'

"Well, I was on that right away. . . . I tried to explain that . . . 'there is this young lady dancing around in such a way that probably distracts attention from the job of the safe handling of a Navy vessel that is powered by a nuclear reactor. Under these circumstances you don't want to encourage that kind of activity.' As soon as that came up, I had to be right on top of it. It was not a period in which anything that happened in the services was going to be shrugged off or laughed off. Everything affected the well-being of the department in the post-Watergate period."

Sometimes, as in the case of Clark Clifford, a single policymaker uses both approaches.

Clifford, who served as an assistant to the president in the Truman White House and then as secretary of defense under President Lyndon Johnson, was not in general an activist in dealing with the press. He said that his approach was to be accessible. He did not believe in background sessions, in the informal sharing and exchange of information with journalists who covered him and the Defense Department during his tour as secretary. He did not try to establish strong personal relationships with key members of the Washington press corps. He was concerned about leaks, and their impact on policymaking, and believes it inappropriate to disclose to the press sensitive matters which affect other countries. Leaking, he said, is "undemocratic," and he disapproves of the practice. Yet, "because of the transcendent nature of the issue and the depth of conviction," Clifford acknowledged aggressively using the press in an effort to change US policy in Vietnam. He began to hold regular press conferences and to seek out opportunities for coverage. It was, in his view, an exception to his general rule, but he said that if he had it to do over again he would spend more time with the press overall and believes that he might have been more successful in influencing administration policy on Vietnam had he done so.

Contrast Clifford's view with that of Melvin Laird, who became secretary of defense after a long career in the House of Representatives. Laird sees a big distinction between the way the press looks to a Congressman and to a senior official in the executive branch. The difference, he says, is that members of Congress need the press to communicate with their constituents, and that this need is direct and immediate. Executive branch policymakers depend less on getting their message out through the media. Yet whether by legislative training or personal conviction, Laird was by his own account just as much of an activist with the press while he was secretary of defense as he had been while on Capitol Hill. Laird's notion was to start out being honest with the press and accessible to reporters. Then he added to that a commitment to work actively on his press relations, establishing good personal connections, and providing reporters with information before they came asking for it. Doing that, he said, would substantially increase the chances of receiving sympathetic treatment and accurate, if not necessarily favorable, coverage. Laird talked about the press as an instrument to be used in policymaking, not a threat to it. From his experience, Laird believes that if a policymaker works straightforwardly to manage relations with the press, coverage can be enormously helpful. Nowhere could this be more true than in the case of Postmaster General Winton "Red" Blount and his effort to reorganize the US Post Office. Recounting Blount's operation in detail provides some sense of just how sophisticated and comprehensive—and successful—an activist strategy for dealing with the press can be.

The Post Office Reorganization

Until August 6, 1970, perhaps no department in the history of the United States had been so shackled by vested interests, stultifying personnel practices, archaic regulations and equipment, and an absence of elementary management practices as was the United States Post Office Department (POD). Nowhere was the sauce of political patronage thicker than in the POD. So it was not surprising that in 1969, Postmaster Blount, with the support of President Richard Nixon, set out to undo two centuries of tradition by removing the Post Office Department from the executive branch control and turning it into an independent government corporation. Blount was capitalizing on a reform movement begun by former Postmaster General Larry O'Brien, but O'Brien had failed to win congressional support for a fundamental restructuring, and no one expected Blount, his successor, to fare any better.

There was little support in Congress for POD reorganization because, to an extent unrivaled anywhere in the executive branch, the Congress ran the department. Each of the 32,000 local postmasterships existing in 1969 had to be confirmed by the Congress, and under long-standing tradition, the person recommended by a loyal member was always the person nominated by the administration. The selection of a postmaster was just about the only piece of patronage available to a member of the House outside of his or her staff. Congress legislated how much postal employees would be paid and under what conditions they would work, how much would be charged for various classes of mail and, in essence, determined where the Post Office would build its facilities. The links between the Congress and the postmasters were very tight, but no tighter than the ties between the Congress and the postal unions. At 88 percent of its employees,[1] the Post Office was the most highly unionized federal agency. The lobbying of the two largest of the unions—the National Association of Letter Carriers (NALC) and the United Federation of Postal Clerks (UFPC)—was legendary. They could produce thousands of their members to visit their respective congressman on Capitol Hill, they were at the top of the list for lobbying expenditures, and their members contributed financially to campaigns. Their efforts had paid off: Congress enacted eighteen pay increases for postal employees in the twenty-five years from 1945 to 1969. The letter carriers saw a congressman's constituents a lot more regularly than the congressman did, and that alone gave them tremendous clout.

Postal reform began to emerge as a concern for federal officials in the late 1960s. The volume of mail had just about tripled since World War II, the deficit from operations had increased to $1.1 billion, and systems and equipment were antiquated. If anyone needed tangible evidence of a problem, they got it when the Chicago Post Office nearly shut down in October 1966.

O'Brien was postmaster general at the time, and he tried to take advantage of the Chicago crisis by warning that a "catastrophe" was approaching.[2] In April 1967, he told a stunned audience from the Magazine Publishers Association that he favored turning the Post Office Department into a nonprofit (and nonpolitical) government corporation. When O'Brien left the government to work for Robert Kennedy in his campaign for president, whatever momentum there was for postal reorganization went with him.

However dismal the prospects seemed, Nixon had made postal reform a campaign promise and he began to make good on his commitment early into his administration. The first step was a dramatic and unpopular one: Nixon and Blount eliminated Post Office political patronage by ending the practice of allowing congressmen to name the postmasters. Republican congressmen, contemplating the fruits of recapturing the White House, were furious, but Nixon and Blount knew that with both the House and Senate controlled by Democrats, there would be no postal reform without Democratic support. If they waited until after filling available postal jobs with friends of Republican congressmen before moving on reform, they knew that the Democrats would never have taken them seriously. The second step, eventually more important but less visible for the time being, was to develop a strategy for convincing the public, and through them the Congress, of the benefits of reorganization. It was really a two-stage process: first the case had to be made that there was a serious and important problem at the Post Office; then, reorganization had to become the solution.

Blount knew that reorganization would not come about without going outside Washington: "Congress owned the Post Office and they liked that old baby just the way it was. We needed the newspaper pressure in the members' districts to shake up things."[3] He decided to set up what POD memos referred to as a "front organization" to push for reform. The idea had three enormous advantages: it provided a way to create a lobbying campaign that federal personnel were prohibited from doing directly or allocating funds for; it created a funding channel to allow those who favored reform to offset the efforts of the unions; and, most important, it permitted the public effort on behalf of the Nixon–Blount bill to be bipartisan.

The key to bipartisanship was O'Brien, the former postmaster general and former Democratic Party chairman who was already on record as favoring both reorganization and a grassroots lobbying approach. After some persuading, O'Brien agreed to co-chair the operation, to be called the Citizens Committee for Postal Reform (CCPR). The Republican half of the team was to be Thruston Morton, retired US senator and also a former national party chairman. The final step at the preliminary stage was to hire a marketing expert; Blount settled on William Dunlap, who did marketing for Procter & Gamble.

Dunlap was given an office at the POD, and two weeks to develop a full-scale plan. He remanded his public salary; P&G continued to pay him while he worked on the reorganization during 1969 and 1970. Dunlap wrote a marketing plan, he recalled, "just the way I would at Procter & Gamble. Essentially I took a packaging goods approach that you use to market a product, and applied it to the government sector." His approach was explicit, thorough, and very sophisticated. The purpose was to "stimulate the maximum amount of active support . . . and to utilize this favorable public reaction as a positive force that could be directed toward the members of Congress."[4] In the twenty-eight-page document he prepared, he laid out plans to utilize all the available media, national and local, print and electronic, in all their available slots: letters to the editor, editorials, news stories, feature articles by the postmaster general, and even appearances on entertainment television such as *The Tonight Show* and *The Joey Bishop Show*. The appeal to the media was to be based on their role as opinion makers, their self-interest as mail users, and their commitment to keep their readers and viewers abreast of the news, namely the news about postal reform. It was a saturation strategy in which press support, or at least press cooperation, was crucial.

Kick-off was set for May 27, 1969. During the preceding week, Blount and a handful of his aides gave background briefings to the editorial boards of papers in six major cities to ensure that all the coverage around the announcement was not from the highly political Washington press corps. On May 27, the president sent the reorganization message to the Congress. Nixon read a statement at the White House and Blount followed with a press briefing and a twenty-two-page press packet outlining the legislation. POD designed a special packet for editorial writers. There was a POD headquarters briefing for staff which was wired directly to three hundred top postmasters around the country. A POD publication called *Postal Life,* sent to every postal employee, explained the legislation in great detail. The Mail Users Council sent a "Memo to Mailers" presenting the reorganization proposal to sixty thousand business executives. CCPR, whose formation had been announced on May 26, issued a press release hailing the bill.

Editorial reaction to the reorganization was enthusiastic. Congressional reaction was cool in general, and absolutely frosty among the senior members of the House Post Office Committee (HPOC). Chairman Thaddeus Dulski (D-NY) had his own modest reform bill which stopped far short of establishing a government corporation to replace the Post Office Department. Senior Republicans on the committee were upset because the White House had eliminated congressional patronage in Post Office jobs. The administration had to reach all the way down to the fourth-ranking Republican Edward Derwinski (R-IL) and Democrat Mo Udall (D-AR) to find co-sponsors.

A confidential recap of a June 10 senior POD staff meeting indicated that reaching the postal employees was to be the number one short-run priority of the public relations campaign. Number two was producing favorable editorials in the home districts of congressmen on the Post Office Committee. Specific efforts toward these objectives were to be supported by continuing national coverage. During June and July, Blount appeared on *Meet the Press, Today,* and two nationally distributed radio programs; plus, he gave several dozen interviews to editorial boards, national reporters, and syndicated columnists. O'Brien and Morton testified together before Congress and appeared together before the National Press Club, drawing editorial praise for CCPR and postal reform as being "above politics." Ads soliciting support for CCPR were taken in the *New York Times* and the *Washington Post* in late June. Blount and other top officials at POD began giving background briefings for editorial boards at key papers around the country. PDO press kits were mailed to virtually all of the nation's newspapers. Many newspapers used large parts of the press releases and editorials supplied by POD and CCPR. Some prestigious newspapers, such as the *Denver Post* and the *Milwaukee Journal,* were almost in front of the bandwagon, writing editorials urging Blount and CCPR to keep up the good fight against, as the *Journal* said, "the traditionalists in Congress."[5]

The activity produced coverage. As early as June 16, Dunlap counted 194 news stories, 232 editorials, 27 op-ed pieces, and 39 cartoons on the reorganization bill. At the end of June, Blount reported that 88 percent of the editorials favored the bill, now numbered H.R. 11750, with 9 percent undecided and only 3 percent opposed.

The pressure from the coverage was beginning to be felt where it counted—in the Congress. At a HPOC hearing near the end of July, Congressman Robert Tiernan (D-RI), originally opposed but thought to be wavering, referred to the "tidal wave" of local press support generated by CCPR. Testimony to Congress by union officials during the summer reflected their frustration at the success of CCPR in building support for the reorganization; they used words like "brainwashing" to describe what was happening.

By the time HPOC took its first vote in early October, there was as much support on the committee for the administration's bill as for Dulski's. In six months, Blount and his friends had taken a solution that almost no one supported to a problem that few people took seriously and made it politically salient and even compelling.

Soon after the committee vote, postal reform became intertwined with another issue dear to the hearts of postal employees: a pay raise. Udall agreed to support a pay raise bill which was far in excess of what the administration said it would accept, and the Udall pay raise bill was rushed through the House on October 14, despite the threat of a presidential veto. The Senate was working on a different pay raise bill, so the unions knew that with the prospect of a conference committee to resolve the differences between the Senate and the House and the possibility of a veto, there would be no quick fix. Nixon tried to tie the pay raise to the reorganization. As John Ehrlichman, the president's domestic policy adviser, recalled, "Nixon knew that sooner or later he would have to give in to the unions [on a pay raise] and he wanted reorganization in return."[6]

While the president and the unions were facing each other in this stand-off during the fall, CCPR went back to the streets. The press campaign was more or less put on hold; something of a saturation point had been reached and there was no coming event to provide hard news coverage. The emphasis was on direct mail, advertising, and appeals to the business trade press. CCPR was making its pitch more narrowly to business interests, emphasizing, for example, the Chicago break-down and suggesting that such disruptions could happen again.

CCPR began to gear up the media campaign as the Senate began its hearings on postal reform in November. The unions attacked CCPR: "One of the smoothest and most massive attempts at public brain-washing since the German glory days of Joseph Paul Goebbels," said NALC President James Rademacher on November 25,[7] while simultaneously taking a page out of the CCPR success story and starting a media campaign of his own.

The objectives of the NALC campaign were to break the connection between reorganization and the pay raise, and to pressure the president into signing the pay raise bill when it reached his desk. It was a three-part initiative. First, ads were run in four hundred newspapers and on three hundred radio stations seeking support for the pay raise bill, and urging people to write to the president. Second, just to make sure the message was received, letter carriers, the ladies' auxiliary, and several unions distributed a total of six million pre-addressed cards with requests that they be filled out and sent to the White House. If Nixon still vetoed the bill, part three of the plan would be implemented: a march on Washington by 15,000 letter carriers, and a television broadcast responding to the veto message. Within a week of the beginning of the NALC marketing blitz the White House received three million pieces of mail in support of the pay raise.

CCPR and the POD struggled over a response. Two ads were run in the *Washington Post* on the theme that the reorganization would deal with the difficult working conditions that the NALC had made the focus of their campaign for the pay raise.[8] While the debate was continuing over whether to make a more broad-based rejoinder, the White

House intervened. White House Special Counsel Charles Colson called Rademacher and asked him to come in to talk. Rademacher and his union had supported Nixon in the 1968 campaign, and the White House felt that there was room to negotiate but that relations between Rademacher and Blount were so strained that the dialogue could not begin at the POD.

With the assistance of Udall, Colson and Rademacher hammered out a compromise in early December, trading substantial collective bargaining provisions and pay raise support, for ending union opposition to the government corporation concept. Rademacher says that he made the deal because he "saw the handwriting on the wall,"[9] but he had made a huge tactical error in not involving the rival postal union, the UFPC, in the White House negotiations. As a result, Rademacher's union was the only one to support the compromise. The Senate and House were ready to ask for a conference to iron out their differences on the pay raise bill, and the White House moved quickly to put the compromise on the record with a December 12 meeting between Nixon and Rademacher. Rademacher had been the most militant union opponent of the administration's bill, and he now found himself explaining his switch to skeptical union members, including some in his own union. The deal, plus the administration's continuing opposition to the pure pay raise, deferred the House–Senate conference while the parties struggled toward a compromise in early 1970. Negotiations were made more difficult because there were public splits and tensions on each side, between Colson and Blount for the administration and between Rademacher's NALC and the other unions for the employees. CCPR and the POD kept a low profile during this period, but by the end of February there was still no agreement. On February 25, Dulski turned up the heat by holding a press conference to say that there was no agreement, and that he and his Senate counterpart, Gale McGee (D-WY), were prepared to move ahead on a pay raise.

Dulski's announcement galvanized the reorganization's supporters into action. With a few days, the POD, Udall, and Rademacher had drafted a new bill with enough changes to be able to say that it was a new compromise. Rademacher threatened a strike if there was no pay raise, and predicted that there would only be a pay raise if there also was reorganization. Rademacher and Blount personally walked

the halls of Congress, lobbying Democrats intensely for the new proposal. According to some newspaper reports at the time, Rademacher
was offering union support and Blount was offering new post offices
and patronage, and holding out the prospect of no Republican opposition in the next election. Whatever they did, it worked. On March 12,
in a stunning upset, several more Democrats deserted Dulski and the
HPOC voted 17–6 to report out the administration's latest version of
reorganization.

Rademacher and Blount met the press and tried to claim that the
victory was in everyone's interest, but the New York postal union
locals were not convinced. A strike vote was taken on March 17, and
on the next day all mail service was halted in New York City as the
first postal strike in the nation's history was underway. At the height
of the strike, on March 21, 152,000 postal workers (a third of the total
postal workforce) walked out of 671 post offices, including nine of the
ten largest in the country. Mail service was virtually at a standstill. It
was a crisis which affected nearly everyone, from the IRS which was
losing one billion dollars a day in unreceived income tax checks to the
elderly individual waiting for a Social Security check in order to pay
for food and rent. Senator McGee called it the "most serious domestic
crisis in forty years."[10] The president went on television to tell the
American people that what was at issue was nothing less than "the
survival of government based on law."[11] Court orders succeeded in
putting a stop to the picketing, but not to the strike. Appeals from
national union leaders went unheeded by the runaway locals.

The media were everywhere, hounding officials as they came out
of meetings and speculating about what might happen next. The vaunted
public relations machines at POD and CCPR, which had put reorganization on the agenda and just gotten a bill out of committee, were
suddenly in a reactive mode, trying to stay on top of the latest event
rather than creating it. Blount and the POD information experts saw
both the obligation to minimize consumer confusion and the opportunity to use the strike as another vehicle for pushing postal reform.
After the first few days of the strike, Blount used press conferences
and personal appearances to send the message that the blame rested
with the Congress, which had the power to pass a postal pay hike and
the reorganization. Reorganization, he argued, would give postal workers

the right to collective bargaining, so that they would not have had to strike to pressure the Congress for more money.

Finally, on March 23, Nixon declared a national emergency, going on television to say that he was sending in the National Guard (which he called a ''supplemental work force'' to soften the blow).[12] In his seven-minute address, he carefully emphasized both that the strike was illegal and that the grievances were legitimate and open to negotiation. What was needed, he argued, was for only the Congress to pass reorganization so that the postal employees would have the right to bargain collectively for their pay raise rather than lobby for it.

Calling in the troops effectively killed the strike. Postal employees began to return almost immediately. Within twenty-four hours Blount was able to hold a press conference to announce that the return to work was significant enough so that negotiations should begin.

While administration officials were exultant over success in what they called the ''domestic equivalent to the Cuban Missile crisis,'' it was not clear that the cause of postal reform had been advanced.[13] Colson recalls that there was concern at the White House that Congress would rush through a pay bill and that the union opposition to reorganization would intensify in response to the administration's having called in the National Guard. The somewhat dormant CCPR bought ads in major newspapers linking pay and reorganization, the White House never backed away from the linkage in their negotiations with the unions, and major media began to editorialize that the need for reform was demonstrated by the strike.

Finally, after several weeks of hard bargaining, a package was worked out which provided for an immediate and retroactive pay hike, with a larger hike to take effect when reorganization was signed into law. The reorganization agreed to was in all essential respects the same as the one reported by HPOC. George Meany, who was by then speaking for the unions, hailed it as ''a tremendous step forward'' because postal employees had won the right to collective bargaining.[14]

The bill passed the House overwhelmingly on June 18. On the Senate side, eight of the twelve members of the Senate Post Office Committee were up for re-election in the fall and didn't want the blood of another postal strike on their hands. David Minton, then counsel to the committee, says that ''reform was a high visibility item in the

media following the strike and that had a very influential role in pushing reorganization through."[15] The Senate passed the bill in essentially
the same form as it had come over from the House. When the House
approved the conference committee report on August 6, reorganization
was on its way to the White House, where, not surprisingly, the information folks at POD had prepared an elaborate bill-signing ceremony
that received enormous and favorable press coverage.

The Impact of the Press

Assessing the impact of the press in the enactment of postal reorganization is complicated. What was produced in the media by the
POD and CCPR press strategies went far beyond news coverage, and
included commentary, editorials, and advertisements. In addition, there
were other elements which played important roles, such as the grassroots organizing and the pressure it generated on members of Congress
and the strike. White House support was obviously important. Winton
Blount's tenacity was crucial. In the view of Congressman Derwinski,
"What got postal reform through was that Blount was an unusually
determined, able man who just bulldogged it."[16] Blount himself sees
the campaign to win the support of the public and the local media as
central to their success, although not solely responsible for it. "There
is no key force or event that created postal reform; it was a lot of forces
and events working together. . . . The campaign to draw media support was enormously important; that's the way you move the Congress
and if we had not had the media support we would have had a bad
time. I don't remember specific incidents where a Congressman would
cite editorial support in his home district as his reason for changing his
position, but you could see that their changes corresponded to periods
when public support for reorganization was voiced. . . . If the public
had been 'ho-hum,' fifty–fifty, I don't think we would have reorga-
nized the Post Office."[17]

Assessing the impact of the press is further complicated by the
understandable tendency to separate news coverage from editorials and
both of them from paid advertisements. One of the insights behind the
Blount strategy is that all those pieces of the media play a role and
have an effect. Advertisements are public relations, not press cover-

age, but Blount and his allies understood that each element of the media has its own constituency and influence, and that all were important in putting reorganization on the agenda, framing the issue, putting pressure on the Congress, and eventually passing the bill. When it comes to advertising, the press is just a conduit. In the Post Office case, officials were able to get news coverage and editorial support for reorganization that was almost as unfiltered as their ads. It is challenging enough to examine what role in general the press played. The task becomes impossible if it has to include distinguishing impacts among different types of newspaper copy. It also becomes irrelevant, because the point is that the POD and CCPR set out to use the mass media, in all its formats, to help achieve their policy goals and they succeeded. The question is how much credit does the entire media campaign deserve for their success.

When the bill was filed in May 1979, the outlook for its passage was bleak. Postal reform was not a salient issue for the editorial writers, never mind the general public. It was a priority for the Nixon administration, but there was strong opposition from powerful unions, a Democratic Congress, Republicans angered by the patronage shutoff, and those beloved letter carriers who delivered the mail.

Then for a few months, the pro-reorganization forces had the field to themselves. The opposition was there, but asleep. During that period, most of whatever appeared in the newspapers about reform was there at the initiative of CCPR and the POD. When the opposition awoke in September, their advantage had been almost completely dissipated. What looked almost impossible in May now appeared to be about to happen. The unions had wanted a pay raise and wanted to keep their future in the friendly hands of the Congress. By mid-September, it appeared that they might get the worse of both possible worlds, no pay raise and a reorganization bill out of their beloved House Post Office Committee. During the interim, the POD and CCPR had been able to achieve two huge objectives. First, they had taken an issue, postal reform, and put it on the national political agenda. That was no mean feat, and it was aided enormously by the willingness of the president to climb aboard and stay there. Without the press strategy it seems very unlikely that, absent an unforeseen external intervening event such as another Chicago-type crisis, reorganization would have ever gained its momentum in the Congress in general or in HPOC in particular. The second great achievement during that period, besides putting reorganization on the front burner, was to frame the administration's bill in such a way as to give it the best shot at success. The framing had three pieces to it: whatever were the grievances with the Post Office, whether they be late mail or underpaid letter carriers, reorganization was an answer, if not *the* answer; support for the proposal was bipartisan; and the administration bill was the only real reform. While the unions and their supporters in the Congress were talking with each other, these three messages were being systematically trumpeted all over the land in a multimedia spectacular aimed directly at the press and the public, and only indirectly to the legislators themselves. When the music stopped, there was a sense out there that the problems in the POD were real, that the Nixon bill was a positive response to them, and that this was an issue above partisanship.

The unions recognized this and responded with their own press campaign, which stemmed the tide, not by directly countering any of those three messages, but by adding two of their own. The first was that CCPR was not what it appeared to be; the second was that the only real issue for the postal employees was pay. The unions appear to have understood that the clear field had given the POD and CCPR the opportunity to put reorganization on the political agenda and to frame it in a way that made the union opposition rhetoric on the merits no longer credible to journalists and editorials writers following the issue. By their own positive campaign, the unions were able to salvage the most they could: reviving the pay raise issue as a high congressional priority, and putting the CCPR and its campaign for reorganization temporarily on the defensive.

There was a third great press campaign in this story: the effort of the White House to try to create a climate during the strike which would help to ensure that whatever happened, reorganization would not be hurt by the walkout. As the strike spread, the White House developed a strategy with four objectives, as recalled by Ehrlichman: "Nixon . . . wanted us to paint the strikers as outlaws who were doing something illegal; . . . to convey to the American public how to use the post office during the strike; . . . to use the strike to sell postal reform; and finally, he wanted to make sure that he came out of this looking like a strong leader.''[18]

The program was straightforward and well executed. Under the direction of H. R. Halderman, a game plan was prepared to convey these messages through a variety of means, including saturating television talk and news shows with administration spokespeople and friendly members of Congress. Herb Klein sent fact sheets to three hundred editorial writers and nine hundred radio and television news directors. Handling the combination of messages was tricky; too much strong leadership and strike-baiting might backfire. Letter carriers were generally among the most popular of public employees, and the polls showed that there was substantial sympathy for the postal workers and their specific grievances. The administration did not want to encourage other unions to join the postal workers, or to encourage the most militant among their number to take control.

This campaign, too, was successful, although once again helped significantly by the firm commitment in the White House to sticking with the issue during the hard bargaining which produced the combined pay-and-reform package that eventually was enacted.

The press campaigns played a major role in the outcome of this policymaking. Campaign is not used casually here; these were not one-time efforts, such as a single press conference or individual leak. They were well planned, complicated, continuing, multifaceted, and well executed. Most important, they worked. One moral of the tale is that Ronald Reagan did not invent the concept of press management, but anyone who remembers Franklin Delano Roosevelt's fireside chats knows that anyway.

What is special in the POD reorganization is that a single department and an outside organization, not the president, were the primary initiators of press coverage. Contrast the performance here with that of Harold Brown and Cyrus Vance in the production and deployment of the neutron bomb. Unlike the positive activist steps taken by Blount, Vance and Brown took a passive reactive posture throughout almost the entire period when their issue was up for grabs. Circumstances were different for them to be sure; the story was begun by a journalist and the president was never fully on their side. Yet it is hard to imagine

Blount sitting back and simply responding to what Brown and Vance felt was a distorting and troublesome picture of the neutron bomb.

Getting out in front does not always allow the policymaker to frame the issue. The Carter administration officials found that out during the relocation at Love Canal, when they thought they were initiating coverage, but end up reacting to the leak of the pilot study report and losing control of the story almost before they began. The Reagan administration fared no better when it tried to frame the decision to restore tax exemptions to Bob Jones University and Goldsboro Christian College as tax issues and not civil rights issues. But the Post Office reorganization story suggests that a comprehensive, well-thought-out press strategy that is well integrated to the policymaking can make a difference.

David Gergen, for example, thought so when he pushed for aggressively counterattacking after the showing of the CBS documentary *People Like Us,* which criticized the administration's policies toward people in need in general and the accelerated Social Security disability reviews in particular. In the White House senior staff meeting where the response strategy was on the agenda, Gergen argued for a tough response and was supported by Meese and Baker. Deaver was not so sure. He noted that the show was third in the ratings, attracting only 17 percent of the audience, and suggested that going after CBS might only heighten the public awareness of the fairness issue. Richard Darman, deputy chief of staff, agreed and suggested they only go after the question of fairness, not CBS or the documentary. Gergen, however, felt very strongly. "The notion that you should let people bang you over the head when you're in the White House is one of the stupidest ideas that anyone can entertain; if you're not willing to speak out when you're being wronged, you're going to get taken to the cleaners politically. We didn't realistically expect a retraction from CBS, but we did think that the next time we'd make them think twice and get a fairer show. . . . No single show like that will lose you a lot of moderate votes, but if you allow those perceptions to harden over time, it's very difficult to turn them around."[19]

The counterattack was launched. Press briefings were held, telegrams of protest were sent to CBS and released to the rest of the media, and several top officials became actively engaged in promoting the administration's defense. Was it successful, or at least worth the effort? Administration officials still disagree. Former SSA administrator Paul Simmons thinks that neither the show nor the controversy about it was very important in the hinterlands, where grassroots attitude toward the CDIs was going to have an impact on the Congress. Gergen, on the other hand, believes that reporters in general were more sensitive and thorough after the counterattack and cites the next CBS story, one on food stamps, as a case where the network acted "very professionally, checked it out quickly, and ran a correction."[20]

Activists and Reactors

Melvin Laird said two things in explaining his overall activist strategy for dealing with the press: first, that good press and good press relations are very useful and important to the policymaker, and second, that good press comes from going out and getting it.

We know from our survey something about those officials who practiced what he preached. Policymakers spending more than five hours a week with the press are twice as likely as the others to have served in the Congress. Those spending more hours with the press are more likely to be liberal than those spending less than five hours a week. Both activists with respect to hours and activists with respect to seeking coverage are substantially more likely to be found in the foreign policy area than are reactors. The reactors are more likely to be found in commerce or agriculture. There is a clear relationship between an activist press strategy and years of federal service. The longer in office, the more likely the activism. For example, 61 percent of those who served less than ten years spent less than five hours with the press, but only 48 percent of those who served over twenty years spent that little time. Similarly, 72 percent of those who served less than ten years sought coverage, whereas 80 percent of those who served at least twenty years did so.

There is also a trend toward activism. Those officials who left government during the Nixon and Johnson administrations were less likely to have spent over five hours a week with the press, although they were no more or less likely than their successors to have sought coverage.

Does activism make any difference? Is it worth the effort? Winton Blount certainly thought so. So did the other activists among the senior federal policymakers we surveyed. Understandably, those who sought coverage initiated a much higher percentage of the stories about their agencies than those who said that they did not try to actively seek or influence coverage. More significantly, those who spent more time with the press initiated a higher percentage of the stories about themselves than others, and reported that they were more successful in getting the coverage they desired than their less active colleagues.

One reason given by some officials for not being more aggressive in seeking coverage was fear of creating an adversary relationship with reporters that would come back to haunt them. That has not been the experience of senior federal policymakers who tried. There is no difference at all among them with respect to the friendliness or hostility of their relationship with the press based on how many hours they spent on press matters or on whether or not they actively sought coverage.

Policymakers appear to favor either an activist or a reactive approach to the press, although many officials may combine both strategies. The Post Office reorganization story illustrates a well-designed affirmative press strategy that produced powerful results.

We considered as activists those policymakers who went out and sought coverage or spent more than five hours a week thinking about and dealing with the press. We found that activists in the survey were distinguishable from their colleagues in their attitudes toward and use of the media. Activists were much more likely than the others to believe that the press had a substantial or dominant impact on policy and on policymaking; perhaps that is why they are more active in trying to shape coverage. They are much more likely to leak, and twice as likely to find informal communications with the press useful.

Those policymakers who take the activist route tend to apply that approach throughout their dealings with the press, not only spending more time at it and employing a wide range of techniques to get better coverage, but also using the press more broadly, in Melvin Laird's words, as an instrument of policymaking.

Perhaps more significant although less surprising, is the clear sense from the survey, the cases, and the interviews that the activist strategy produces better coverage than the reactive. Better coverage leads to more success for the policymaker in achieving his or her policy goals; there is broad consensus among senior officials on that point. That would strongly suggest that the activist strategy is a way toward success in policymaking, although that is not to equate successful policymaking with either good policymaking or good policy.

CHAPTER SEVEN

DISPELLING THE LEAK MYSTIQUE

T HE LEAK IS a dramatic example of the activist use of the press. But in the dialogue between reporters and officials, leaks are a complex, confusing, and controversial subject. There are arguments about what is a leak, whether or under what circumstances officials should leak, how and why leaks occur, and what is the impact of leaks on policymaking.

The *American Heritage Dictionary* defines a leak as a "secret or accidental disclosure of confidential information."[1] That definition rests heavily on one factor, the confidentiality of the information. The essence of confidentiality is the assumption that the information held would not be revealed. Reporters and officials identify additional elements as important in defining leaks and distinguishing them from other forms of journalist–policymaker communication. Among them are the confidentiality of the source, the nature of the information, and the initiation of the contact. Leaks have a negative connotation and therefore are subject to different definitions depending on where people sit and their own standards of practice. One person's leak is another's profile in courage. That is one reason why talking about them with reporters and journalists is complicated.

On the question of confidentiality of the source, few journalists and reporters would classify as a leak information where the source is revealed, although under the dictionary definition an accidental leak conceivably could be one in which the source is named as part of the story. Anonymity seems an inevitable element of the traditional leak, even though technically it might not be essential.

All leaking by definition is trafficking in confidential information, but there are differences in the nature of the confidentiality. There are at least three types of confidentiality. First is information which is confidential only in the sense that it is not widely known. An example of a leak of such information is the official who gratuitously slips a reporter a copy of an obscure public record that discloses something embarrassing to someone. Most people would call that a leak even though the information itself is theoretically already available to the press. Second, there is information, such as classified documents and grand jury testimony, which is protected by laws, regulations, or oaths. Transfer of that information to a reporter would almost always be considered a leak and would be condemned out of hand by most officials in all but extreme circumstances. The third category of confidentiality covers the huge area of typical and more routine leaks, where the information is thought of as confidential by someone and the official knows that life would be difficult if he or she were disclosed as the reporter's source.

There is also confusion about the distinction among a leak, information on background, and a confidential source. The words mean different things to different people, yet the overlap is substantial. What is common to them is the anonymity of the informer. All the leakers in the Agnew case were anonymous sources; are there anonymous sources who are not leakers? When journalists make the distinction, they often are referring to the process of getting the information: a leaker is more regularly someone who takes the initiative with the journalist; an anonymous source is a person the journalist contacts, often routinely, for information and insight. In the words of Albert Hunt, Washington bureau chief for the *Wall Street Journal,* "Leaks are stories that are instigated, sometimes by the government for a purpose, sometimes for a good purpose, sometimes for a sinister purpose, sometimes for a selfish purpose, whatever." Confidential sources, on the other hand, are often labels for the people reporters go to and rely on.

Yet there is usually something more subtle to the process than that; sometimes it is aggressive reporting more than an aggressive policymaker that results in a leak. Leaks often take months to generate. Leaks also often happen by accident, as when an official lets information slip without thinking about it or incorrectly assumes a reporter already knows a particular piece of information.

When policymakers make this distinction they may be basing it on the nature of the information or its level of specificity. It is a point that officials sometimes make when they try to separate leaking from their own well-honed practice of providing anonymous background and source information to reporters. Officials argue that they don't leak because the only information they provide to journalists is general direction, suggestions as to other sources, and the like. Yet the element of anonymity still exists; the officials want it that way. The line drawing by officials seems as artificial as that based on who initiates the contact which has been suggested by reporters. It may be common usage and common practice to make the distinction among practitioners, but most anonymous source activity seems to fit well within the dictionary definition of a leak. Officials could only explain away such conduct as something other than leaking to an audience of colleagues or reporters. Anyone else would find it a distinction without a difference. Conventional wisdom and usage would argue that there are only two essential elements of a leak, if we want to include all those communications that people might reasonably call leaks: that the information is considered confidential under a broad definition of the term, and the leaker does not want people to know he or she is the source.

Finally, there is the negative connotation of leaking which makes it difficult to discuss no matter how widespread the practice. Here is a revealing exchange between a group of senior officials in the national security field and a teacher with experience in both government and journalism. The professor started by asking how many in the room had leaked. No hands went up (except his). Then he said, "Okay, forget classified information. How many have leaked nonclassified information?" Still no hands. Then he asked, "How many have ever told a reporter something you wouldn't want your boss to know you had disclosed?" Nearly half of those in the room raised their hands. Cyrus Vance called leaks "childish" and "naive," but that would be too mild for a lot of middle level managers in the federal government. For many of them, leaking confidential information is unethical, disloyal, and just plain wrong. Yet for many senior federal officials and nearly all journalists, most leaks do not carry that negative moral baggage.

They are at worst an annoyance. Schlesinger called leaks "mainly a source of irritation" and President Ford described them as a "real pain."

While the arguments about leaks continue, so do the leaks. Forty-two percent of the officials who responded to the survey said they leaked, and it is reasonable to assume that the figure is, if anything, understated. Leaks played a significant role in nearly every one of the cases we studied in detail, although we did not choose any of them for that reason. In the neutron bomb story, for example, Richard Burt of the *New York Times* was leaked the information that President Carter had decided to cancel production of the bomb. He went with the story, and the publication may have played a crucial role in softening Carter's final position. In the Love Canal relocation, the leak of the report on chromosomal damage began the process of undoing the carefully worked-out schedule for assessing the validity of the study. It contributed in a major way to the abbreviated process by which the decision to relocate was made. In the Bob Jones University tax exemption decision, a series of leaks occurred following the media criticism of the decision to restore the tax exemptions. First there were leaks from the White House designed to put the responsibility for the policy shift on Edwin Meese. Then, when that created its own brouhaha in the press and in the White House, someone leaked the notation on the president's log, indicating that Reagan had encouraged or endorsed the policy shift before the decision was public. That leak refocused attention on the president and his views on the issue, and eventually resulted in his taking full responsibility for the whole matter. When the Reagan administration was fighting legislation to reform the accelerated Social Security disability eligibil-ity reviews, White House officials used leaks to try to get the message out that bureaucratic changes were underway. Later, when it seemed inevitable that some legislation would be passed, the Department of Health and Human Services (HHS) began drafting its own legislative package, working with both key members of Congress and the White House staff to gain support. After the story broke about Roy Benavi-dez, the Vietnam war hero who was thrown off the disability rolls, a draft of the HHS legislative package was leaked. The leak made it appear that the department was simply responding to the criticism stemming from the treatment of Benavidez and undermined Secretary

Heckler's quiet negotiations with the chief congressional spokesperson on the issue, Congressman Jake Pickle.

Leaks were never more central to the story, however, than in the investigation and prosecution of then Vice-President Spiro Agnew. The leaks seemed to be coming from every direction every day, and the leaks themselves became a public issue in the case.

The Leaks and the Agnew Resignation

Quite appropriately, the story begins with a leak. On August 5, 1973, George Beall, the United States attorney for Maryland, received a phone call from Jerry Landauer, an investigative reporter for the *Wall Street Journal*. Landauer told Beall that he was planning to write that Vice-President Spiro Agnew was being investigated on charges of bribery, extortion, and tax fraud.

Agnew had been a target of an investigation for about three months. By the time of Landauer's call, the prosecutors had several contractors who were willing to testify that he had participated in a kickback scheme. To protect the secrecy of the investigation, Beall and his prosecutors working on the case had taken a number of unusual steps. They did not tell the IRS investigators working with them that Agnew was a target. They did not tell their colleagues in the US attorney's office. They postponed until the latest possible time sending subpoenas which covered the period during which Agnew was in office. According to Aaron Latham in his exhaustive piece in *New York* magazine, they concentrated on taking evidence on Agnew only from those who were also prosecutable in connection with the pay-offs, and therefore unlikely to run to the press. Finally, there was the issue of informing the incoming attorney general, Elliot Richardson, who had taken office in May 1973, after the resignation of Richard Kleindienst. When Beall and Richardson met on June 12, Beall says that they discussed the importance of keeping the investigation out of the press, and that they agreed to "make sure that there was no paper flowing back and forth" between their offices and to keep "to a very tight circle the people who knew of the investigation."[2]

What Beall remembers most about that phone call from Landauer on August 5 was how much specific information the reporter knew. It was clear that Landauer had seen the letter which had been sent to Agnew on August 1, advising him that he was a target of the investigation. Beall says that he would neither confirm nor deny the existence of the letter or even of the investigation, and that he tried to discourage Landauer from going ahead by suggesting that the reporter's reputation would be in jeopardy.

There was no story the next day, Monday, August 6. Landauer was trying to get more information and pressing Agnew's staff for a reaction, while Richardson was being briefed by Beall and was then himself briefing President Nixon. Richard Cohen of the *Washington Post* had been close to breaking the story as well. On Monday evening Agnew and his press secretary learned that the *Journal* story was going to run in Tuesday's paper. Because the *Post* has a later deadline, Cohen was able to give Agnew time to write and issue a statement that would make it into his story for Tuesday's *Post*. This meant that the *Post* would have something the *Journal* did not have, and Agnew would benefit by the Washington community reading his denial at the moment they learned of the investigation. At eleven that night, Agnew issued a statement which said, in part, "I will make no further comment until the investigation has been completed, other than to say that I am innocent of any wrongdoing, that I have confidence in the criminal justice system of the United States and that I am equally confident that my innocence will be affirmed."[3]

The next round of articles, appearing on Wednesday, August 8, included the charges, the meeting between Richardson and Beall, and the names of some of the witnesses who were prepared to testify. Later that day, the vice-president held a press conference and went on the attack, breaking his vow of silence thirty-six hours after he had taken it. He again proclaimed his innocence, and indicated particular annoyance that all the information was attributed to sources, as in "sources indicated yesterday," "informed sources have said," and "sources close to the investigation emphasized."[4]

From then on the investigation became a daily national drama, and the responsibility for the disclosures a continuing theme. Many of the country's major metropolitan newspapers assigned reporters to the story; the others followed it using the wire services. Often the stories just added background; sometimes they provided new information.

Much of the new anonymous information seemed to come from people closer to the president or to Agnew than to the Justice Department. For example, there were stories reporting details of the meeting between Agnew and President Nixon and stories outlining the strategy Agnew's lawyers were planning to use in his defense. However, much news about the case continued to be published with attribution to "sources close to the investigation."

The leaks were a special problem for the prosecutors. Leaking is not considered proper prosecutorial conduct, and so the sources and ethics of the leaks were quickly becoming a subject of press coverage themselves. That put the onus on the Justice Department to find out who was leaking, to stop it if it was coming from them, and to get the word out if it was not. The prosecutors in the US Attorney's office took the extraordinary step of issuing a press release saying they were not the source. Some were not convinced. Charles Morgan, director of the national office of the American Civil Liberties Union (ACLU) sent a letter to Richardson saying that the leaks about the evidence raise "serious questions about the due process being accorded the Vice-President"[5] and that it seems that "some of the information which has appeared in the newspapers could only have come, directly or indirectly, from law enforcement officials."

On Sunday, August 19, Richardson appeared on ABC's "Issues and Answers."[6] He defended the performance of his department, spoke of his "distress" at the leaks, and said that he would discipline anyone found to be responsible for them. The next day, however, *Time* (in advance copies of the issue dated August 27) included a long piece on the Agnew investigation which implicated the Justice Department directly. *Time* reported a previously undisclosed witness against the vice-president, the substance of that witness's forthcoming testimony, the view of "Justice Department officials in Washington" that an indictment "appears inevitable," and two direct quotes attributed to anonymous sources at Justice.[7] The leaks appeared to have become a tidal wave.

Agnew wasted no time. On August 21 he charged in a prepared statement that the Justice Department leaks were a "clear and outrageous effort to influence the outcome of possible grand jury deliberations." He asked the news media to "urge Mr. Richardson and the

Justice Department to conduct such an investigation [of the leaks] diligently wherever it may lead." Richardson said he "shared the Vice-President's concern," urged the media to exercise "restraint in what they report," and reiterated that he would pursue any lead implicating Justice Department officials.[8]

President Nixon involved himself publicly, ordering Justice to conduct an internal investigation. Then he held his first press conference in five months, saying the leaks were "completely contrary to the American tradition." He added that anyone from the Justice Department, the prosecutor's office, or the grand jury who has leaked "will be summarily dismissed from government service."[9]

While both the president and the vice-president were putting the attorney general on the hot seat, there was at least one unexpected effort to relieve some of the heat. In his page one story on the Nixon press conference, William Kovach of the *New York Times* wrote "While both Mr. Agnew and Mr. Nixon restricted their complaints to leaks of information from Federal sources, a good deal of information made public came from other sources. So widespread has been the investigation—which began last year—and the number of people involved so large that a reservoir of information is available to the press outside the Federal system, *including lawyers and friends and enemies of those under investigation* [emphasis added]."[10]

The next day, August 23, Richardson ordered Glen Pommerening, the acting assistant attorney general for administration, to undertake an internal investigation. Richardson's aides say that Nixon may have affected the timing, but the attorney general was already committed to the investigation. Agnew had sent Richardson a letter urging the probe, and now Richardson wrote back, outlining the steps he was taking and making it clear that there were plenty of other reasonable suspects: "As you know, a considerable number of people in and out of government are aware of some details of the investigation. Its outlines are known to a number of witnesses, individuals under investigation, their lawyers, select members of my, your, and the White House staff, and certain investigative personnel of the Internal Revenue Service. For this reason, there may be no fully effective means of stopping the cynical rumors and conjectures all too evident in recent weeks. We can, however, continue to insist that those in our employ behave with extraordinary circumspection."[11] Also on the twenty-third, the United Press International carried a story on the leaks, with "Justice Department sources"[12] suggesting that the White House might be doing the leaking. Finally, the American Civil Liberties Union chimed in again with a second letter, this one pointing to the newspaper and magazine attributions as evidence of Justice Department leaks and criticizing Richardson for suggesting that reporters ought to exercise restraint in what they publish.

During early September, the prosecutors began to discuss when and how to present the evidence. On September 10, Richardson received a call from White House counsel J. Fred Buzhardt, who had been acting as liaison among Justice, the White House, and Agnew's lawyers. Buzhardt said that Agnew was willing to open negotiations on a plea bargain.

For ten days, Richardson, Beall, and Assistant Attorney General Henry Petersen met with Agnew's three lawyers to try to hammer out a deal. The prosecutors were determined to make the evidence a matter of public record in order to increase general understanding about the case against Agnew. Agnew wanted to avoid that kind of broad disclosure, and to avoid a jail term if there was a guilty plea.

The relative calm during the first few days of the negotiations was broken on September 18. David Broder, the highly respected columnist for the *Washington Post,* wrote that Agnew was considering resignation and quoted a "senior Republican Party leader" as saying that Agnew would almost certainly resign.[13] The next day, the prosecutors met with Richardson to discuss what progress was being made. A grand jury session was scheduled that day, and the prosecutors feared that if they cancelled it the press would figure out that actual plea bargaining was going on. They sent the deputy US Attorney to stay with the grand jury for an hour and then release them, telling them not to reveal that they heard no testimony. Still, the *New York Times* reported the following morning that a source had said that "crucial negotiations" had halted the investigation.

The talks began to stumble over the issue of what Agnew would say in court. Richardson was pressing for an acknowledgment of the connection between the building contracts and the pay-offs. Agnew's lawyers balked and on September 22 they broke off the negotiations.

That morning, the *Post* reported that the bargaining was taking place, attributing its information to "informed sources," "two sources," and "a source who says he has talked with Agnew several times recently." That same day, Fred Graham reported the negotiations on CBS News. The Graham story, attributed to "a source close to the negotiations," said that the government's strategy was being determined by Henry Petersen; Graham quoted the source as quoting Petersen as saying, "We've got the evidence, we've got it cold."[14] Agnew was furious and most press commentators overlooked the point that the Petersen quote was attributed to an anonymous source and not from Petersen directly to Graham. Petersen was subjected to harsh criticism, particularly in the *Times* and in *Time* magazine.

On September 28, Agnew moved to bar the grand jury from hearing any testimony against him, on the grounds that impeachment was the only constitutional way of proceeding and that the leaks had made it impossible for him to get a fair trial. The Justice Department issued a statement the same day, strongly suggesting that Agnew and his friends were responsible for the leaks, pointing out that there was no coverage of the case until the August 1 letter from Beall to Agnew and the letter itself "was brought to public attention by the Vice-President."[15] Here was the ideal conflict story for the press, one that required no initiative on its part to keep it going.

Agnew was working both the courtroom and the court of public opinion. A September 28 column by James Reston of the *New York Times* laid out Agnew's impeachment and fair trial arguments, although Agnew was not revealed as the source. Reston repeated the Petersen incident, again attributing the quote to Petersen directly. On the twenty-ninth, Agnew spoke before Republican women in Los Angeles and renewed his attack. He charged that the *Wall Street Journal* had a copy of the Beall letter before he had seen it, that Petersen was "unprofessional and malicious and outrageous," and that because of the "tactics which have been employed" he would not resign if indicted.[16] His oratory brought down the house.

After the speech, Nixon asked for assurances from Richardson that Petersen had not leaked, which Richardson gladly provided. On October 1, a letter from Graham to the *New York Times* clarified the record on the Petersen quote and implied that Agnew's lawyers were the source: "It is clear from the broadcast that the quote from Mr. Petersen about the strength of the evidence was said at [a negotiation session] to Mr. Agnew's lawyers—not to me."[17]

Buoyed by the reception in Los Angeles, Agnew told Republican officials that he regretted he had not also denied that he had either initiated plea bargaining or that he was interested in a deal. His staff dutifully reported this to the press. Next, Agnew's press secretary said that the vice-president planned to go after the Justice Department again in a speech scheduled for Chicago on October 4. The White House, however, was becoming increasingly concerned that Agnew's rhetoric would force the president to have to choose publicly between his vice-president and his attorney general. Based on pressure from the president's men, Agnew fired his press secretary and did not deliver the planned speech. NBC News on October 2 quoted Justice Department officials as charging directly that Agnew's lawyers leaked the Petersen quote. Agnew responded immediately. He said his attorneys were willing to sign statements to the effect that they were not the sources of the information, and challenged Graham to be "decent enough" to confirm that they were not the leakers.

During an unusual informal appearance in the White House press room on October 4, Nixon told reporters that he supported Petersen. Agnew was beginning to fold his tent. In Chicago, he said that "a candle is only so long before it burns out."[18]

While the public relations war was winding down, the legal battle was not. Judge Walter Hoffman, who was presiding over the grand jury, called for an evidentiary hearing on the leaks. Agnew's lawyers issued subpoenas to nine reporters and four senior Justice Department officials. The Justice Department's position was to urge the judge to quash the subpoenas for the newsmen while not objecting to the subpoenas issued to the officials at Justice. By this time, Pommerening had completed another report, which said that he had received further confirmation that the original Landauer story had come from Agnew's people, and that "a person on the Vice-President's staff" had been the likely source of other leaks.[19]

Meanwhile Agnew, back in Washington, instructed his lawyers

to reopen negotiations. Buzhardt was in Florida. Agnew's lawyer flew there, rather than have Buzhardt return to Washington where he might be recognized by a reporter.

The next day, Sunday, October 7, Justice Department lawyers had a major strategy conference. According to Aaron Latham, in his piece in *New York* magazine, this was a difficult meeting. Richardson and Petersen were prepared to compromise both on what Agnew would be required to say in court and on any recommendation the department might make with regard to whether or not Agnew should go to jail, but the prosecutors from Baltimore wanted a tougher line. Latham quotes Petersen as saying: "This man is the goddamn Vice-President of the United States. What do you want to do? Make him crawl on his belly?" The answer from one of the prosecutors, according to Latham, re-emphasized that Agnew's reputation was not the only one on the line. Assistant Attorney General Barney Skolnik responded to Petersen, "It isn't a question of making him crawl on his belly. It is a question of how what we are doing is going to be perceived."[20]

What everyone hoped would be the final negotiating session was scheduled for Monday with the judge in a room he had taken at the Olde Colony Motor Lodge in Alexandria, Virginia. Reporters found the site and the two teams of lawyers walked into the motel under the glare of television lights. Most of the deal was cut then; the most important issue still unresolved was whether Justice would make a recommendation on a jail sentence. On October 9, the last negotiating meeting took place. When it became clear that without a recommendation from Justice against jail there might be no deal, Richardson agreed. The arraignment was set for the following day.

Just before 2:00 P.M., the Justice team and Agnew's lawyers entered the courtroom. Then came the vice-president. When all parties had been seated, Agnew authorized a phone call to be made to a lawyer who was waiting outside the secretary of state's office to deliver Agnew's resignation. When it was confirmed that the resignation had been received, and therefore that Agnew would not go down in history as the first sitting vice-president to plead to a felony, the proceedings began. Agnew pleaded nolo contendere to one count of tax evasion. Richardson spoke, emphasizing the importance not only of the agreement between the parties *being* just and honorable, but also *being per-*

ceived as just and honorable. He presented a forty-page exposition of the evidence against Agnew.[21] Agnew then spoke. Among other things, he said that if a trial were held, the "intense media interest" in the case would "distract public attention from important national problems."[22]

There was one last leak. Before Judge Hoffman's locked courtroom was opened, the resignation was already out. Back in Agnew's office, one of his secretaries, Lisa Brown, had told reporters what was going on.

The Impact of Leaks

The leaks in the Agnew case became more than a casual annoyance to the prosecutors and the Justice Department. Without the leaks the public would have known a lot less for a lot longer about the investigation. Typically in political corruption cases, there are so many people involved and so much information around that some material about the investigation does get reported. Here, however, in spite of the careful plans of the prosecutors to keep the investigation quiet, there was an extraordinary amount of detailed information reported regularly, from the time Agnew was informed of the probe until his day in court. This was a two-month continuing news story. Arguably some of the leaks, such as those about the plea bargaining, were as much under the umbrella of politics and public policy as the administration of justice, and thereby subject to less restrictive standards of confidentiality. But most of the information that was published from anonymous sources consisted significantly, although not exclusively, of the material which most everyone would consider to be properly confidential to the investigatory process. While some of what was published was not accurate, on the whole the picture painted by the coverage told a fair story of what was happening.

If we are to take the principals at their word, all were unhappy that the information was published. Leaks always make information known to the public which would otherwise be secret. Leaks from criminal investigations always raise questions about due process and fair trial for the suspect, but they also often have an impact on the capacity of officials to administer justice in the public interest. In the

Agnew case, the leaks had several notable effects on the people, processes, and products involved in policymaking.

First, the leaks turned the lives of the Baltimore prosecutors upside down. Reporters from around the country flocked to their offices. Beall installed a door blocking access to the lawyers' and investigators' working areas. Reporters were required to wait in the reception room, and the traditionally open feeling in the office was replaced by an atmosphere that more closely resembled a state of siege.

Rather than simply go about their prosecuting business, they had to learn how to deal with the press and how to cope with the public suspicion that they were acting unprofessionally. They knew from the moment that Agnew became a target of the investigation that part of their job was to convince the public that they were acting fairly and responsibly. The leaks made that substantially more difficult to do. In addition, the leaks and Agnew's trying to use them to his advantage forced the prosecutors not only to try to stop the leaks but to develop their own press strategy designed to counteract Agnew's tactics. The leaks affected the senior Justice Department officials in much the same way, although Richardson, Petersen, and some of the others had previous experience dealing with leaks, and extensive experience dealing with the press under stress. All of them devoted a lot of time and energy to the problem. A third set of policymakers, those in the White House, were also affected by the leaks, which began to complicate their own problems arising out of Watergate and required them to get involved as part of their own strategy for survival.

Second, the leaks forced the Department of Justice officials to add a new factor to their strategy discussions. They had to take steps to secure their own information channels and to reassure the public that they were not only doing their jobs, but that they were trying to find out whether there were any culprits within their midst. The leaks and the fear of future leaks caused the prosecutors to put less in writing and to limit the number of people who could be informed about the case and therefore available for help in policy judgments. One of Beall's team members, Barney Skolnik, says that the press as a whole caused them to expend a lot of diversionary effort: "If it hadn't been for the press . . . we would not have had to waste as much time and energy persuading people to come in through the basement and all the other rubbish we had to go through to get people to talk to us."[23]

Third, the leaks themselves became an issue of great importance, challenging the credibility of the prosecutors. This heightened the prosecutors' sense of the difficulty they faced in convincing the public that they were being fair and procedurally responsible. They were being held accountable not only because the press was watching, but also because their integrity was at issue.

Fourth, the leaks themselves did not exacerbate relations between officials and reporters institutionally, but there was increased tension between some individual reporters and officials because of the problems stemming from them. Richardson challenged the press briefly, calling for restraint on their part in deciding whether to print what had been leaked to them. He did not push the point and on the whole, both Agnew and the people at Justice went out of their way to acknowledge and accept the journalist's perspective that stopping leaks was not the job of the press. Everyone involved seemed to understand leaks as part of the daily routine of the interaction, but that was not enough to keep all the waters calm here because this was hardly routine business and the stakes were very high.

The most important issue is whether the leaks significantly shaped the way the government did its business or the outcome of the case. The leaks did affect the process of policymaking, leading the prosecutors to put less in writing and to involve fewer people in the process. Also, the whole process probably took less time than it otherwise would have because of the intense press coverage in general, and the fear of leaks in particular. Constant publicity creates its own pressure to act. Beall himself believes that the amount of focus from the media was in part responsible for the speed with which they worked. "I think the press attention forced a resolution of the matter earlier than might otherwise have been the case. For example, if this had been a typical criminal case, the plea bargaining would have taken place after the charges were placed. . . . Of course here the whole prenegotiation process took place before the charges were filed. Everyone was on a faster track. Part of it was because we were dealing with the vice president of the United States. But part was also because of the tremendous public attention that was attracted."[24]

Beall speaks of the overall coverage, but since there would have been far less coverage if there had been no leaks, it was the leaks that created most of the problem for him.

What about the substance of the policies? Perhaps Agnew got a better deal than he would have had otherwise because of the pressure on the prosecutors created by the issue of the leaks. The contrary is also possible: perhaps the prosecutors were tougher on Agnew than they might have been because the spotlight on the case made them particularly sensitive to the charge of letting the vice-president off easy. Charles Colson, who was part of Agnew's defense team, believes that the coverage hurt the vice-president's chances of making his best defense. ''If it had not been for the glare of publicity, there would have been many more negotiations. There would have been more efforts to produce witnesses who would contradict the government's witnesses. . . . The ultimate decision to resign was because in that public climate you could not judicially resolve the situation. It's possible that four months later, without the stories, it might have come to the same conclusion. But the press coverage made it impossible to follow what would have been normal investigative processes and normal defense maneuverings.''[25]

Richardson believes that the coverage had no impact on the outcome, only on the steps they all took near the end to preserve the secrecy of the negotiations. Jonathan Moore, Richardson's associate attorney general and chief political adviser, speculates that it is at least conceivable that the government would have pressed a harder position without the coverage. ''A public sense of confidence and trust in the outcome was one of the things we cared about. The press plays a role in influencing what the public psychology is and, therefore, without the press playing a part we would have had a much easier time maintaining public confidence, perhaps even if we had pressed for a stronger position.''[26]

Stronger negotiating posture or not, ultimately it seems that the outcome would have been basically the same because Agnew held the vice-presidency, the trump card which he appeared to be willing to use whenever the negotiations got tough. The prosecutors were committed to getting him out of office without the time required or the uncertainty of outcome with either a trial or an impeachment. His presence would have affected the ongoing Watergate crisis in ways that they believed were clearly not in the national interest. Agnew knew this, or sensed it, and that gave him the leverage to drive a hard bargain.

There is a pattern of leaks affecting the process of policymaking much more than they affected the substance of the policies. In the decision of the Carter administration to relocate over seven hundred families from Love Canal, the leak of the results of the preliminary study of chromosomal damage among residents there in and of itself had no effect on what officials in retrospect believe to have been the inevitable policy choice. But there is no doubt that the leak was one of the key factors in making the policymakers feel that they had to act more quickly than they would have preferred. The leak advanced the story ahead of the policymakers' schedule and put them of the defensive, forcing them to explain themselves and make future commitments to demonstrate that they were on top of the situation. Similarly, in the Bob Jones University tax exemption story, the leaks were used, presumably by White House officials, to try to fix responsibility for the decision on Meese. They did not add very much momentum to what already existed for back-tracking and reversing what had taken place. And in the case of the Social Security disability reviews, the leaks were used by government officials as an unsuccessful and last-ditch effort to stave off congressional action by suggesting that the administration was taking sufficient steps on its own.

The only leak that occurred in the cases we studied in depth which seemed to affect policy as much as process was in the neutron bomb case. On March 27, 1978, President Carter had made what appeared to be his definite and final decision to cancel the neutron bomb. Some of his key people, including principally National Security Adviser Zbigniew Brzezinski and Secretary of State Cyrus Vance, continued to urge Carter to reconsider. For several days, the cancellation decision was kept under wraps. Stories appeared, but they were remarkably off base, most of them predicting that Carter would move ahead with the weapon. Both Richard Burt of the *New York Times* and Walter Pincus of the *Washington Post* were tipped off that Carter had decided on cancellation. Pincus discarded the information because, he now says, he ''just couldn't believe that after all these months with everybody saying everything was go, Carter was going to cancel.'' Pincus's information had come from a congressman by way of his editor.

Burt says he was told by a "non-American," who had learned about the cancellation from a senior US official and mentioned it to Burt "in a normal, passing encounter." Burt confirmed the story with three officials and then went to print. On April 4, the *Times* led the paper with Burt's story, under the headline "Aides Report Carter Bans Neutron Bomb; Some Seek Reversal." Burt's scoop was accurate, and some administration officials assumed he got it from a proponent of the bomb, such as Brzezinski, who would have leaked it in a last-ditch effort to generate enough support for production to turn Carter around.

At the State Department and the Pentagon there was general bemusement, and surprise that the story had not leaked earlier. But with the West German foreign minister due in town to talk with Carter about the bomb and other matters that very morning, the White House was extremely upset. The decision was made to deny. Within twenty-four hours, Vance, Hodding Carter, Harold Brown, Jody Powell, and West German chancellor Helmut Schmidt's spokesperson Klaus Boelling all unequivocally denied that a decision had been made and said the story was wrong. Even President Carter, who had been telling his own advisers that he had decided not to go ahead, was now telling leaders in Congress that he had not made up his mind.

News reports covered the Burt article and the denial as a story in itself. Some even speculated that the "misleading information was leaked to Burt by an opponent of the bomb in the administration who was trying to put last-minute pressure on the president not to go ahead. The story and the rebuttal unleashed a wave of protest from Congress, from Republican leaders George Bush, Ronald Reagan, and Gerald Ford, and from a large number of the nation's leading newspapers, all outraged at the idea that Carter was even considering cancellation. Even the *Washington Post*, which had started the whole process with Walter Pincus's story almost a year before, urged the president editorially to "make a forthright, no-nonsense decision to proceed," [27] in light of the strain on relations with the allies and the questions about his leadership.

It is impossible to know for sure what impact the Burt story denial had on Carter, but circumstantial evidence suggests it played an important role. Carter began to reevaluate his position that morning. By his own account, within two or three days, and right in the midst of the protests from the politicians and the press spurred by the story and denial, he had moved from cancellation to deferral. In the *Post,* Walter Pincus gave the Burt article credit for the change, although Powell and NSC Deputy Director David Aaron deny it. During a background session for the press just after the deferral was announced, Brzezinski himself said that the "fourth estate played a significant role." When asked point blank whether the Burt story and the reaction to it made the president shift his stand, Brzezinski said, "I think there may be something to that, but you'd have to ask the president to be sure."

Part of the whole strategy for presenting the new decision to defer had to include the notion that the Burt story was dead wrong, that there never had been a decision to cancel. Otherwise, the president would appear to have changed his mind twice, first going ahead, then cancelling and finally deferral. The administration was fairly successful in making the point. Both *Time* and *Newsweek*[28] characterized Burt's story as false; with the exception of an Evans and Novak column, no one in the press seems to have challenged the administration's denial. One of the consequences of this leak was that the administration felt that it had to resort to a bald-faced lie to counter it.

At a press briefing with Burt in the room, Powell characterized the story as "bad reporting." Burt was incensed, and at the conclusion of the briefing he cornered Powell, whom he had never met before, to express his displeasure. Powell ushered him into the office and, in a disarmingly friendly way, explained how much difficulty the story had caused. Burt says he learned a lesson from the experience: "What Jody was saying was that when you're protecting the president, all is fair in love and war."[29]

Ironically, the one leak in our cases which seemed to affect the policy outcome was, if Burt is to be believed, inadvertent. In the Agnew resignation story, where leaks were a central focus of the policymaking and appeared to be clearly advertent, they seemed to have little impact on the final result although substantially affecting the process of getting there. Despite the prevalance of leaks, the impact on policy is hard to discern and thereby even harder to predict. We cannot say that leaks do not affect policy outcomes, just that the impact is tough to anticipate, may be less than imagined, and probably is more on process than on policy. This conclusion from the cases is confirmed by the conversations with senior officials and the results of the survey.

When officials are asked about the impact of leaks, they talk about process, rather than substance. The impact of leaks is better understood as having changed the routines of policymaking over time, then in terms of the effect of any single leak in a particular case. Policymakers expect leaks, anticipate their impact, take preventative measures, and use them strategically themselves. As Sam Hughes said, "Anybody who is in . . a fairly significant position in an agency is out of his mind if he puts anything on paper that he's not willing to see published. It complicates decision-making processes. [Not putting anything on paper] complicates communication processes. And I think it probably complicates the process of public education." Our responses from senior federal officials suggest that by and large they have taken Hughes's advice. Three quarters of those officials who worried about leaks limited the number of people involved in decision making and put less information in writing as a result of their concern. On the other hand, just over 20 percent of our worriers said that leaks caused them to narrow the range of policy options that they considered, and even fewer of them said that their concerns on this score caused them to increase the range of policy options or to reshape their options.

Among the questionnaire respondents, officials who served in the Johnson and Nixon years were just as likely to leak as those who served later, yet the anecdotal evidence we have from the policymakers we interviewed suggests that leaks are much more of a factor now than they used to be. One explanation for this apparent inconsistency is that different information now is leaked, and the leaks themselves are more significant in substance.

Theodore Sorensen believes that leaks are a more serious issue in the 1980s than they were for President Kennedy. Respected policymakers who served in the earlier era, such as Dean Rusk, Elmer Staats, and Wilbur Cohen, said that leaks were not a problem for them, and discounted their significance. Rusk said that the only leak he had any difficulty with in all his years as secretary of state was when someone released his comment made in the midst of the Cuban missile crisis that "they were eyeball to eyeball and the other fella just blinked." "It should not have been leaked," Rusk said, "because it might have had some effect on old man Khrushchev, who was impulsive and unpredictable.''

Those who served in recent years were much more likely to worry about leaks than those who served more than a decade ago (75.5 percent to 57 percent). Officials who served in the 1970s and 1980s talked more about the importance of leaks and about what they did to adjust to leaks as a continuing part of policymaking. Elliot Richardson, for example, said that his defense against leaks was to open up the process of decision making. That way there would be enough people involved and aware of what was going on that the number of secrets to be leaked would be kept to a minimum and fewer people would feel that they had to leak to air their point of view. Others used very different tactics. Brzezinski excluded people from meetings in order to prevent leaks. Peterson said that during his time in the Nixon White House, ''they were so upset about the leaks and the effect the leaks were having on policy that they specifically forbade White House people or senior staff members from talking to certain members of certain institutions of the media.'' Predictably, officials we recontacted who had said they had not leaked were critical of the impact of leaks, suggesting for example, that less information is now put in files, leaving successors less well equipped to understand what went on before them.

If advertent leaks are often unsuccessful in changing policy, there must be other motives that lead officials to provide confidential information to reporters. For example, each of the potential leakers in the Agnew case had different possible reasons for leaking.

The prosecutors might have believed that unless the fact of the investigation were public, the White House and the new attorney general would find a way to protect the vice-president. Thus, the seemingly never-ending flow of leaks during the Agnew investigation could reasonably have been ascribed to the prosecutors or to those who worked with them in Washington or Baltimore: it was information the prosecutors knew best, their reputations were being challenged by Agnew, and they thus appeared at this stage to have an interest in the public understanding the seriousness of the charges and the quality of their evidence. The stories often hinted or suggested directly that they were the sources. Furthermore, the prosecutors from Baltimore were logical suspects because they were concerned, especially early on, that Richardson would not aggressively pursue the investigation. Keeping the heat on him through publicity, one could hypothesize, would force him to proceed, or more precisely, to let them proceed without interference.

Agnew charged that the Justice Department was leaking because officials there wanted to restore a tarnished reputation. That argument does not hold up well. The reputation of the department was much more likely to be restored by steadfastly and professionally pursuing the evidence than by making the case in the newspapers. Later in the story, when the integrity of the department was at issue because of the leaks, not because of backing off the case, and when sympathy for Agnew was at its peak, the department had an interest in getting information out which showed that the prosecutors were on solid ground in their investigation, and that there were other, more likely, leaking suspects.

Almost as soon as the leaking became an issue, Richardson suggested publicly that there were other more reasonable suspects. Glen Pommerening's internal investigation of the leaks at the Department of Justice provided support for Richardson's notion. Pommerening had asked each of those involved in the Agnew investigation for the names of any employees of the department who might know anything about the case. Having developed that list, he took sworn statements from each of them, under penalties of perjury. Pommerening found only nineteen persons who said they knew of the investigation before the Landauer story, with only eight of them having in-depth knowledge of the case. If Pommerening is right in his numbers, and if Agnew is right that the first leak came from Justice, the source was no minor functionary. In addition to the interviews, Pommerening tried to correlate what each person knew with the information in particular stories in the press. His preliminary report said that the 134 Justice Department people interviewed had signed sworn statements saying that they were not the source of leaks and did not know who was.[30] Pommerening had analyzed the news reports against who knew what when, and had concluded that there was a strong correlation between the time information was conveyed to the White House and to the vice-president and when it appeared in print. He raised the possibility that stories attributed to Justice Department sources may have actually been from people outside the department who themselves were attributing to the department the information they were conveying to reporters.

What about the White House? The vice-president's problems posed problems for the president. As the evidence mounted against Agnew while his public relations effort seemed to be gaining momentum, the White House might have seen Agnew's continued presence as further tarnishing the administration. The president had supported Agnew publicly for a long time. It was not until September 25 that he openly backed away, after he had been briefed by Richardson on the evidence. The White House issued a statement that day which was substantially cooler toward the vice-president than anything the president had said before, calling on the American people to ''accord the vice-president the basic, decent consideration and presumption of innocence that are both his right and due.'' But Agnew's associates believed that the White House had been responsible for some damaging leaks before then. Once Nixon put some distance between himself and Agnew, it was in his interest that there be an increasing public awareness of just how strong the case was against the vice-president, who was still very popular within the Republican Party. Colson says that from mid-September on, the ''White House was running a campaign to pressure Agnew out'' and that White House at that point had a motive for leaking ''just like the prosecutors.''[31]

There were also several potential leakers who were not among the policymakers in the case. Agnew first charged that others under investigation had leaked information to the press. They had an interest in turning the investigations away from themselves and probably had less experience in dealing with the press than the officials and thus were more vulnerable to sophisticated and aggressive reporters.

Finally, of course, there was the vice-president, his lawyers, and staff. The Justice Department investigation of the leaks pointed in that direction by analyzing who knew what when, and when information was reported. It was the vice-president who stood to gain the most by having the public believe that he was being subjected to unfair treatment by the prosecutors. There is a strong sense that Agnew was the source of the long Reston column on September 28, and after all, the original letter from Beall to Agnew apparently was not leaked until Agnew had received it.

Each of these possibilities assumes an independent rational tactical or strategic motive. However, leaks are not always, maybe not even usually, the product of a rational calculation by the leaker. Leaks may also be elicited by a clever reporter or may come from a person who does not realize the significance of the information imparted. Leaks may occur by accident as well as by design. When by design, they may be just as likely intended for some unrelated purpose—such as ingratiating oneself with the reporter or inflicting harm on an enemy— as to affect the outcome of the issue at hand.

In the Agnew case, the leaks became an issue. The leak of the pilot study report did not cause such a furor in the Love Canal relocation story. Why here? There seem to be three reasons why leaks became a story in themselves in this case. First, the leaks raised questions about whether the constitutionally protected rights of an individual were being served. Second, the leaking would have been a violation of law for some of the potential leakers. Third, one of the principals wanted to put leaks on the agenda as part of his effort to undermine the credibility of his antagonists.

Leaks also became an issue near the end of the neutron bomb story. What made the leak to Richard Burt a public, albeit minor, issue in that case? There was no constitutionally protected right at stake, as there was with Vice-President Agnew, and while issues of national security were involved in the policymaking, there was no national security risk in the leak. There was no potential violation of law. What made it an issue was that, as in the Agnew case, one of the story's principals—here, the White House and there Agnew—had an interest in falsely discrediting a basically true story. It was the official challenge to the substance of the leak—the denial—that made the leak an issue in each case.

There is another point about this story that ought not to be lost in comparing it to the Agnew case. There was a lot of speculation during the Agnew investigation about who did the leaking. It was based on trying to establish motives, as well as to connect who had the information with the content and timing of the leaks. Once again, the assumption of a high degree of rationality and purposefulness may have been misplaced. A leak is usually thought of as a single discrete communication of specific and confidential information from official to reporter. Yet most of what are called leaks do not occur that way, and most of the anonymous communication that does occur between officials and reporters analytically looks like a leak, whether or not the parties involved choose to label it so. Jerry Landauer had been working on the Agnew story for a long time, investigating leads and doing his own research into the contract-awarding business in Maryland when Agnew was county executive there. The person who leaked the Beall letter to him might have been someone he had been talking to for months or even years. In the case of the neutron bomb leak, if Burt is to be believed, the leak came from someone who was not a part of the administration and was talking with Burt "more out of bewilderment and shock" than out of a desire to get him to write about it. Burt followed up the information with three other sources, all of whom presumably confirmed the basic information and added something themselves to provide Burt with enough detail to justify the lead story placement by the *Times*.

Bernard Gwertzman, veteran diplomatic correspondent for the *Times*, believes that officials and the public think leaks are more planned and willful than is usually the case: "There are books that credit me with all kinds of leaks. There's Bill Sullivan, who was our ambassador to Iran . . . saying I got tremendous leaks from the State Department. It's kind of amusing because I think in his vision he had some official reading the cables and then calling me up. . . . Whereas in fact some of the best stories I've got occurred in the following fashion: It was December–January, '78–'79, when the Shah was kind of on the ropes. I remember having lunch with a friend of mine at the State Department in which we weren't really talking about Iran. This was a guy who was senior enough to know what was happening. We got talking about Iran and I said, 'Gee, it must be tough on Sullivan. What does he tell the Shah? Does the Shah ask him for advice?' And the guy agreed. 'Yeah,' he says, 'it is tough. The Shah is a Hamlet-like figure. He doesn't know whether he should use force or not use force, and he asked Sullivan for advice, but we can't decide what to tell Sullivan. And so we tell Sullivan not to tell him anything.'

"I checked this out with a couple of other people, and nobody said, 'That's not right.' So I write a story more or less saying that, that Sullivan's reporting that the Shah is indecisive and he can't get [clear signals]. What I didn't realize when I was writing this was that this was a very top secret. I'm not sure the guy who told me this even knew that Sullivan had been sending these cables. He was just a friend of mine. He had no particular axe to grind with Sullivan. He was sympathetic to Sullivan. I think Sullivan thought somebody in Washington was trying to knife him. It's a funny kind of system."

Gwertzman's story has the ring of truth to it. We tend to assume more rationality, purposefulness, and logic from others than we do for ourselves. The "system," as Gwertzman refers to it, is probably a lot more accidental than orchestrated. Journalists get leaks when they are not expecting them, and what appears in print as a leak from a single source, perhaps confirmed by others, is often the result of a lot of conversations out of which the reporter gets what Gwertzman calls a "mosaic" of what is happening.

The idea that leaks may be less systematic than they appear does not eliminate intent on the part of the leakers. Almost all the leak suspects in the Agnew story had a reasonable motive at some point for trying to get some of the information out anonymously.

In the leak of the report in the Love Canal case, motivation is more subtle. It seems likely there that the leaker either talked to Jack Watson or was someone who had attended the key Friday meeting that Watson chaired, where the strategy for releasing the report was developed. Since it was going to be released the next day anyway, why would anyone leak it to the *New York Times*? A likely explanation, perhaps the most likely, is that the leaker was someone who had an existing relationship with the *Times* reporter, similar to the example offered by Gwertzman. The leak may have come because the reporter pursued his source and because the leaker saw it as an opportunity to do a favor for a reporter from a very important news organization. It does not seem to have been a leak designed to affect policy as much as a leak which was a part of a reporter–source relationship. That type of leak is called either a self-interested leak or an ego leak, and is distinguished particularly from a policy leak.[32] It often occurs when the policymaker is trying to show the reporter that he or she is important by being privy to important information. In a policy leak, the clear purpose is to try to influence the outcome of a particular decision-making process.

There are two variations on the ego leak. In the goodwill leak, the leader has no professional interest in the policy area or in the particular information involved, but is trying to curry favor by providing information that the reporter will find useful. In the casual or no-purpose leak, the transfer of information comes as a by-product of a personal relationship between the reporter and the leaker which is characterized by ongoing conversation and mutual trust. Richard Burt's explanation about the leak in the neutron bomb case may fit into this category.

Another leak is the trial-balloon leak, where the details of an initiative are surfaced to see what the reaction will be. There is also the whistle-blowing leak, usually when a frustrated official, without routine access to the press, leaks information about some alleged wrongdoing in government. Then there is the grudge leak, when an official releases negative information, often personal and embarrassing, to settle a score or damage someone else. The leaks in the Bob Jones University tax exemption fracas which tried to pin the blame on Edwin Meese are a good illustration.

Finally, and most esoteric, there is the reverse effect or reverse blame leak. For instance, someone may leak material which on the surface appears to be damaging or negative to himself or herself, but serves to get some important information out while minimizing the possibility of being identified as the source. When Alexander Haig was secretary of state, notes from one of his early morning inner staff meetings were leaked to the *Washington Post*. The notes included some personal and uncomplimentary comments by Haig about world leaders. At first blush, the leak would seem to be intended to undermine Haig; but on further reflection, as pointed out shortly after the incident by William Safire in the *New York Times*, Haig was under criticism at the time for not being tough enough for the job, and the notes presented him as a confident and independent official with his own point of view.

These types of leaks represent a range of disinterestedness and different degrees of moral justification. If you ask leaders why they leaked, as we did, you cannot expect them to respond with the more mean-spirited or self-interested reasons which we know do exist. Yet with that limitation, the answers they did give us provide some additional insight into leakers' motivations.

For example, nearly four out of five of the leakers identified countering false or misleading information as the reason they leaked. In their eyes, at least, they were assisting the process of getting at the truth, of helping the reporter do the job, of keeping the public informed. Nearly as many leaders, almost three out of four, said they leaked to put something on the agenda, to gain attention for an issue or policy option. The other two reasons chosen by more than half of the leaders from the list we offered were to consolidate support from the public or a constituency outside of government (64 percent) and to force action on an issue (53 percent). If Agnew and his friends leaked in their struggle for survival in 1973, it was for outside support; and if there was a policy rationale for the leak in the Love Canal case, it was undoubtedly someone sympathetic to the plight of the families at Love Canal who did it to force action, in the belief that by making the report a *New York Times* exclusive, there was sure to be a significant and positive response from the Carter administration, whatever the concerns about the quality of the study, the availability of the funding, and the legal authorization to act.

Developing good relations with the press was indicated as a reason for leaking by just about 40 percent of our leakers. This number is probably underestimated, both becasue this is a rather candid admission for an official to make, even anonymously, and becasue experience indicates that it is standard reportorial practice and simple human nature to hold out the hope of good relations as a possible benefit of cooperating on a story.

Six other reasons for leaking were mentioned by about a third of our leakers. Three are clearly policy leaks: to send a message to another branch of government (32 percent), to stop action on an issue (31.5 percent), and to slow action on an issue (29 percent). One is the trial balloon: to inform other officials of a policy consideration or action (30 percent). A fifth may be a combination of policy and ego: to protect one's position (30 percent). The sixth is clsoe to what we earlier called the accidental leak: the result of an enterprising reporter shrewdly eliciting the information (29 percent).

What we can glean from this data is that those who admitted leaking most often leaked for policy-related reasons of putting items on the agenda and sending a message to those outside of government. Leaks are often, if not usually, given more space and time by news organizations because they are exclusive stories. It follows that leaks can be particularly effective in accomplishing those purposes. The other most often-cited reason for leaking, correcting the record, may have a range of goals behind it. It may be a way to further policy interests or a way of trying to earn the gratitude of the reporter. Leaking ''the truth'' to correct a mistake may help the journalist without embarrassment to anyone. If the reporter's original story was inaccurate, by providing a corrective leak the official can enable the reporter to fix the mistake in such a way as to draw the least possible amount of attention to the original error. On the other hand, if the error was made by one reporter, giving a competitor an exclusive on the right information can help guarantee that it will get the biggest possible play.

However much the cases and the survey results suggest that leaks may be less systematic than officials and the public suspect, there is nothing to suggest that they are less prevalent. On the contrary, everything we have found argues that leaks as broadly defined are a routine and generally accepted part of the policymaking process. There were leaks in five of the six cases we studied, and both journalists and officials with whom we talked confirmed the view that they are a pervasive element of the interaction. There was disagreement over the importance, the propriety, and the value of leaks, but not whether they were a large fact of life in Washington.

Nearly 74 percent of the senior government officials we surveyed said they were concerned about leaks affecting policy they were working on or responsible for. It is even more remarkable and surprising that over four out of ten officials admitted leaking. The actual percentage must be even higher than that; some who did would presumably not admit to it and others would define leaks narrowly enough so as to exclude their own practices.

It is reasonable to make two assumptions about the senior federal officials who said they leaked. First, they probably did. And second, while they may have had varying definitions of a leak, most of them meant something broader than leaking information which was classified or otherwise protected by law. We found some important differences between the admitted leakers and their more tight-lipped colleagues.

Who Leaks?

First, the self-described leakers are active in their dealings with the press. They spent more time with the press than did the nonleakers. About 62 percent of the nonleakers spent five hours or less a week dealing with the press or thinking about press matters, compared to only 41 percent of the leakers. On the other end of the spectrum, only 12 percent of the nonleakers spent between ten and forty hours a week dealing with the press, whereas 20 percent of the leakers were that active. As another measure of their level of activity, leakers were much more likely than nonleakers to have sought out coverage for themselves, their policies, or their agencies. Almost nine out of ten leakers (89 percent) sought coverage; less than two out of three (65 percent) nonleakers did so.

Leakers used the press as a resource. They were much more likely than nonleakers to rely on the mass media and on the trade press for information about their own policy area. Similarly, they saw informal and unofficial communications with reporters (not recessarily leaks) as an asset in doing their jobs. There was a dramatic difference between leakers and nonleakers here: only 22.5 percent of the nonleakers thought that these informal communciations were more than somewhat useful to them, whereas 44 percent of the leakers felt that way.

Second, leakers tended to be more confident about their grasp of the relationship between the press and government. For example, 72 percent of the leakers thought they spent the right amount of time with the press, whereas only 64 percent of nonleakers did. And while most all officials believed they understood how the press operates, the nonleakers fell significantly below that average and the leakers were well above it. Similarly, the more successful senior policymakers seemed to be less interested in stopping leaks and tracking down the leakers than others. They often saw leaks as an "annoyance" in President Ford's words, but did not divert energy and resources to trying to eliminate them.

One who was somewhat famous for trying just that now has some doubts. Sitting in his New York office long after he had left the government, Henry Kissinger mused aloud about leaks and shared some second thoughts on his own celebrated efforts to root out the leaders: "When you're in government, you know the motive of the guy who leaked it, and so obviously it creates extremely bad feelings that a colleague will use this method to achieve his objective. In retrospect, I think our reaction—no doubt, my reaction—was excessive. You see, most of the leaks—if you are philosophical about it—go away. I mean, they're unpleasant, but so what? If you ignore them, most of them are not of that huge significance."

Third, leakers were more successful than nonleakers in their dealings with the press. They were much more likely (45 percent to 29 percent) to have been successful in getting the coverage that they sought. They were much less likely (55.5 percent to 70 percent) to have had most of the stories about themselves or their offices initiated by reporters rather than by themselves. They saw themselves as having better press relations: about 75 percent of the leakers and less than two thirds of the nonleakers characterized their press relations as more positive than negative.

Fourth, leakers believe that the press has discrete and definable impacts on the policymaking process. When asked what kind of stories had the greatest impact, more nonleakers than leakers said personality stories (30 percent to 21 percent) and leakers more than nonleakers said policy stories (51.5 percent to 42 percent). Support for the notion that leakers had a more discriminating view of the role of the press comes from their answers to the question of whether stories had different impacts when published at the various stages of the policy process: problem identification, solution formulation, policy adoption, implementation, and evaluation. A significantly higher percentage of the leakers than the nonleakers said there was a large or dominant effect at *every* stage, other than implementation where there was no difference between the two groups. Similarly, when asked about various impacts of positive and negative press, both in the trade and the mass media, it was always the leakers who saw impacts significantly greater than nonleakers where there was any difference between them. There was no category in which the nonleakers thought there was a greater impact than the leakers did.

We asked the officials whether they would say that positive or negative coverage in the mass media, or positive or negative coverage in the trade media, had no effect at all. Across the board, the nonleakers were more likely than the leakers to say that there was no effect. The difference was particularly significant on the negative mass and trade press, where the nonleakers were *twice as likely* as leakers to say that there was no effect. This is not surprising. If leakers did not believe that the press has a big impact, they would not be making the effort.

Leakers see the press in strategic terms, as a tool for getting the job done, as a resource for themselves. There is a huge difference between leakers and nonleakers in their views about the nature and extent of particular impacts of the press. On every dimension we tested, leakers saw more impacts and bigger specific impacts than did their nonleaking colleagues.

Finally, it is these attitudes toward the press and their strategy for dealing with the press that separates leakers from nonleakers more than demographic characteristics or policy area. There is hardly any relationship between leaking and ideology—conservatives are just as likely to leak as moderates. Liberals are just slightly more likely to admit doing so. Congress, trade or economic policy, and foreign policy produce slightly higher percentages of leakers, and law enforcement slightly lower, than other areas. There is no correlation between length of service and propensity to leak. Even more important, those policymakers who served in the Johnson and Nixon years were just as likely to leak as were their successors who served under Ford, Carter, and Reagan.

Why Do Nonleakers Not Leak?

To try to understand the nonleakers as well as the leakers, we went back to a few of our respondents who said they never leaked and asked them why.

Three themes emerged. First, leaks were more conventional among political appointees than among career civil servants, even those career bureaucrats who rose very high in the government. Second, a minority of those we called back said they didn't leak becasue it was an unethical way to behave. Third, a majority of those we questioned said that they didn't leak becasue they simply didn't think it was effective.

On the difference between career civil servants and political appointees, one person with whom we talked said that it "boils down to having more discipline and the adverse affect on one's career." Another said career people only leak for very important situations, such as where a whistle needs to be blown, but not as a matter of routine. Stuart Eizenstat, who handled domestic policy for the Carter White House, was one of those senior political appointees who believed in the efficacy of leaks. Eizenstat was an advocate of what he called the "conscious planned leak" or the trial balloon. He believes that they could have been used more when he was in government to seek public and congressional reaction to possible presidential decisions. On the other hand, Brzezinski, who served in the same White House said that he did not leak, that "someone at my level never leaks."

Some of the officials we talked with at length took the moral view of leaks. Clark Clifford said there was "something disloyal" about them. Cyrus Vance said that he never leaked, that leaking was "one of the most corrosive practices that goes on in Washington." Among the nonleakers whom we recontacted, one said that leaking "erodes the democratic form of government." Another declared firmly that leaking is unethical: "I don't even think about it. . . . There are certain rules you just abide by." While this was a distinctly minority view, it did put those who held it at odds with the journalists, all of whom saw leaks as part of the routine ongoing relationship between the government and the press. As Knight-Ridder national correspondent James McCartney said, "Leaks are what it's all about. They can have different motivation, but leaks are the way in which people who oppose policy in the formation stage surface it so that a public debate can be created about it."

Are leaks effective? Nonleakers do not think so, but certainly some leaks, such as the trial balloon, can be useful in assessing reaction to a policy initiative or an appointment. Effectiveness is a function in part of motive. Thus, one kind of effectiveness is illustrated by the folklore from in the administration of Lyndon Johnson about people leaking the names of forthcoming appointees because they knew that Johnson would kill the appointment if it was made public before he was ready to announce it. And the testimony of those officials who did leak and gave us their reasons for doing so would suggest that they found leaking a useful device. It is not at all clear that the leaks in the Love Canal and Agnew stories changed the policy outcomes there, although there is a strong sense that the reaction to the leak to Richard Burt of Carter's decision to stop production of the neutron bomb played an important role in his softening his position. In that case, however, Burt says that the leak was not even intended to raise a ruckus, although at the time there was strong speculation that the leak had come from someone who wanted to see that decision reversed, and people in and out of the White House operated as if that were the case. All of our cases suggest that the impact of leaks on the substance of policy is hard to predict. Yet the fact that leaks are so widely used, and that journalists consider them so integral to their jobs, would suggest that officials who think that leaks are not integral to *their* jobs are simply wrong.

Perhaps the most important point to be made about leaks is that journalists see them as indispensable to their work. That is true of so-called authorized leaks—trial balloons and the like—where the reporter is aware that he or she is being used by the official in return for a scoop. It is true of the rare but classic spectacular leak, Deep Throat in the parking garage. And it is particularly true of the more routine leak, the day-to-day gathering of information about what is going on in government by the press from sources whose bosses would be unhappy if they knew the communication as taking place.

CHAPTER EIGHT

TOWARD BETTER POLICYMAKING

You can't do your job without the press.
—ELLIOT RICHARDSON

T HE PRESS HAS substantial and specific impacts on policies and policymaking in the federal government. The influence of the media in determining how Americans govern themselves has grown and intensified over time, particularly in the past two decades.

There are many reasons why this has been the case. Poliltical parties used to be the testing ground for candidates and ideas; they served to mediate the public policy dialogue by providing internal incentives for consensus and compromise and a structure for the debate. As the role of the political parties has diminished, the press has stepped in, sometimes eagerly and sometimes not. Television and other advances in communication technology have provided new formats for the conduct of public affairs, new challenges and opportunities for policymakers and reporters in doing their jobs. There have been vast increases in the size of government and the size of the Washington press corps. As a consequence, both the public and the policymakers increasingly rely on what is published and broadcast for information about public affairs.

Therefore, in order to make policy well, officials increasingly have to take into consideration the press and public relations aspects of their programs and decisions. Everything we have learned here thus drives us to the conclusion that policymakers will be more successful at doing their jobs if they do better in their relations with the press. To put it more provocatively, having more policymakers who are skilled at managing the media will make for better government.

Officials who are adept communicators are often taken to task, particularly by reporters, for controlling the news. But there is a crucial distinction between managing the news—for example, trying to put the best possible face on an issue or setting the agenda—and lying or deliberate misrepresentation.

The evolution of the relationship between government and the press over the past two decades has made this challenge of communicating much more difficult for officials than it was before. Interaction between reporters and policymakers is marked less by cooperation and shared interest than by competing to convey pictures of reality to the American people.

Many officials have not kept pace with the changing role of the press and changing relationship between policymakers and reporters. Some officials still don't believe it, don't want to believe it, or believe it but think it is wrong. They operate as if the era of a cooperative press still held, or at least still ought to hold. They resent the intrusion of the press, and think of coverage as undermining consideration of the issues on the merits. They underestimate the degree to which they can influence press coverage.

As a result, they often get the kind of coverage (or noncoverage) that diminishes their chances of getting their priorities accepted, their policy choices adopted, and their programs implemented. We have seen in this study that by leaving the public communication aspects of policymaking out completely or by bringing them in only at the end, policymakers decrease their effectiveness and undermine their own policy goals. Failure to consider press aspects of policy choices can often lead to policy failure down the road. People with less stake in the policy than in its communication are valuable early on in the policymaking process, not just after the policy decision has been made.

Successful officials, those who see themselves and are seen by colleagues as successful in policymaking, tend to be activists in their press relations, more engaged in the struggle over what reality is presented to the viewing and reading public. Even many of them, however, often deal with the press on a case-by-case basis and do not have a coherent press stragegy. They have not gone through the process of establishing goals for their press relations and assessing the available means for reaching them, as they often have done for their legislative relations and for their policy areas.

Ad hoc and unsystematic press relations undermine successful policymaking. As the influence of the press on government grows, the need for officials to understand the press and to be competent in their dealings with reporters grows as well. Increasingly, it is part of the job. Good government requires good press relations and good press management.

People who want to make government work better should be encouraging policymakers to develop skills at communications and press relations and should value officials who possess those abilities.

For many government officials, the increasing impact of the press on policymaking challenges their assumptions about the role of the press. They must develop a new professional relationship with journalists. A professional relationship does not mean that reporters and officials are partners in policymaking. They do different jobs. They have different interests. Policymakers usually have personal and professional stakes in the outcome of policy debates. Journalists are like stockbrokers who care less whether or not the market moves up or down than whether or not it is moving. Unlike Walter Pincus in the neutron bomb story, most reporters have no stake in a particular policy result, but have a huge interest in the continuing story . . . and in the story continuing.

Dean Rusk characterized this difference by suggesting that "the press operates in a field of opinion and officers of government operate in a field of decision." There is more overlap between those fields now than there was in the 1960s when Rusk was secretary of state, but the fundamental distinction still applies. No matter how much they can and do influence each other, the press does not make the policy decision, and the policymaker does not write the news.

If officials think about reporters as colleagues in public affairs, they will be more open to understanding the media and working within he constraints under which reporters function. If policymakers know the conventions of the press, they will be better able to develop their own ways of dealing with journalists so as to maximize their chances of achieving their policy goals.

A Question of Perspective

The first element of a professional relationship with the press is embracing a realistic perspective on the press and its role in government. Midlevel federal policymakers moving up the bureaucratic ladder typically have not had regular and direct dealings with the press, but nevertheless have very strong views about the press. Their views are overwhelmingly negative, and have been formed by stories they did not like and journalists whose methods they question. When they talk about the press the image they often describe is the reporter from *60 Minutes* sticking a microphone into the face of some frightened and outmanned bureaucrat. The image is not representative of very much of the real-life interaction between reporters and officials and carrying it around undermines the potential for a professional relationship.

There is a lot of public rhetoric from both officials and journalists about how adversarial their relationship is and ought to be. Here, for example, is a straightforward statement from Knight-Ridder's James McCartney: "I believe in the adversary relationship between the press and the government. I believe it is my job to try to test them against every abstract standard I can think of to see if they're doing what they say they're doing. . . . I believe it's my job to assume that they may very well be lying and misrepresenting because all of my experience suggests they probably are."

It is not clear from reporters' actions what they are really talking about when they speak of an adversary relationship. There are two senses in which they judge the relationship as adversarial. One is in answer to the question of what is their relationship *with* one another, that is, how well do they get along? The other is a question of their relationship *to* one another: are they combatants, do they have competitive and conflicting professional requirements?

To hear some journalists and officials talk, one would believe that they exist in a state of perpetual conflict on both counts, with constant tension and mutually exclusive interests. Depending on whose side you are on, in this rendering journalists are either dedicated to holding officials accountable or looking for headlines. Yet the real life interaction which we found between officials and reporters looks much different. It confirms our assumptions that the idea of an adversarial relationship does not go very far toward explaining the impact of the press on policymaking. And it follows that by assuming or adopting an adversarial posture, a policymaker will not be establishing the kind of relationship which will advance his or her programs and goals.

Even in the dramatic case of the neutron bomb, the mood between government and the press was not very hostile or difficult. There was tension in the relationship between Don Cotter and Walter Pincus to be sure, but Pincus was almost in the category of a policy protagonist at that point and the tension between them did not extend institutionally to their colleagues in government or the press respectively. The other journalists covering the story felt no stake in the outcome; they were following events, trying to get hold of the truth. Similarly, in the case of the relocation at Love Canal, hostility or adversariness are inappropriate ways to characterize what was going on between reporters and officials. The leak of the report undermined the government's strategy, and the coverage changed the decisionmaking process, but those consequences did not affect the relative friendliness of the relationships between them.

Other officials tend to confirm the more benign view of the nature of the relationship. Over 70 percent of the senior federal officials who responded to our questionnaire characterized their relationship with the press as more friendly than not. This is true over time and throughout the highest levels of the federal government. There was not much difference across policy areas, although those who worked in foreign policy had somewhat more positive press relationships than the rest, and those in defense and those in congressional leadership slightly less so. Even in those groups which had the least friendly relations, conservatives and those who were unsuccessful in getting the coverage they sought, a majority or near majority had good relationships with the press.

Successful and respected policymakers tended to share this basically positive view. President Gerald Ford said his relationships with the press were "friendly," and that the press was not the enemy. Wilbur Cohen talked about his "close relationships" developed over the years with reporters who covered the Department of Health, Education, and Welfare. Former Secretaries of State Dean Rusk and Cyrus Vance lauded the press and the job they did. James Schlesinger, who had some difficult times dealing with the press, talked about "plugging away" without animus to get reporters interested in Carter's national energy plan. Their memories may have selectively reconstructed the past to an extent, but these were policymakers who were selected as successful and they generally shared their perspective in this regard.

Of all the policymakers we talked with at length, only Laird used the word adversary in describing the press. Laird distinguished adversary from antagonist, and characterized the press as a resource and opportunity which could be used by the sophisticated policymaker in the service of policy goals. Brzezinski said the press has "developed a more adversarial style," by which he said he meant that reporters are more inclined to seek and use leaks without regard to national security consequences. (Brezezinski also pointed out that his relationship with the press changed and became more difficult, and more adversarial, when his role in the administration changed from providing background information to being a public advocate for particular policy options. As advocate, he was often part of a policy conflict story and he had to be more careful in what he said to reporters.) Henry Kissinger said that he "genuinely liked" the reporters who covered him.

While time might have healed whatever wounds existed and policymakers might well be hedging a bit for public consumption, it is significant that not one of these successful officials described a relationship which was characterized by tension and hostility. What we know from their public records is not inconsistent with their characterization.

The journalists corroborated that view. As David Broder, the respected syndicated columnist from the *Washington Post,* said about presidents who have successful press strategies: "They accept that there are built-in conflicts in the roles of the two institutions and the two sets of people." Officials who do not do as well with the press tend to have a different and less realistic perspective about reporters. Robert Pierpoint, the veteran correspondent for CBS, put it this way: "They don't like the process of being examined by reporters. They want the policy process to be final and finished before it is exposed. Then they can trot out the policy and say 'here it is, it's wonderful, and here's why it is wonderful' and the agonies of how they reached that and what they left out of the policy, or what they neglected, or what they're ignoring or what they're hiding is something they don't want to discuss with the press.''

Being an activist in relations with the press does not undermine a positive press relationship. Those who did not seek coverage, did not spend much time with the press, and did not leak had no more friendly relationships with the press as those who did. It is not the amount of time, but the quality of time that counts. Quality of time here means treating journalists as fellow professionals with an important job to do and nurturing the relationships informally so that they can stand the test in a crisis. Journalists understand that it is the job of policymakers to try to have the best face on their policies presented to the public and they do not resent appropriate actions by officials to try to bring that about.

Thus the reality of the interaction between journalists and officials does not square with the rhetoric of the adversary relationship. The myth of the adversary relationship, insofar as it describes personal or institutional hostility, dies hard becasue policymakers and reporters have an interest in keeping it alive. For the official it is a way to explain bad press without accepting any responsibility for it; for the journalist, it is a way of asserting independence in the face of enormous interdependence. Reporters and officials who work in Washington know that the day-to-day relationships are civil and positive on the whole. They need each other too much and know each other too well to have it any other way.

Having a positive, friendly and thereby professional relationship does not mean being friends. There is a world of difference between friendship and friendliness. There is no excuse for not trying to be friendly. Otherwise, officials do themselves, their programs, and the public interest a disservice. But there are great dangers in trying to be friends with reporters. Eizenstat pointed out, ''You can't have friends in the press in the sense that you cannot expect to take them into confidence and share with them your innermost thoughts, unless you are explicit with them about not going on the record. And even if you are, you are courting danger because they're human, and it's almost unfair to them.''

A professional perspective on the press also requires a fundamental respect for the role and responsibilities of journalists. That means treating reporters' inquiries as part of their doing their jobs, not as intruding on the policymaking job. It means that good policy is not determined solely by the technical merits but that the press relations merits must also be taken into account. In the neutron bomb story, Cotter and other Defense Department weapons experts could not understand how the bomb appeared from the perspective of Pincus or their European antagonists. They attributed opposition to a misunderstanding of the bomb. The lawyers at the Treasury and Justice departments made the determination that the tax exemptions for Bob Jones University did not have an adequate statutory base and thought that their conclusion was enough to justify a policy change. What they failed to think hard enough about was the impact on the president once the decision became public. They did not confront the reality of how blacks would see the policy because, among other things, no blacks were consulted during its development. And the administrators in Health and Human Services focused enormous attention and energy on correcting "misinterpretations" of the accelerated Social Security disability eligibility review program that could have been anticipated much earlier if the communications issues had been treated as seriously as the substantive policy issues.

Part of a professional relationship with the press comes from accepting the idea that whether or not a policy can withstand press scrutiny may itself be a test of good policy. Eizenstat again was particularly strong on this point: "If you can't articulate and convince people that what you have done is right, maybe what you did isn't right. And if you can't answer questions adequately, put to you by the press, about why you made the decision and why you didn't make the opposite decision, then perhaps you made the wrong one."

Finally, the professional relationship includes a responsibility to help journalists do their jobs well when it is possible to do so. Staats talked about "tipping off" reporters the day before he was going to issue a big report at GAO so that they could meet with his staff and get background information. Richardson said that "where I could help I did." Hughes added, "The more things you can tell them the better. That is not to say that you can tell them everything all the time, but the more they know about our business . . . the better off the world tends to be." It is a question of collegiality, of realizing that even if, as Rusk says, press and policymakers are in different fields, both fields are in the same arena. Kissinger believed that he "benefitted enormously" from his treating the press with respect, and from their sense he could also "do a good press briefing."

Richardson had a wonderfully cryptic view of the nature of a professional relationship with the press which captures much of what has been said by others about particular aspects of that relationship: "I tried to deal with them on the basis of the understanding that I know that you know that I know that you know what you are doing and you know what I am doing."

Seeing journalists as colleagues in public affairs, maintaining friendly relations in spite of frustrations and disagreements over coverage, and respecting the journalistic role as journalists understand it to be, all are components of an attitude on the part of policymakers which will help create a professional relationship.

A Matter of Knowledge

The second element of a professional relationship is understanding the press. That means knowing and accepting the media's constraints and conventions, though not necessarily endorsing them. There is an implied contract here: the benefits to policymakers of a professional relationship with the press can only come if the policymaker is aware of the constraints under which journalism operates and works within them, rather than dismissing them, or fighting them.

The experience of respected policymakers who have had some success in their press relations is instructive. From conversations with them and with reporters, four facets of newspersons' professional lives emerge as particularly important for policymakers to keep in mind: the pressure of time, the need for information, the demand for brevity, and the peculiar character of news.

The idea that print and electronic news organizations live under enormous time pressures is not news. But for policymakers, internalizing that idea means being accessible to reporters in the same way they are accessible to key colleagues in the executive and legislative branches of government. It means answering their phone calls even if the official is not able to answer the question or provide the information. Eizenstat believes that this is among the most important qualities for a good relationship with the press: "The average working reporter develops a mutual respect for someone who . . . recognizes his deadlines."

Accessibility has an availability dimension as well as a time dimension. Laird said that every key press person had his home number. He argues from his experience that reporters will treat policymakers fairly if the policymakers will talk to them. In the Agnew investigation, Justice Department officials overcame traditional reluctance to talk about pending matters with the press because the integrity of the investigation and the department had become an issue. They realized that once they were under fire, they could not expect the public to maintain confidence in the administration of justice unless they were willing to try to convince reporters of the correctness of their handling of the case.

A second constraint which policymakers must address is the media's need for information. Very often for the policymaker, no news is good news. For the reporter, it is just the reverse. Journalists need information and they depend on accurate information. A professional relationship requires openness and candor.

Openness is a particularly sensitive issue for policymakers. Some information is legally secret. Beyond that, officials often have facts and knowledge that journalists need in order to do a complete story, but one that the officials would prefer to keep under wraps or whose release they would like to time. Officials want to preserve their discretion; journalists want to have all the available and relevant information, and they are good at digging it out.

When an official has information that a reporter is seeking and the reporter knows that, the official's stake in withholding that information has changed. The policymaker's timetable has been affected by the journalist's pursuit of the story, and the policymaker's interest in providing the information has increased. To some extent, this is what happened in the Social Security disability reviews. The senior officials at the Department of Health and Human Services were focusing on the policy goals alone, and that led them to deny publicly that the problems existed even after they themselves knew better, and after the reporters knew better as well. Acknowledging the problems and revealing what they were doing to try to deal with them would have reflected a different, more professional, attitude toward the press and its role. In this case, it might well have enhanced their chances of achieving their policy goals.

In Schlesinger's view, openness results in the press giving the policymaker the benefit of the doubt. He thought he was "on the side of the angels" at the CIA because he had opened up the agency to reporters in a way his predecessors had not done.

A policymaker with an undue obsession about secrecy in press relations is vulnerable to manipulation by other officials. Laird tells a story of how this worked in the 1968 presidential campaign. Laird was a member of the Republican leadership team in the House of Representatives at the time and working hard for the election of Richard Nixon. He had learned that Vice-President Hubert Humphrey, the Democratic nominee for president, was about to announce a Vietnam withdrawal plan being prepared by the Defense Department. He told that to reporters who wrote about it. Predictably, Johnson then denied it and a Humphrey campaign initiative, if not an actual Vietnam policy initiative, was lost.

Policymakers' intense concern with keeping things secret also is manifested in worrying about leaks. The problem of leaks looks worse to them when they are in office than afterwards. Consistently, policymakers told us that looking back on their experience they worried about leaks more than was warranted and that the unauthorized release of confidential information usually presented fewer problems than imagined. One way for officials to deal with sensitive information that they know is going to become public if it sits around for a while is to release it themselves. Both John Gardner and Sam Hughes emphasized an attitude which Gardner summarized as "When in doubt, get it out."

Since reporters often must rely on officials for information, they can easily be misled. But an official who tries to take advantage of this vulnerability puts the success of his or her policymaking at risk. Time and time again officials emphasized that one of the secrets to an effective relationship with the press is never lie to them. There is a very fine line between misleading a reporter and allowing a reporter to come to his or her own wrong conclusion. Eizenstat, for example, trod that line very carefully in dealing with Judy Woodruff, who was then covering the White House for NBC, over the decision on the B–1 bomber. It was, Eizenstat recalled, a "very hot, closely held decision." It was June 30, 1977, when the president gave Eizenstat the responsibility to inform Defense Secretary Harold Brown that the B–1 was going to be scrapped. When Eizenstat returned to his office, Woodruff called.

As he tells it: "Judy and I had been next door neighbors in Atlanta and she said, she put it very interestingly, 'Would I be getting out on a limb if I reported that the President was going forward with the B–1 bomber?' And I said, 'Judy, you have to make your own decision. I can't answer that.' And she said, 'Well, can you just tell me whether I would be embarrassed if I said that?' Now, I could have very easily said, 'You would be embarrassed.' I just said, 'Look, you have to make your own decisions. I cannot give you any guidance on it.' "

As it turned·out, another key Carter staff person, Hamilton Jordan, told Woodruff that no decision had been made. Based on that misinformation, Woodruff stopped trying to find out which way Carter had in fact decided to go. The next day Carter announced the cancellation. Woodruff never forgave Jordan for misleading her, but she held no grudge against Eizenstat for the way he had handled the situation.

Part of never lying involves policymakers being willing to tell reporters that they don't know the answer, or that they know the answer but simply cannot reveal it. Clifford believed that telling reporters that he could not answer a question was crucial to their fair treatment of him: "I determined that when I went to the Pentagon at no time was I going to lie to the press. I either was in the position where I could tell the truth, or I would be in a position where I couldn't say anything. . . . My relationship with the press proved to be excellent. . . . Now there were a number of times that I would say, 'I understand why you asked that question, but I cannot answer it.' And often times they didn't like that, but at least I wasn't giving them a false steer." One of the ways a reporter will acknowledge and demonstrate respect for an official who does not mislead them is by reporting the official's failure to answer in a way that does not suggest deception, or by not reporting it at all.

Candor also includes correcting a mistake if you make one. Laird remembers once running down to the press room at the Department of Defense and recalling the reporters when he realized that a general from the Joint Chiefs of Staff had unintentionally incorrectly identified the source of a piece of pipeline picked up in Laos during the Vietnam War.

Gardner emphasized that lack of candor not only runs counter to reporters' needs but is an ineffective tactic because good journalists are particularly skilled at recognizing it: "Journalists have a very keen sense of who double talks and who doesn't, a very keen sense of public officials who are disingenuous and foxy with them." And officials pay a price for being that way. "You never tell a reporter something that isn't true," says Robert Ball. "That's just dynamite."

Admitting mistakes, acknowledging that the answers exist but cannot be revealed, an official's willingness to say that he or she probably should know the information but doesn't, all are consistent with the reporter's need for maximizing openness and minimizing secrecy.

A third element is brevity. To take the most dramatic and obvious example, television correspondents are often only able to use a very brief comment from an official in a policy story. Perhaps there is an opportunity only for a fifteen- or thirty-second quote in a story that will have between a minute and two on the air. For a policymaker who has been struggling with the details of a complicated decision, framing it in a few seconds for an audience of millions of people may seem foolish, irresponsible, or simply impossible. Yet it is the responsibility of the policymaker to try to meet the need of that reporter. The reporter knows how difficult that challenge may be. Even under those pressures the policymaker can have some measure of influence over the message by thinking hard, before speaking, about just how to say whatever can be said in that brief a period. The officials can also maintain some control by providing only one quote for the reporter so that at least it is the policymaker's choice of the best message possible under the time constraint that gets out, and not that of the reporter.

However, when a policymaker does not want to be forced into taking a precise position, making the answer more complicated than necessary may be a way to avoid being quoted without being unresponsive. Elliot Richardson said that when he wanted to avoid coverage, he would use too many words. When he got an inquiry that might put him in a position to say something "ill-considered" if he were to answer concisely and to the point, he would, in his words, "smother the question with saliva'' so as to leave the reporter with nothing suitable to report.

Finally, part of understanding the press is accepting the idea that ''news'' has particular qualities: it needs to be new, timely, and dramatic; it helps if it there are elements of conflict and if it has short-term rather than long-term interest. Policymakers are not required to embrace enthusiastically the conventional definition of news, just to know it and accomodate to it if it is possible and responsible to do so. As Califano put it, ''Look, the reality is that the press is more interested in controversy than in still waters.''

Echoing that view, Staats talked about how much easier it was to get coverage at the General Accounting Office where investigative and often critical reports were issued regularly than at the Bureau of the Budget where his ''news'' was more positive than not. Peterson lit his daughter's doll on fire to demonstrate the potential for nonflammable materials. McNamara recalled an instance where he created a conflict in order to get coverage for an issue the press was not inherently interested in: ''I wanted to talk on population, and I wanted it covered in the *New York Times* and the *Washington Post*. . . . Now how you get on the front page of the *New York Times* talking about population is damn difficult. So, frankly, what I did was go to Notre Dame and spoke on the subject of population at a Catholic University.''

Information must also be current and new to be news. The press needs a ''news hook'' for information. McNamara described how he was able to get *Newsweek* to cover the substance of an article he wrote on population for *Foreign Affairs* magazine by encouraging them to tie his article to a draft of a White House policy position on a related subject which had just been leaked.

Laird emphasized the importance of internalizing the needs of the press in this area, rather than fighting them. So did John Gardner: ''There's no doubt that you can say things in a very abstract way or you can say them in a more dramatic way. You can make a comment out of the blue without a context or you can save it and make it when some critical event happens. You can make use of these things: brevity, hooking things to events, stating them more dramatically.''

An Issue of Strategy

A professional attitude toward and sophisticated knowledge of the press creates the opportunity, but only that, for a policymaker to deal with the press—and, yes, to manage relations with the press—so as to best serve the interests of policy goals. The views and experiences of hundreds of officials who have served at the highest levels of the federal government during the past twenty years strongly suggest that to be successful in their jobs policymakers must move toward a theory of press relations which is deliberative and strategic in character. That means they must establish goals for their press relations and assess various means of achieving them. There are lessons to be learned not only from the anecdotal testimony of former policymakers but also from the related disciplines, such as general public management, private sector public relations, and political campaigning. A full-blown theory of public press management is beyond the scope of this book, but there are some broad and tentative ideas about strategic thinking in press relations which come directly out of this research.

If there is any clear message running through the policy decisions which we examined in detail it is that the failure to consider the press aspects of a policy can often mean trouble down the road. That was most dramatically illustrated in the Bob Jones tax exemption story, where the lawyers at the Treasury and the Justice departments focused solely on the legal issues until the decision was made and only then involved their colleagues who were experts in public relations, not tax law. Only two of the lawyers, Peter Wallison and Edward Schmults, seemed to have some inkling in advance of the public relations disaster that they were bringing on themselves. It is easy in retrospect to wonder how they could have not seen what was coming. The more important point is that had someone with expertise and a focus on the press been involved from the beginning it is very possible that another course would have been taken. At the very least, they would have known more about what they were getting into.

Much the same was true in the handling of the Social Security disability reviews. There the administrators of the program, both of whom had extensive experience dealing with the press in other circumstances and one of whom was actually a former journalist, were so confident of their program that they could not assess the volume or the quality of the growing critical drumbeat until it drowned out all their explanations and complaints about coverage. When the White House intervened, it was primarily the communications people, not the substantive program people, who got involved. They could see that this was a program heading for disaster, a personal disaster for many recipients and a political disaster for the administration. They were the ones who, in the end, spurred several of the reforms.

One of the difficulties for policymakers in bringing the public relations or press aspects of the policy into the policymaking early on is the question of which policies are likely to become public issues. There are hundreds, perhaps thousands of decisions made by the federal government every year. Must each of them be scrutinized in this way? Are there ways of thinking about policy choices that would trigger the need to involve press people whenever it is appropriate? One way might be to adopt a longer view of thinking about the press and developing tools for analyzing policies which will begin to identify communications consequences.

Some of the officials with whom we talked had indeed developed longer-term approaches. Kissinger said it became a policy of his to "spend a lot of time with the press when I didn't need them. . . . I thought it was worthwhile to see senior journalists when they could do absolutely nothing for me at a given moment on the theory that, when I really needed to talk to them, they might listen to me." Kissinger also offered another longer-range strategy: going out of Washington and dealing with the local press. This was not something he did very much, but he did it at least once and it is a notion that others have used as well. The idea was suggested to him when he was secretary of state and under heavy criticism from the Washington press corps in 1974: "Hubert Humphrey [then having returned to the US Senate] came to see me and said: 'Listen, don't let Washington spook you. You're a big man in the rest of the country. Go out into the country. Go from state to state. All the media will cover you in that state. You won't get national attention, but you'll get a lot of attention in that state, and that will influence us here in the Congress.' . . . I did that, and wherever I went I had press conferences. . . . I went to thirty-seven states. And when you go to thirty-seven states and dominate the news for two days in that state, you must have an impact.'' Gardner and Richardson also talked about going out into the country and dealing with the local press while they were at the Department of Health, Education, and Welfare.

A second piece of long-range thinking comes from Laird, who believed that having long-term policy goals and repeatedly telling the press about them would result in the goals being reflected in their stories. He argued that it is important for policymakers not to think only in terms of a given day's stories. They should think of stories appearing over a six- to twelve-month period and let the press know about the long-term plan. Reporters will communicate the plan and furthermore will realize that the policymaker is sophisticated in dealing with reporters and is insisting on reacting to more than just breaking news or what they're interested in in a given day.

Richardson suggested that policymakers ought to think about the tactical problems of dealing with the press differently depending on two factors: whether or not the policymaker wants the information out; and whether or not the journalist wants the information. There are three relevant combinations: when the policymaker wants it out and the journalist is interested in it; when the policymaker wants it out and the journalist isn't interested; and when the policymaker doesn't want it out and the journalist would be interested. Each of these situations obviously presents a substantially different problem for the policymaker, and requires substantially different techniques for solution.[1]

A fourth long-range notion is that there are some issues which by their nature can be expected from the very beginning to become public issues. Perhaps, for example, any change in policy with regard to nuclear weapons, no matter how inconsequential or noncontroversial from the policymakers point of view, is in that category. Those issues are either so sensitive that they ought to be subjected to public debate or so inherently volatile that they ought to be subjected to the scrutiny of their public relations aspects before a decision is made.

If the Ford administration, which originally gave approval for the production and deployment of the neutron bomb, had thought about the public communication aspects of the policy, could they have made a difference in its acceptance? What could they have done had they been prescient enough to anticipate what might happen? Leslie Gelb's deputy, David Gompert, has pointed out that there was a quite accurate and nonvolatile way to describe the weapon which might not have produced the brouhaha. Here's Gompert's lead sentence:

> The US, as part of a long-standing modernization program of nuclear weapons in Europe, is about to begin production of a low-yield nuclear weapon, designed to kill enemy soldiers in Russian tanks through radiation, at the same time reducing collateral damage from blast in civilian areas. [2]

There are two essential differences between Gompert's ''story'' and Pincus's story. First, in Gompert's story, there is no exposure of a ''secret.'' The government is revealing the information itself. Second, the story characterizes the weapon in a way that is as least as true to the facts as in the *Post* story, but is also consistent with the government's perspective on the policy. Had the story been presented that way early on, there would have been no Pincus revelation, and very likely there would have been an entirely different outcome of the policy debate.

There is another element of the Pincus story that is missing in the Gompert version. It does not include those fateful words, ''kills people but leaves buildings intact'' which were to haunt the bomb until it was deferred. Those words were in Pincus's first story and undoubtedly gave it, along with the secrecy angle, much of the drama that landed it on page one and enabled it to have the impact that it did. But they were not Pincus's words; they came from the government, from an anonymous nuclear weapons expert who undoubtedly thought he was providing innocuous information to an inquiring reporter.

Preventing the anonymous government expert from putting his foot in his mouth raises another issue of strategic thinking about the press. One way of combatting the problem is to try to limit the number of people who are allowed to talk to the press. This is a policy adopted by many senior managers in government. It has succeeded at times and often for a time, but it also courts disaster. It creates a challenge for reporters to break through the barrier, and it leaves the silenced employee unprepared for what will happen when they do. It is like riding on treadless tires: it is a policy that will work until the very moment it fails. Journalists are trained in finding out who has information and then ferreting it out. Good journalists are experts at dealing with unsuspecting individuals and inducing them to say something they later wished they had kept to themselves. And of course the policy of silencing employees does little to prevent the employee who wants to say something embarrassing to the administration from doing so anonymously.

This example also raises another possibility. Could that anonymous nuclear weapons expert have been better prepared? Some very successful policymakers talked about how their success with the press came in spite of their lack of training. Kissinger is thought to have been an expert at press relations. He came to high levels of government from academia, unprepared for his public role. He seems surprised himself at how well he did. "Because there has been so much talk about my masterful handling of the press, it is usually forgotten that I never had a press conference before I came to Washington in 1969. I had no view on how to handle the press. I had no experience. I slid into it by means of background briefings requested by Nixon on a monthly basis, on a case-by-case basis. So I slid into press relations, not with any particular policy, but really almost accidentally."

Wilbur Cohen, who came to his cabinet job through the bureaucracy felt equally ill equipped. "When you get to be secretary, nobody teaches you how to deal with the press. An interesting phenomenon of being the highest ministerial officer in the government, and yet you have no real training for that. You have learned by osmosis, and you have learned by various other factors. But there are many times when you are caught unprepared." Cohen and Kissinger were successful perhaps because they were born with the skills necessary for dealing with the press, but recent American history is littered with the remains of officials at the senior levels who suffered in their personal and policy goals in part at least because of their inept press relations. There are a lot of people, perhaps including Pincus's anonymous expert, who wish they could take back what they said.

Senior officials regularly receive help in managing their employees, managing their time, and managing their congressional relations. But training policymakers in press management is often considered risky, potentially embarrassing, and even somewhat dirty business. Part of the risk probably stems from concern that no one knows what the subject is about. Part undoubtedly comes from a concern that officials will be portrayed—in the press and by the press—as being trained in press manipulation or in controlling the news. Whatever demeaning jargon is used to describe the enterprise, it is a bit disingenuous but not surprising for reporters to be critical of an effort to give officials better resources for dealing with them and their colleagues. And whatever the criticism, policymakers cannot be expected to develop thoughtful and strategic press relations unless they learn how.

Thinking about the press as an integral aspect of thinking about the policy, thinking about the press before there is a crisis of the moment, and thinking about how to deal with the press well in a systematic way that can be conveyed and understood by other officials all are part of what is meant by strategic thinking about the press. None of this can come, however, unless it follows a more positive attitude toward the press and its role and a more sophisticated and even sympathetic understanding of the pressures under which reporters do their jobs.

Criticizing officials for being effective at getting their messages out is wrongheaded and shortsighted. By being successful with the press, policymakers will do better at contributing to the public policy debate, at advancing their policy goals, and at creating understanding and support for their programs. Everyone of us has an interest in government working better. That is why it is in everyone's best interest that policymakers do better at press relations than most of them are doing now.

It is increasingly true that policymakers can't be good at their jobs without being good at dealing with the press. Policymakers can't make policy, at least for very long, without it.

EPILOGUE

THE NEXT QUESTIONS

A FRIEND OF MINE is fond of telling his students that it is not necessary to say everything in order to say something. That is the spirit in which this study was undertaken and it is therefore not surprising that this book has raised as many questions as it has answered. What is most obvious is that understanding and thinking about the role of the media in public affairs is important work that has just begun.

There are two categories of questions on the agenda. There are those which we expressly did not address, and those which we did not anticipate but which flowed out of the findings. Some are particularly directed to the press.

1. From the beginning, we made a decision to limit the scope of the work to the press–government connection in Washington. We realized both that Washington is unique and that there is a world of interaction between reporters and officials at the state, county, and municipal levels of government. We do not know whether the impact of the press in those environments parallels what we found in Washington or not. We do know that it is very important and its effects may be even more immediate and substantial than at the federal level.

2. We also limited our study to the policymakers' point of view. We benefitted enormously from the interviews with fifteen distinguished journalists, which were designed to be a kind of reality check on what the policymakers were telling us. Inevitably, what the jour-

nalists said raised a whole new set of questions about the impact of the press on government from the perspective of the reporter and the editor.

3. While we made some effort to look at the trade press, we did not go very far in that direction. Our sense is that the trade press plays an important role, much different than that of the mass media and perhaps much different from agency to agency.

4. The findings suggest that the effect of the press is in general more substantial in foreign policy than in domestic policy. We are not at all sure why this is so, or what are the consequences for both of the specific differences.

5. We knew going in to the work that television is playing an increasingly important role in policymaking. What we found suggests its impact is vast and not well understood. Policymakers suggested several problems as a consequence of the presence of television, but the evidence is primarily anecdotal and there is countervailing evidence from policymakers who have seen television as a resource for policymaking rather than a burden.

6. In chapter eight, we identified a substantial piece of work that is yet to be done, that of starting with the understanding that dealing with press is part of the policymakers' job and then developing a comprehensive and strategic theory of public management of the press which will enable officials to do their jobs better than they have before.

7. If officials become more sophisticated about the press, its role and its impact, the media will have to think hard about their own ways of dealing with officials. Policymakers who are more professional in their dealings with the press will under some circumstances pose new challenges for reporters covering them.

8. What are the implications for the press of the awareness that there are serious and substantial new consequences for public affairs from their own values, methods, conventions, and constraints and from

the predictable ways that officials respond to what they do? How should they use the power which they now possess, whether or not they sought it or enjoy it? Walter Lippmann developed the first coherent theory of the role of the press in public affairs in his book *Public Opinion,* written over half a century ago. It is still relevant today in its analysis of the limits of the capacity of journalism to communicate ''objective facts,'' and the limits of the public at large to absorb and make use of the information that is available about public affairs. But the factors we have identified as having changed the policymaker's world have changed the reporter's world as well and given journalists a scope far beyond what Lippmann had imagined it. It is time to begin where Lippmann left off, to identify those changes and their implications, and to chart the course for the role and responsibility of the press in public affairs in the years ahead.

DESIGNING
AND CONDUCTING
THE SURVEY

by WENDY O'DONNELL

The goal of including a survey in our study of the role of the press in federal policymaking was to provide some baseline information about the interaction between the press and senior federal officials against which we could compare the data we generated in the interviews and the case studies.

In designing the questionnaire, we determined that we wanted the survey instrument to provide us with four general categories of information:

1. How the official conducted his or her press relations, including the amount of time the official spent with members of the press each week or thinking about the press issues, and the amount of influence the official was able to exercise over press coverage. This inquiry comprised the first four questions on the form.

2. The effects of the press on policy processes and formation, including the impacts at different stages of the policy process, whether positive and negative coverage had different effects, whether there were distinctions between mass media and the trade press, how much information the media provided to the official in the conduct of his or her job, and whether the official was concerned about leaks or leaked information. This appears as the second, and longest section of the questionnaire, covering three of the form's eight pages and eleven separate questions.

3. The nature of the relationships between the official members of the press corps—whether the official believed his or her relations with the press were predominantly hostile or friendly, how much influence the members of the press brought to bear on issues, and instances in which the media had the effect of advancing or inhibiting a policy goal. In the six questions in this section, we also asked whether the official believed the media had the ability

to help groups outside of government—such as interest groups—gain federal attention, and how well the official thought he or she understood the operations of the press.

4. Background data on the official, such as the length of service in government, the area of government served, ideology, and the official's patterns of viewing and reading the media—television, newspapers, magazines, radio, and trade press—was the last section on the form.

Once the general categories were determined, we began the task of drafting the working of the questions with an eye to clarity and lack of bias, while at the same time, giving the official the greatest possible latitude in providing us relevant information.

A draft of the survey, containing a total of thirty-seven questions, was pretested on several former officials (from three different presidential administrations and one former member of Congress) to determine if the form really did elicit the kind of data we wanted. The individuals who consented to help us with the pretest were: Philip Heymann, Robert Seamens, Charles Haar, and Andrew Maguire. Those tests revealed some problems, including that the survey was too long, and the document was revised a final time down to thirty-one questions.

In the final form, we provided as many check-off or scalar answers to questions as possible in order to make the survey easy to complete. For example, in the question on how much time the official had spent thinking about and dealing with press matters, three possible answers were provided: too much time, the right amount of time, and too little time. The official had only the check the one that came nearest his or her perception. For a later question on how the official characterized his or her relations with the press, we provided a five-point scale, ranging from hostile at one end to friendly at the other, giving the respondent the opportunity use interim points to reflect other than an absolute position.

We did, however, include four brief essay questions in our survey: asking the official to describe the types of informal or unofficial communications that took place with members of the press; to give examples of situations in which the press advanced and inhibited a policy; and to describe the impacts in his or her policy area if the media did not exist.

At the same time we were developing the questionnaire, we were also working to construct a picture of the universe of present and former senior federal officials. We knew that the scope of our research was to take in approximately twenty years, the Johnson through the first Reagan administrations. We decided to survey all those individuals who actually made or were in a position to directly affect the shaping of policy in either the executive or legislative branches during that period. For the executive branch we finally settled upon officials of cabinet departments at the level of assistant secretary and above, and the heads of certain executive offices and independent agencies appointed by the president. For the Congress, we selected the leadership of both parties and the chairmen and ranking minority members for the major standing committees in both houses.

The following the positions comprised our universe:

All the cabinet departments were included: Agriculture, Commerce, Defense, Education, Energy, Health and Human Services (and its predecessor Health, Education, and Welfare), Housing and Urban Development, Interior, Justice, Labor, State, Transportation, and Treasury. Within these departments, we surveyed people who held the following positions: secretary, deputy secretary, undersecretary, and assistant secretary for all departments, as well as the general counsel for Commerce, Housing and Urban Development, Interior, Transportation, and Treasury. The latter were included to balance off a low number of assistant secretaries or a lack of more senior personnel relative to the department's size. There were a few other inclusions specific to certain departments for purposes of balance, comparability, or policy responsibility: in Defense, the chairman of the Joint Chiefs of Staff, and the chief of staff and secretary for each military branch; in HUD, the general deputy assistant secretary for housing and the president of the Government National Mortgage Association; in Justice, the associate attorney general; the director for public affairs in Justice and Transportation (in the other departments, the chief public affairs person occupies the rank of assistant secretary and was included on that basis); in Treasury, the commissioner of the IRS; and in the State Department, the UN representative.

In the executive office of the president, we included the presidential press secretary, the assistant to the president for national security affairs, the chairman of the Council of Economic Advisors, and the director of the Office of Management and Budget and its predecessor, the Bureau of the Budget. Finally in the agencies, we included the chairman or administrator of each of the following independent agencies: the Board of Governors of the Federal Reserve, the Environmental Protection Agency, the Federal Communications Commission, the Federal Trade Commission, the National Aeronautics and Space Administration, the Nuclear Regulatory Commission and its predecessor, the Atomic Energy Commission, the Occupational Safety and Health Administration, the Securities and Exchange Commission, and the Veteran's Administration.

The individuals who made up our sample from the Congress were fewer in number than those in the executive branch. The responsibility for day-to-day implementation of policy rests on the executive branch. While the Congress shares in problem identification and policy adoption, relatively few members of Congress have formal senior policy responsibilities and, hence, a lower number fit our criteria for senior federal officials. In the Senate, we decided to include: the president pro tempore, the majority and minority leaders and whips, and the chairman and ranking minority members of the committees on appropriations; armed services; banking, housing and urban affairs; budget; commerce, science and transportation; energy and natural resources; finance; and foreign relations. In the House of Representatives, our sample included the speaker of the house, again the majority and minority leaders and whips, the chairmen of the Democratic Caucus and the Republican Conference, and the chairmen and ranking minority members of the committees on appropriations; armed services; banking, finance and urban affairs; budget; education and labor; energy and commerce; foreign affairs; judiciary; rules; and ways and means.

Together, the individuals who served in these positions during the time of the Johnson, Nixon, Ford, Carter, and Reagan administrations numbered 1,002. Once we had eliminated those who were unavailable to us for one of several reasons (death for the most part, but also ill health, no current address available despite repeated attempts and cross-checking several sources, or the individual was already being contacted to be interviewed), our total universe of available present and former officials totalled 957.

From this sample, we set a goal of a 50 percent response rate. We achieved that goal, in an effort that lasted the better part of a year and involved four separate rounds of contact with the individuals identified. In the first wave, we mailed the questionnaire to all the individuals in our sample along with a mass-produced letter addressed "Dear Friend." While this gained us more responses than might be expected, it did not get us near our goal. We were received answers from just under 20 percent of our universe.

Our second approach used a letter signed by a member of the study group who had had some contact with the individual, and for those whom no one knew directly, a letter signed by either Jonathan Moore, the chairman of the study, or Martin Linsky, the project director. The response to these letters moved us to a fraction below a forty percent response rate.

Round three concentrated on those individuals who still had not responded but whom one or more of us knew. They received yet another letter, not only signed by their friend or acquaintance but including a note urging them to participate in our study. This last round of mailings brought us to 44.6 percent of the total sample, still short of our target. We tried one more strategy: phoning the people who had not yet responded, encouraging them to complete the questionnaire, and offering to send them yet another copy.

We found many of the present and former officials responsive to this approach, especially once it was explained how important their response was to our research. The result was that this last effort brought in enough completed questionnaires, and we ended with a sample population of 483, or 50.47 percent of the universe of present and former senior federal officials who were available. We checked the returns against the sample as a whole and found that our respondents accurately represented the universe of senior federal officials.

Using the Statistical Package for the Social Sciences (SPSS) program package, we generated the frequencies (or raw numbers), as well as the raw and adjusted percentages of the total population for each response with the exception of the essay questions which could not be coded for computer analysis.

We also performed cross-tabulations on each of the responses, comparing the answers to certain questions or sets of questions where our hypotheses suggested there might by significant correlations. For strong correlations we looked for a significance factor of .05 or less (indicating less than 5 in 10,000 likelihood that the relationship we described could have happened purely by chance rather than by correlation). For trends, we looked for a significance level around or below the .10 level (less than or equal to 1 in 1,000 likelihood the relationship existed by coincidence). Findings at these significance levels gave us reasonable certainty that the answers reflected a real relationship and not a random occurrence.

In the end, the survey did what we hoped it would do, giving us an outline of information about the relationship between policymakers and the press on which we could color the detail and shadings provided by the interviews and the cases.

The questions for the survey with the adjusted percentages of responses for each of the nonessay questions follow in Appendix C.

APPENDIX B

THE INTERVIEWS

There were three purposes of the interviews we conducted with reporters and officials: to determine their attitudes and perceptions regarding the role of the press in the policymaking process in their experience; to detail their own behavior in the press–government interaction; and to compare their views on the impact of the press. The journalists and policymakers selected for interviews were nominated by panels of their respective peers. Our goal was to use this process to a generate list of twenty-five policymakers and fifteen journalists to talk with at length about the impact of the press on policymaking.

We designed the panels to have nominators whose collective experience would cover the period from 1963 to 1983. For policymakers, we wanted nominators from a broad range of policy areas and from both the executive and legislative branches. For journalists, we wanted representation from both the print and electronic media, and from those who covered the bureaucracy, the Congress, and the White House.

Each member of the policymakers' panel was asked to nominate ten persons "who have been respected, successful senior policymakers at the federal level during the last twenty years." Each member of the journalists' panel was asked to nominate five persons "who have reported on the federal government with fairness and competence during the last twenty years."

Those whom we asked to nominate policymakers were Richard Bolling, Edward Brooke, William Bundy, Anne Gorsuch Burford, Joseph Califano, Frank Carlucci, Richard Cheney, Clark Clifford, George Christian, Wilbur Cohen, William Colby, William T. Coleman, Jr., Barber Conable, John Connally, John Culver, Richard Darman, John Dunlop, Stuart Eizenstadt, David Gergen, H. R. Haldeman, Patricia Roberts Harris, Phillip S. Hughes, Roger W. Jones, Nicholas Katzenbach, Bert Lance, Laurence E. Lynn, Jr., John W. Macy, Jr., Frederic Malek, Harry McPherson, Daniel P. Moynihan, Paul

O'Neill, Elliot Richardson, Jack Rosenthal, Donald Rumsfeld, Dean Rusk, James Schlesinger, Charles L. Schultze, Donna Shalala, William Simon, Elmer Staats, Herbert Stein, John Volpe, Charls Walker, Charles Weltner, Anne Wexler, Robert C. Wood, Andrew Young, and Barry Zorthian.

Those who we asked to nominate journalists were Dom Bonafede, Hodding Carter, James Doyle, Elizabeth Drew, Joseph Durso, Jr., Rowland Evans, Max Frankel, James F. Hoge, Jr., Norman Miller, Morton Kondracke, William Kovach, Joseph Kraft, Stuart Loory, Robert C. Maynard, Walter Mears, Loye Miller, Roger Mudd, Walter Pincus, William Rusher, Charles Seib, William Small, Lesley Stahl, Sander Vanocur, and George Watson.

We determined who were the twenty-eight policymakers and eighteen journalists who received the most nominations, adding an additional three in each category on the assumption that we would not be able to arrange interviews with everyone. In cases of ties, we selected those nominees who would provide us with more balance over time, among policy areas, among areas of government, and for the journalists, in types of media and news organizations. Those chosen as having been nominated most often as successful and respected policymakers were Howard Baker, Robert Ball, Richard Bolling, Zbigniew Brzezinski, Arthur Burns, Joseph Califano, Clark Clifford, Wilbur Cohen, Stuart Eizenstat, Gerald Ford, John Gardner, Phillip Hughes, Henry Kissinger, Melvin Laird, Russell Long, Robert McNamara, Wilbur Mills, Richard Nixon, Peter Peterson, Elliot Richardson, Walt Rostow, Dean Rusk, James Schlesinger, George Shultz, Theodore Sorensen, Elmer Staats, David Stockman, and Cyrus Vance. We were not able to arrange interviews with Baker, Burns, Long, Nixon, Rostow, Shultz, and Stockman.

Those nominated as fair and competent journalists were David Broder, Elizabeth Drew, Bettina Gregory, Bernard Gwertzman, Robert Hager, John Hebers, Albert Hunt, John Lindsay, James McCartney, Walter Mears, Morton Mintz, Roger Mudd, Jack Nelson, Ron Ostrow, Robert Pierpoint, Art Pine, Helen Thomas, and Sander Vanocur. We were able to arrange interviews with all but Drew and Pine.

The interviews were held from October 1983 to January 1985 by people associated with the project. Those who conducted interviews were Martin Linsky, Jonathan Moore, Wendy O'Donnell, Gary Orren, David Whitman, and Lewis Wolfson. The interview with Henry Kissinger was done jointly by John Chancellor and Wendy O'Donnell. All the interviews were taped with the exception of the interview with Melvin Laird, which he insisted be done without recording. The interviews were all on the record.

All quotations in the book from interview subjects which are not footnoted are from the interviews. Transcripts of the interviews are on file at the Institute of Politics, John F. Kennedy School of Government, Harvard University.

QUESTIONNAIRE

I. Press Relations

1. On average, weekly, how many hours did you spend thinking about and dealing with press matters?

	0–5:	52.9%
_____ hours	5–10:	27.4%
	10–40:	15.6%
	over 40:	4.0%

2. How would you describe the amount of time you spent thinking about and dealing with press matters in terms of accomplishing your policy goals? *(Check only one answer)*

Too much time	15.1%
The right amount of time	67.3%
Too little time	17.6%

3. Did you try to seek or influence news coverage regarding your office or agency?

Yes   75.2%
No   24.8%   ——*Proceed to question 4.*

IF YES:

a. Specifically, what did you do to try to seek or influence coverage?

1. _____

2. _____

3. _____

b. Which of the above were most often successful?

_____

_____

_____

c. Overall, how successful were you at getting or influencing coverage of your office or agency?

(Circle one number on scale)

0%	9.3%	53.7%	36.4%	0.6%
1	2	3	4	5

Never Successful   Sometimes Successful   Always Successful

4. In general, what percentage of the stories which dealt with your office or agency were initiated by the news reporters themselves, what percentage were initiated by you or your staff, and what percentage were initiated by a third party?

	0–25	25–50	50–75	75–100
a. Initiated by reporters:	13.2%	23.6%	33.9%	29.3%
b. Initiated by you or your staff:	46.2%	27.8%	20.7%	5.2%
c. Initiated by a third party:	74.3%	17.7%	6.4%	1.6%

II. Effects of the Press on Policy and Process

1. In your experience, which kinds of stories generally had the most impact on you and your job?

(Rank order the following story types from 4 for the greatest impact to 1 for the least impact. If you believe story type had no effect, mark no difference.)

	1	2	3	4
a. Stories about personalities, reputations, hirings and / or firings	29.0%	23.7%	20.3%	26.9%
b. Stories about how your organization worked and how policy was made	16.2%	38.0%	30.8%	14.9%
c. Stories about immediate policy issues facing you	19.1%	14.7%	20.5%	45.7%
d. Stories about long-term problems in your area	30.9%	29.2%	25.2%	14.5%
e. No difference	19%			

2. In your experience, how significant was the impact of the press at each of the following stages of policy making?

(Check one answer for each stage.)

Stages of Policy Making	No Effect	Small Effect	Large Effect	Dominant Effect
a. Identification of the problem	19.5%	41.6%	35.8%	2.7%
b. Formulation of solution	22.7%	61.6%	15.3%	0.5%
c. Adoption of policy	13.1%	48.4%	36.2%	2.3%
d. Implementation	19.8%	47.6%	29.9%	2.8%
e. Evaluation	14.4%	42.9%	38.3%	4.4%

3.a. When an issue in your office or agency received what you saw as positive or negative coverage in the *mass media*, did that coverage:

(Check those which occurred most frequently in each category of coverage.)

	Positive Coverage	Negative Coverage
Increase your chances for successfully attaining your policy goals regarding the issue	78.5%	6.4%
Decrease your chances for successfully attaining your policy goals regarding the issue	4.8%	71.4%
Increase the speed with which the issue is considered and acted upon	38.8%	36.0%
Decrease the speed with which the issue is considered and acted upon	9.9%	36.2%
Make action on the issue easier	63.1%	9.6%
Make action on the issue more difficult	5.7%	67.9%
Increase the number of policy options considered	18.3%	27.8%
Decrease the number of policy options considered	15.8%	27.5%
Reshape the policy options considered	10.3%	39.9%
Cause you to reassess your policy position on the issue	7.6%	49.0%
Galvanize outside support	50.1%	18.6%
Undermine outside support	5.7%	65.7%
Move responsibility for the issue to a more senior official or officials	9.7%	43.0%
Increase the importance of the issue within the bureaucracy	26.2%	49.0%
Cause the public and / or other officials to assume the information contained in the coverage is accurate	31.7%	33.8%
Have long term effects on your career	23.2%	22.1%
Affect your credibility on other issues	22.3%	32.6%
Have no effect	16.8%	9.0%

3b. When an issue in your office or agency received what you saw as positive or negative coverage in the *trade press*, did that coverage:

(Check those which occurred most frequently in each category of coverage.)

	Positive Coverage	Negative Coverage
Increase your chances for successfully attaining your policy goals regarding the issue	63.6%	3.4%
Decrease your chances for successfully attaining your policy goals regarding the issue	2.3%	55.0%
Increase the speed with which the issue is considered and acted upon	28.7%	23.0%
Decrease the speed with which the issue is considered and acted upon	7.8%	28.4%
Make action on the issue easier	52.7%	4.7%
Make action on the issue more difficult	3.1%	51.4%

	Positive Coverage	Negative Coverage
Increase the number of policy options considered	16.5%	24.3%
Decrease the number of policy options considered	11.9%	18.3%
Reshape the policy options considered	9.6%	31.0%
Cause you to reassess your policy position on the issue	8.8%	40.3%
Galvanize outside support	43.7%	12.7%
Undermine outside support	3.9%	48.6%
Move responsibility for the issue to a more senior official or officials	7.8%	29.5%
Increase the importance of the issue within the bureaucracy	20.4%	36.2%
Cause the public and / or other officials to assume the information contained in the coverage is accurate	28.4%	20.9%
Have long term effects on your career	20.9%	13.7%
Affect your credibility on other issues	17.8%	24.0%
Have no effect	24.5%	16.5%

4. Approximately what percentage of all the issues you dealt with were reported by the press?

0–10	10–20	20–30	30–40	40–50
10.4%	11.9%	14.0%	7.0%	2.9%

50–60	60–70	70–80	80–90	90–100
10.8%	6.3%	10.8%	9.2%	11.8%

5. To what degree did you rely on the following types of media organizations for information about your policy area?

	Very much	Somewhat	Very little
a. The mass media	30.9%	38.8%	30.4%
b. The trade press	30.2%	44.8%	24.9%

6. To what degree did you rely on the mass media for information about parts of government outside your policy area?

Very much	15.3%
Somewhat	38.8%
Very little	45.8%

7. a. How useful were informal / unofficial communications from members of the media to you in performing your job?

(Circle one number on scale.)

11.9%	18.7%	37.7%	20.5%	11.2%
1	2	3	4	5

Not Useful   Somewhat Useful   Very Useful

237

b. Please describe the type(s) of informal / unofficial communications and how it
was or they were useful to you.

_____

_____

_____

_____

8. While in office, were you concerned about leaks affecting policy you were working on or responsible for?

Yes   73.9%

No   26.1%   ——*Proceed to question 9.*

IF YES:

	of all	of leaks
a. Did that conern: *(Check as many as apply.)*		
Cause you to limit the number of people involved in decision making	55.3%	76.8%
Cause you to increase the number of people involved in decision making	1.8%	2.4%
Expand the range of policy options that you considered	10.8%	15.0%
Narrow the range of policy options that you considered	15.0%	20.8%
Reshape the policy options that you considered	11.5%	15.9%
Reduce the amount of information that you put in writing	54.0%	74.9%
Increase the amount of information that you put in writing	1.5%	2.1%
Other (please specify):	9.3%	12.8%

9. Did you ever feel it appropriate to leak information to the press?

Yes   41.9%

No   58.2%   ——*Proceed to question 10.*

IF YES:

	of all	of leaks
a. Why did you feel that it was appropriate? *(Check as many answers as apply.)*		
To gain attention for an issue or policy option	29.7%	73.4%
To force action on an issue	21.4%	52.7%
To slow action on an issue	11.7%	28.8%
To stop action on an issue	12.8%	31.5%
To consolidate support from the public or a constituency outside government	25.8%	63.6%
To inform other officials of a policy consideration or action	12.3%	30.4%
To divert press or public attention from another issue	2.6%	6.5%
To reveal your bargaining position on an issue	5.7%	14.1%
To protect your position	12.3%	30.4%
To undermine another's position	7.5%	18.5%

IF YES:	*of all*	*of leaks*
To develop good relationships with members of the press	16.1%	39.7%
To counter false or misleading information	31.7%	78.3%
The reporter was enterprising in soliciting information	11.7%	28.8%
To send a message to another branch of government	13.0%	32.1%
Other (please specify):	4.2%	10.3%

10. Overall, how great do you believe the effect of the media is on federal policy? *(Circle one number)*

0.2%	3.1%	40.0%	49.0%	7.5%
1	2	3	4	5
No Effect		Some Effect		Dominant Effect

11. Imagine that the media did not exist. Describe how you think your job and the process of policy making in your area would have been different without the media. *(Use a separate sheet of paper if you wish)*

_____

_____

_____

_____

_____

_____

_____

_____

III. Evaluation of Press and of Press-Government Relations

1. On balance, how would you characterize the relationship between you and the members of the press who were covering your office or agency? *(Circle one number on scale.)*

0.4%	2.9%	26.1%	40.7%	29.9%
1	2	3	4	5
Hostile		Mixed		Friendly

2. In your experience, to what degree did reporters use formal news channels (e.g., official press releases, on-the-record interviews, press conferences) as their source for news? *(Circle one number on scale.)*

0.2%	8.8%	40.0%	31.1%	20.0%
1	2	3	4	5
Never		Sometimes		Often

3. In your experience, did the ability of an individual or group outside of the government to gain attention in the media:

(Check those answers which occurred most frequently)

Magnify the individual's or group's influence	81.2%
Gain attention from higher level officials for the individual's or group's views	67.8%
Have no effect	5.9%

Other (please specify): _____

4. From your experience, describe a situation in which the press had a significant effect in advancing your policy goals.

_____

_____

_____

_____

5. From your experience, describe a situation in which the press had a significant effect in undermining your policy goals.

_____

_____

_____

_____

6. Do you feel you have a good understanding of how the press operates and why they do the things they do?

Yes	93.8%
No	6.2%

IV. Background Information

1. Are you serving and / or have you served in:

The Executive Branch	80.8%
The Congress	9.6%
Both	9.6%

2. Generally, do you consider yourself to be:

A Liberal	20.0%
A Moderate	57.4%
A Conservative	22.6%

3. What was your primary policy area or areas?

Commerce / Agriculture	16.2%
Defense	19.8%
Trade / Economics	22.2%
Human Services	18.2%

Foreign Policy	22.4%
Environment / Scientific	12.7%
Legal / Law Enforcement	16.2%
Other, please specify:	20.7%

4. How many years have you served in federal office(s)?

0–5	5–10	10–20	20+
29.5%	24.8%	20.5%	25.2%

5. This question is for those no longer serving in the federal government. All others, please proceed to question 6.

   How long have you been out of the government?

0–5 years	53.2%
5–10 years	27.6%
10–15 years	13.8%
15–20 years	5.5%

6. Did the programs you administered serve a specific constituency rather than the general population?

Yes	29.9%
No	60.6%

7. Was your primary responsibility in the area of public affairs and / or media relations?

Yes	10.5%
No	89.0%

8. How often, while in office, did you read, watch or hear the following types of media reporting?

   (Circle one number on each scale.)

	Never		Sometimes		Often
a. Network News and Public Affairs	1.9%	7.2%	15.2%	16.1%	19.5%
	1	2	3	4	5
b. Newspapers	0.2%	0	1.2%	7.7%	90.8%
	1	2	3	4	5
c. News magazines	1.5%	6.8%	16.7%	20.1%	55.0%
	1	2	3	4	5
d. Trade publications	3.7%	15.0%	20.9%	17.7%	42.6%
	1	2	3	4	5

9. Please list the three specific news programs or publications that you relied on most for information.

1. _____
2. _____
3. _____

10. All responses to this questionnaire are strictly anonymous. However, if you are willing to be contacted so that we may ask you further questions about the interaction between the press and government, please provide your name and an address and telephone number where you can be reached on the lines below. If you do not wish to be contacted, leave these lines blank.

NAME: _____

ADDRESS: _____

_____

TELEPHONE NUMBER: _____

NOTES

Much of the material in this book comes from in-depth interviews with twenty senior federal officials and eighteen Washington-based journalists, each of whom was selected by a panel of their peers as having been particularly competent professionals. See Appendix B for a more complete discussion of the interview portion of this research. Whenever any of the interview subjects are quoted from the interview done for the project, there is no footnote. Footnotes are added only where the quotation came from another source.

Thinking About the Press and Government

1. According to James Q. Wilson, "The bureaucracy as we know it today is largely a product of two events: the Depression of the 1930s (and the concomitant New Deal program of President Roosevelt) and the Second World War." "The Rise of the Bureaucratic State," *The Public Interest,* Fall, 1975, p. 77. Also see James Q. Wilson, *American Government* (Lexington, MA: D.C. Heath, 1983), p. 354.

2. Hugh Heclo, "Issue Networks and the Executive Establishment," in Anthony King, ed., *The New American Political System.* (Washington: American Enterprise Institute, 1978), pp. 89–91.

3. William L. Rivers, *The Other Government: Power and the Washington Media* (New York: Universe Books, 1982), p. 172.

4. Dom Bonafede, "The Washington Press—It Magnifies the President's Flaws and Blemishes," *National Journal,* May 1, 1982, pp. 767–771. Also see William J. Lanouette, "The Washington Press Corps: Is It All That Powerful?" *National Journal,* June 2, 1979, pp. 896–901; and Howard Penn Hudson and Mary Elizabeth Hudson, eds. and pubs., *Hudsons' Washington News Media Contacts Directory,* 1968 through 1984 editions. One of the earliest tabulations appears in Leo Rosten, *The Washington Correspondents* (New York: Harcourt Brace, 1937).

5. Hugh Gregory Gallagher, *FDR's Splendid Deception* (New York: Dodd, Mead, 1985).

6. David Herold, "Historical Perspectives on Government Communication," in Lewis M. Helm, Ray Eldon Hiebert, Michael R. Naver, and Kenneth Rabin, eds., *Informing the People* (New York: Longman, 1981), pp. 14–21. According to data supplied by the U.S. Office of Personnel Management, in 1961, 626 people were employed by the government as writer-editors at a cost of $4.6 million. In 1983, those numbers had increased to 2037 and $55.7 million. Over the same period, the number of public affairs specialists in the federal government grew from 538 persons costing $5.2 million to 2667 persons costing $88.1 million. Compared with the growth of all civilian employees in the federal government, the expansion rate was more than twice as fast for editor-writers and over four times as fast for public affairs specialists. (Special thanks are due to Hon. Michael Stinziano, who assisted with this research).

7. See Kenneth Rabin, "The Rising Role of Advertising," in Helm *et al,* p. 144.

8. The historical linkage between media technology and American politics is developed more fully in Gary R. Orren, What's New About the New Media?" *Discussion Paper,* John F. Kennedy School of Government, August, 1984.

9. Hamilton referred to the *National Gazette* as Jefferson's "faithful and devoted servant"; Jefferson labeled the *Gazette of the United States* "a paper of pure Toryism, disseminating the doctrines of monarchy, aristocracy and the exclusion of the influence of the people." See Culver H. Smith, *The Press, Politics and Patronage: The American Government's Use of Newspapers,*

1789–1875 (Athens, GA: University of Georgia Press, 1977), pp. 14–16, 39; Michael Schudson, *Discovering the News: A Social History of American Newspapers* (New York: Basic Books, 1978), p. 15; and Wilson, *American Government,* p. 233. The most complete history of print journalism in the U.S., including its relatioship with government and politics is Frank L. Mott, *American Journalism* (New York: Macmillan, 1941). Mott's book covers the period from 1690 to 1940.

    10. Letter to W. T. Barry, August 4, 1822. James Madison. *Letters and Other Writings of James Madison, Fourth President of the United States* (Philadelphia: Lippincott & Co., 1865), vol. 3, 1816–1828, p. 276.

    11. Quoted in Robert L. Bartley, "The Press: Adversary, Surrogate Sovereign, or Both?" In George Will, ed., *Press, Politics and Popular Government,* (Washington: American Enterprise Institute, 1972) p. 24.

    12. Walter Lippmann, *Public Opinion* (New York: Macmillan, 1922) and *The Phantom Public* (New York: Harcourt Brace, 1925).

    13. Joseph Schumpeter, *Capitalism, Socialism, and Democracy* (New York: Harper and Row, 1942).

    14. In Key's view, the opinions of the public were not mandates but instead operated as "a system of dikes which channel public action or which fix a range of discretion within which government may act or within which debate at official levels may proceed. This conception avoids the error of personifying 'public opinion' as an entity that exercises initiative and in some way functions as an operating organism to translate its purposes into governmental action." V. O. Key, Jr., *Public Opinion and American Democracy* (New York: Knopf, 1964), p. 552.

    15. *Ibid.,* p. 556. Also see Key, *Politics, Parties, and Pressure Groups* (New York: Thomas Crowell, 5th ed., 1964), especially chapters 8 and 24; and *The Responsible Electorate* (Cambridge: Harvard University Press, 1966).

    16. E.E. Schattschneider, *The Semi-Sovereign People* (New York: Holt Rinehart, and Winston, 1960). p. 137. In Schattschneider's words, "The classical definition of democracy left a great unexplored, undiscovered breach in the theory of modern government, the zone between the sovereign people and the government which is the habitat of the parties." *Party Government* (New York: Holt, Rinehart, and Winston, 1942), p. 15.

    17. See, for example, Sidney Kraus and Dennis Davis, *The Effects of Mass Communication on Political Behavior* (University Park, PA: Pennsylvania State University Press, 1976).

    18. James David Barber, personal communication.

    19. See Donald L. Shaw and Maxwell E. McCombs, *The Emergence of American Political Issues: The Agenda Setting Function of the Press* (St. Paul: West Publishing Co., 1977); and David H. Weaver, Doris A. Graber, Maxwell E. McCombs, and Chaim H. Eyal, *Media Agenda Setting in a Presidential Election: Issues, Images, and Interest* (New York: Praeger, 1981).

    20. See Graham Allison, Jr., "Public and Private Management: Are They Fundamentally Alike in All Unimportant Respects?" in *Setting Public Management Research Agendas* (Washington: Office of Personnel Management, 1980).

    21. Anthony King, ed., *The New American Party System* (Washington: American Enterprise Institute, 1978).

    22. Nicholas von Hoffman has defended this kind of reporting. Arguing that news cannot be presented properly "without adopting a point of view," Von Hoffman criticized the role of the modern White House correspondent for assuming "a task closer to stenography than journalism." *New Republic,* September 6, 1982, pp. 19–21.

    23. This view was prominently expressed in the aftermath of the highjacking of TWA Flight 847 and taking of American hostages by Lebanese Shiite Muslims in the summer of 1985. Many claimed that news coverage, especially on television, influenced the unfolding of those events, significantly affecting policy options and government decisions.

    24. While press–government relations are often described as unfriendly, they are rarely described as belligerent. Dom Bonafede's description is typical: "The principal function [of the news media] is to inform, expose and elucidate. In so doing, it will continue to be an adversary— but not necessarily an enemy of government." (Bonafede, p. 771) Similarly, the interests of the press and government are viewed by some as complementary, but the two are seldom portrayed as outright allies. However, there have been times when the press and government have been

244

allies, such as in the early nineteenth century when most newspapers were the capitve propaganda organs of political factions.

25. Tom Wicker, *On Press* (New York: Viking Press, 1975), p. 259.

26. Max Frankel, quoted in William L. Rivers and Michael J. Nyhan, *Aspen Notebook on Government and the Media* (New York: Praeger, 1973), p. 48.

27. Daniel Patrick Moynihan, "The Presidency and the Press," *Commentary*, March, 1971, pp. 41–52.

28. *The Adversary Press* (St. Petersburg, FL: Modern Media Institute, 1983), p. vii.

29. Some people suggest that the press is adversarial because journalists hold views which differ from government officials. The press is typically accused of having a liberal bias. The suspicion of bias deepens when one discovers that members of the national media do have more liberal views than the general public. However, recent studies have questioned whether journalists' personal opinions actually color their reporting in a significant way. See for example, Michael J. Robinson and Margaret Sheehan, *Over the Wire and on TV: CBS and UPI in Campaign '80* (New York: Russell Sage, 1983), chapter 3; Michael J. Robinson, "Just How Liberal is the News? 1980 Revisited," *Public Opinion*, February / March, 1983, pp. 55–60; and Maura Clancey and Michael J. Robinson, "General Election Coverage: Part I," *Public Opinion*, December / January, 1985, pp. 49–54.

Similarly, some claim that government officials do battle with the press for ideological reasons—essentially because they disagree with the content of press stories and hope to refute or silence them. This certainly was the most popular explanation for the Nixon administration's attack on the press. This was even more clearly the source of adversarial rivalry in the early days of the republic. The Federalists who controlled the government at the time were incensed by the pro-Republican, anti-Federalist views expressed in the papers, and they launched an ideological assault against them.

Others argue that adversarial news reporting stems from the media's advocacy of a distinctive point of view, but not one expressed mainly in left–right terms. Several media-watchers have claimed that the American press subscribes to an anti-government, anti-establishment ethic. For example, Moynihan argues, in the article referred to earlier, that the elite national press is hostile toward major social institutions, including government, not primarily for liberal or conservative reasons, but in response to the intellectual's inner need to criticize (see footnote 27). Irving Kristol has traced American journalists' adversarial style to their long-standing "populist" bias, a bias reflecting not so much liberal or conservative preferences as a deep-seated distrust of government generally. See Irving Kristol, "Crisis for Journalism: The Missing Elite," in George Will, pp. 48–49.

30. Quoted in Will, p. 35.

31. Quoted in Ithiel de Sola Pool, "Newsmen and Statesmen: Adversaries or Cronies?," in Rivers and Nyhan, pp. 11–12.

32. Rivers, p. 18.

33. Michael Baruch Grossman and Martha Joynt Kumar, *Portraying the President: The White House and the News Media* (Baltimore: Johns Hopkins Press, 1981), p. 1. Perhaps the best-known recent example of this friendly linkage was the Stockman-Greider affair. David Stockman, the former director of the Office of Management and Budget was interviewed (in 18 tape-recorded sessions) by former *Washington Post* reporter William Greider on how the Reagan administration's economic policies developed during its first year in office. Reflecting on their candid conversations later, Greider noted:

> At the outset, Stockman and I were participating in a fairly routine transaction of Washington, a form of submerged communication which takes place regularly between selected members of the press and the highest officials of government. Our mutual motivation, despite our different interests, was crassly self-serving. It did not need to be spelled out between us. I would use him and he would use me. The fancy name for this is symbiosis, which perhaps gives it more dignity than it deserves. But symbiosis is an elementary mode of operation in the ecology of Washington affairs . . . the functional politics of the city involves complicated webs of such information relationships, transactions for sharing access and information which largely go unobserved. (William Greider, *The Education of David Stockman and Other Americans* (New York: Dutton, 1982), p. xvii.)

Stockman miscalculated the benefit he would derive from this symbiotic arrangement. His views were recounted by Greider in an *Atlantic Monthly* article (which appeared sooner than Stockman anticipated) that nearly cost him his job, and probably cost him much of his reputation and authority. William Safire, the *New York Times* columnist, joined the chorus demanding Stockman's resignation, condemning both the specific instance and the generally accomodating style of press–government relations: "His [Stockman's] chastened departure will put a torpedo into the pernicious symbiosis between men in power and reporters whose job is to check that power. The two must remain adversaries." First Symbiosis Furor," *New York Times,* November 15, 1981 p. E21.

34. William Lanouette, p. 899.

35. The resulting blend of amicability and hostility may reflect a psychological balancing act. According to Pool, journalists are aware of and troubled by the seductions and dangers of co-optation, and their wariness fortifies their adversary posture. "To do his job [the reporter] must grow close to politicians and win their trust, but his job is also to publicly expose them. To do his job he must develop confidential relations with sources and protect those sources, but his job is also to strip the veil of privacy from everyone else's business." Consequently, press behavior becomes "a reaction to the very compromises and concessions" that the reporter must make, "a brave assertion that wards off guilt." Pool, p. 15.

36. Quoted in Martin Linsky, ed., *Television and the Presidential Elections* (Lexington, MA: Lexington Books, 1983), p. 40.

37. On journalistic ideals see Commission on Freedom of the Press, *A Free and Responsible Press* (Chicago: University of Chicago, 1947). Also, see Fred S. Siebert, Theodore Peterson, and Wilbur Schramm, *Four Theories of the Press* (Urbana: University of Illinois Press, 1956).

38. For two recent discussions of the professional norms of public administrators see Mark Moore, "A Conception of Public Management," September, 1983, unpublished manuscript; and Herman B. Leonard, "Theory S and Theory T," November, 1984, unpublished manuscript. These norms, as traditionally conceived, leave little room for the marshalling of support outside the government through the press.

39. A survey of leaders in the United States, Japan, and Sweden asking how much influence they attributed to various groups, found that of all the groups and institutions—business, labor, farming, political parties, intellectuals, feminists, bureaucrats, racial and ethnic groups—the media were consistently held to be the most influential. Moreover, while nearly all other leaders denied that their groups wielded great influence, media leaders concurred with the others' appraisal of the major influence of the press. Sidney Verba, Steve Kelman, Gary Orren, G. Donald Ferree, Jr., Ikuo Kabashima, Ichiro Miyake, and Joji Watanuki, *Equality in Comparative Perspective* (forthcoming). Also see Sidney Verba and Gary R. Orren, *Equality in America: The View From the Top* (Cambridge: Harvard University Press, 1985) chapter 9.

40. Thomas Carlyle, "The Hero as Man of Letters," in *On Heroes, Hero Worship, and the Heroic in History* (London: Chapman and Hall, 1840), p. 152.

41. Quoted in Will, p. 27.

Chapter One

1. David Whitman, "The Press and the Neutron Bomb," Kennedy School of Government, case C94–84–595, p. 28.

2. Ibid.
3. Ibid., p. 9.
4. Ibid., p. 29.
5. Ibid., pp. 40–41.
6. Ibid., p. 41.
7. Ibid., pp. 14–15.
8. Ibid., p. 15.
9. Ibid., pp. 15–16.
10. Ibid., p. 16.
11. This letter was dated July 20, 1977.
12. The article was published in *Vorwearts*, July 17, 1977.
13. Whitman, p. 66.

14. Ibid., p. 68.

15. Ibid., p. 79.

16. Ibid., p. 96.

17. United States Information Agency, ''Neutron Bomb Debate,'' *Foreign Media Reaction, Current Issues* 5, March 1, 1978, page 1.

18. Whitman, pp. 102–103.

19. Ibid., p. 105–106.

20. Ibid., p. 121.

21. Ibid., p. 104.

22. Ibid., p. 105.

23. Philip Geyelin, ''A Bum Rap on the 'Neutron Bomb,' '' *Washington Post,* September 18, 1981, op-ed page.

24. Whitman, p. 43.

25. Ibid., p. 150.

26. Roger Morris, ''Eight Days in April: The Press Flattens Carter with the Neutron Bomb,'' *Columbia Journalism Review,* November / December 1978, page 30. Also see James Burnham, ''The President and the Bomb,'' *National Review,* May 12, 1978, p. 579.

27. Zbigniew Brzezinski, *Power and Principle* (New York: Farrar, Straus, and Giroux, 1983), p. 301.

Chapter Two

1. In his brilliant biography of Walter Lippman, Ronald Steel reports on more than one occasion of Lippman being privately solicited for advice by those in power. For instance, Lippman recommended changes in John F. Kennedy's inauguration address and then wrote favorably about the speech after it was delivered (Ronald Steel, Walter Lippman and the American Century [Boston: Little Brown and Company, 1980], pp. 524–525). Kathleen Turner's recent book (Kathleen J. Turner, *Lyndon Johnson's Dual War,* [Chicago: University of Chicago Press, 1985]) recounts in unsparing detail LBJ's efforts to woo the press which included, sometimes unsuccessfully, soliciting their advice and awaiting favorable coverage it was acceptable.

2. See Appendix C for the full questionnaire.

3. Martin Linsky, ed., *Television and the Presidential Elections* (Lexington, MA: Lexington Books, 1983), p. 55.

4. David Whitman, ''Television and the 1981–84 Review of the Disability Rolls (B),'' Kennedy School of Government, unpublished draft case, p. 3.

5. Ibid., p. 10.

6. Ibid., p. 12.

7. Statement issued by CBS News, April 21, 1982.

8. ''CBS, Reagan, and the Poor,'' *Newsweek,* May 3, 1982, p. 22.

9. Lars-Erik Nelson, ''Politically, There's No Antidote for an Anecdote,'' *New York Daily News,* April 23, 1982.

10. Don Irwin, ''CBS Rejects White House Request to Rebut Broadcast,'' *Los Angeles Times,* April 23, 1982.

11. Statement on Social Security Disability by HHS Secretary Schweiker and SSA Commissioner Svahn, HHS NEWS, April 29, 1982, p. 1.

12. Transcript of CBS Evening News, December 6, 1982, p. 12.

13. Senate Special Committee on Aging, Social Security Reviews of the Mentally Disabled, S.HRG. 98–170, hearings, 98th Congress, 1st session, April 7, 1983, page 8.

14. Whitman, case B, pp. 25–26.

15. Ibid., p. 25.

16. Ibid., p. 27.

17. Ibid., p. 30.

18. D'Vera Cohn, ''White House: We're Sympathetic,'' UPI dispatch, May 27, 1983.

19. Whitman, case B, p. 31.

20. House Select Committee on Aging, Social Security Disability Reviews; A Federally Created State Problem, Comm. Pub. 98–395, hearing, 98th Congress, 1st session, June 20, 1983, page 55.

21. HHS News release, April 13, 1984, page 2.

22. Lloyd Cutler, "Foreign Policy on Deadline," *Foreign Policy,* issue 56, Fall 1984, published by the Carnegie Foundation for International Peace, Washington, D.C.

Chapter Three

1. Martin Linsky, "Shrinking the Policy Process: The Press and the 1980 Love Canal Relocation," Kennedy School of Government, unpublished draft case, p. 14.

2. Donald McNeil, Jr., "Upstate Waste Site May Endanger Lives," *New York Times,* August 2, 1978.

3. The letter is from Dr. Dante Piccino to Frode Ulvadel of EPS's Healthfix Division, dated May 5, 1980.

4. Linsky, draft case, pp. 21–22.

5. See the *New York Times, May 17, 1980.*

6. *Irwin Molotsky, "1710 More Families at Love Canal May Be Relocated Following Tests," New York Times,* May 18, 1980, pp. 1 and 37.

7. Linsky, draft case, pages 28–29.

8. Memo from Watson to President Carter, May 17, 1980.

9. Linsky, draft case, p. 41.

10. For a more complete discussion of the scientific aspects of the problem and this review of the chromosome study in particular, see Adele Levine, Love Canal: Science, Politics, and People (Lexington, MA: Lexington Books, 1982), pages 150–151. The report is generally referred to as the Rall report after Dr. David Rall, Director of the National Institute of Environmental Health Sciences, who had empanelled the review committee at the request of Jack Watson.

11. Linsky, draft case, p. 46.

12. Ibid., p. 30.

13. Two or three on a scale of one to five, with one being no impact and five having a dominant effect.

Chapter Four

1. See transcript of Martin Linsky's interview with Helen Thomas, May 3, 1984. Also see Keith S. Collins, ed., *Responsibility and Freedom in the Press: Are They in Conflict?,* The Report of the Citizen's Choice National Commission on Free and Responsible Media, 1985, pp. 64–65.

2. David Whitman, "The Press and the Neutron Bomb (Abridged)," Kennedy School of Government, case C14–84–608, pp. 50–51.

3. Ibid., pp. 13–14.

4. See Martin Linsky, "What's Happened to News from Iran?" *Boston Globe,* May 3, 1980.

5. Cited, among other places, in Dr. Bob Gray, "Use of Tax Power to Shape Religious Thought Repugnant," *Florida Times Union,* May 15, 1982, op-ed page.

6. David Whitman, "Ronald Reagan and Tax Exemptions for Racist Schools (Abridged)," Kennedy School of Government, case C95–84–609A, page 11.

7. Ibid., pp. 11–12.

8. Transcript of interview with Reagan on PBS' "Tony Brown Journal," February 18, 1982.

9. Whitman, Reagan Abridged case, p. 13.

10. Ibid., p. 14.

11. Martin Schram and Charles Babcock, "Reagan Advisers Missed School Case Sensitivity," *Washington Post,* January 17, 1982, p. 9.

12. Whitman, Reagan Abridged case, p. 10.

13. Ibid., p. 24.

14. See "Tax-Exempt Schools," *Dallas Times Herald,* January 12, 1982, editorial page; Glenn Fowler, "Private Schools Assail Tax Shift," *New York Times,* January 10, 1982, p. 1; "Groups Decry Government Move in Bob Jones case," *Greenville* ((S.C.) *News,* January 10, 1982, p. 1; "Pat: Feds Immoral on School Tax," *New York Daily News,* January 10, 1982; and

"NAACP Blasts Private School Tax Ruling Reversal," *Muskegon* (Mich.) *Chronicle,* January 9, 1982, p. 1.

15. Whitman, Reagan Abridged case, p. 29.
16. Ibid., p. 30.
17. Ibid., p. 31.
18. Ibid., p. 32.
19. Ibid., p. 33.
20. David Whitman, "Selling the Reorganization of the Post Office (A)," Kennedy School of Government, case C14–84–610, pp. 16–17.
21. "Postal Reform Unit Organized," *Syracuse Herald-Journal,* August 26, 1982, p. 2.
22. David Whitman, Post Office Sequel case, p. 9.
23. Allan Cromley, "Television News Angers Reagan," *Daily Oklahoman,* March 17, 1982, p. 1.
24. Whitman, Post Office Sequel case, p. 30 and Appendix C.

Chapter Five

1. David Whitman "Ronald Reagan and Tax Exemptions for Racist Schools (Abridged)," Kennedy School of Government, case C95–84–609A, p. 37.
2. Ibid., p. 23.
3. Justice Department transcript of Attorney General Smith meeting with the press on the Voting Rights Act, January 28, 1982, page 13. Smith also stated that *Bob Jones* "represents not the slightest retreat from the President's position with respect to the overall question of racial discrimination. . . . In that case, the question was not racial discrimination. It was whether or not an unelected administration official should have the authority to determine tax exempt status on the basis of his idea of public policy."
4. Whitman, Abridged case, pp. 38–39.
5. Tom Wicker, "Where the Buck Stops," *New York Times,* January 19, 1982, p. 27.
6. Many people have tried to develop a typology of leaks. This discussion draws heavily on one of the best of those, that constructed by Stephen Hess in his excellent book on press officers in the federal government. See Stephen Hess, *The Government / Press Connection: Press Officers and Their Offices* (Washington, D.C.: The Brookings Institution, 1984).
7. Whitman, Abridged case, p. 56.
8. Ibid., p. 58.
9. Wendy O'Donnell, "The Role of the Press in the Investigation and Resignation of Vice-President Spiro T. Agnew," Kennedy School of Government, unpublished draft case, p. 1.
10. Robert Manoff, deputy director of the Center for War, Peace, and News Media at New York University, is currently working on a history of the coverage of nuclear weapons issues which focuses on the relationship between the press and government, for example.

Chapter Six

1. David Whitman, "Selling the Reorganization of the Post Office (A)," Kennedy School of Government, case C14–84–610, p. 5.
2. Ibid., pp. 2–4.
3. Ibid., p. 9.
4. Ibid., pp. 11–12.
5. Ibid., p. 20.
6. Ibid., p. 31.
7. Senate Post Office and Civil Service Committee, Postal Modernization, hearings, 91st Congress, 1st session, 1969, page 800.
8. Whitman, case A, p. 36.
9. Ibid., p. 38.
10. Text of statement by Senator Gale McGee, issued March 29, 1969.
11. White House transcript of President Nixon's nationally televised comments, March 23, 1970, p. 3. Also see Appendix B of David Whitman, Post Office Sequel case.
12. David Whitman, Post Office Sequel case, p. 5 and Appendix B.

13. Ibid., p. 5.
14. Post Office Department transcript of Winton M. Blount / George Meany press conference, August 5, 1970, pp. 1 and 2.
15. Whitman, Post Office Sequel case, p. 7.
16. Ibid., pp. 7–8.
17. Ibid., pp. 8–9.
18. Ibid., p. 4.
19. David Whitman, "Television and the 1981–84 Review of the Disability Rolls (B)," Kennedy School of Government, case 0485, p. 17.
20. Ibid., pp. 20–21.

Chapter Seven

1. From the *American Heritage Dictionary of the English Language*, paperback edition, based on the hardcover edition (New York: Dell Publishing, 1976).
2. Wendy O'Donnell, "The Role of the Press in the Investigation and Resignation of Vice-President Spiro T. Agnew," Kennedy School of Government, unpublished draft case, p. 8.
3. Richard Cohen and Carl Bernstein, "Agnew Is Target of Kickback Probe in Baltimore, Proclaims His Innocence," *Washington Post*, August 7, 1973, p. 1.
4. "Transcript of Agnew News Conference Dealing with Investigation by Grand Jury," *New York Times*, August 9, 1973, p. 20.
5. "ACLU Demands End to Agnew Inquiry Leaks," *New York Times*, August 16, 1973, p. 27.
6. ABC News, "Issues and Answers," August 19, 1973.
7. "Heading Toward an Indictment?" *Time*, August 27, 1973.
8. "Agnew Press Comments and Richardson Reply," *New York Times*, August 22, 1973, p. 24.
9. Bill Kovach, *New York Times*, August 23, 1973, p. 1.
10. Ibid.
11. Letter from Elliot L. Richardson, Attorney General to Vice-President Spiro T. Agnew, Washington, D.C., August 23, 1973.
12. O'Donnell, unpublished draft case, p. 23.
13. Ibid., p. 31.
14. See Richard M. Cohen and Lou Cannon, "Agnew Lawyers Bargain on Plea," *Washington Post*, August 22, 1973, p. 1; and Fred Graham, text of story reported on CBS Evening News, August 22, 1973, taken from attachment to letter from Fred Graham to the editors, *New York Times*, October 1, 1973.
15. Press release, Department of Justice, Washington, D.C., September 28, 1973.
16. Spiro T. Agnew, *Go Quietly . . . or else* (New York: Morrow, 1980), pp. 179–180.
17. O'Donnell, unpublished draft case, pp. 42–43.
18. Ibid., p. 45.
19. Ibid., p. 46.
20. Aaron Latham, "Closing in on Agnew: The Prosecutor's Story," *New York*, November 26, 1973, p. 72.
21. Statement of U.S. Attorney General Elliot L. Richardson, U.S. District Court for Maryland, October 10, 1973.
22. Agnew, pp. 16–17.
23. O'Donnell, unpublished draft case, p. 60.
24. Ibid.
25. Ibid., p. 61.
26. Ibid., p. 62.
27. "The Neutron Decision," *Washington Post*, April 6, 1978, editorial page.
28. "Furor over the Neutron Bomb," *Newsweek*, April 17, 1978, pages 35 and 38; and "The Neutron Bomb Furor," *Time*, April 17, 1978, page 10.
29. David Whitman, "The Press and the Neutron Bomb," Kennedy School of Government, case C94–84–595, p. 129 (see asterisk at the bottom of the page).
30. O'Donnell, unpublished draft case, Appendix E.

31. Ibid., p. 27.

32. This typology of leaks is not original. Many others who have studied the relationship between press and government have examined the various motivations of leakers. One of the best such efforts, and the one on which this section draws most heavily, is from Stephen Hess, *The Government/Press Connection* (Washington, D.C.: The Brookings Institution), Chapter 7, see especially pp. 77-78. Mr. Hess was a member of the study group for this project.

Chapter Eight

1. Richardson's three options were expanded upon and analyzed in an unpublished policy analysis exercise done by Robert T. Shepardson in partial fulfillment of the requirements for a master's in public policy degree at the John F. Kennedy School of Government in 1985.

2. David Whitman, "The Press and the Neutron Bomb," Kennedy School of Government, case C95–84–595, p. 150.

INDEX